T0339453

Social Media Theory and Communications Practice

Fusing the academic with the applied, this book provides a comprehensive introduction to social media for future communications professionals.

While most social media texts approach the subject through either a theoretical, scholarly lens or a professional, practical lens, this text offers a much-needed linkage of theory to the practical tactics employed by social media communicators. Concise and conversational chapters break down the basics of both social media theory and practice and are complemented by sidebars written by scholars and industry professionals, chapter summaries and end-of-chapter exercises.

This book is ideal for introductory social media courses in communication, public relations and mass communication departments, as well as courses in digital media and public relations.

Online resources include social media writing templates, sample posts and content calendar templates. Please visit www.routledge.com/ 9781032185873.

Whitney Lehmann, Ph.D., APR, is an associate professor in the Department of Communication, Media, and the Arts at Nova Southeastern University, USA. Her industry experience includes working for Seminole Hard Rock Hotel & Casino, Miami International Airport, Barry University and the Miami Herald.

Social Media Theory and Communications Practice

Whitney Lehmann

Routledge
Taylor & Francis Group

NEW YORK AND LONDON

Designed cover image: DigitalVision Vectors/© Getty Images

First published 2024
by Routledge
605 Third Avenue, New York, NY 10158

and by Routledge
4 Park Square, Milton Park, Abingdon, Oxon, OX14 4RN

Routledge is an imprint of the Taylor & Francis Group, an informa business

ISBN: 9781032186832 (hbk)
ISBN: 9781032185873 (pbk)
ISBN: 9781003255734 (ebk)

DOI: 10.4324/9781003255734

Typeset in Bembo
by Apex CoVantage, LLC

Access the Support Material: www.routledge.com/9781032185873

To Colton, Charleston and Belle:
My heart, my home, my reason for it all

Contents

Contributors

Kimberly Cohane is an award-winning digital and social media marketing professional. She worked as a digital marketing professional for over 10 years at Nova Southeastern University (NSU). During this time, she led innovative ways to amplify NSU's brand through a multi-tiered strategy, including digital advertising, Pay Per Click (PPC) ads, social media and virtual reality (VR) tours. She currently works in EdTech and completed her Ph.D. in Conflict Analysis and Resolution at NSU researching how social media bots impact and disrupt online communities.

Megan Fitzgerald Dunn, an associate professor at Nova Southeastern University, earned her Ph.D. in Communication from Florida State University, her M.A. in Journalism from Syracuse University, and her B.A. in Communication from Stonehill College. She teaches a variety of communication and journalism courses, including media regulation, multimedia writing and public speaking. She also serves as the faculty adviser for the university's student-run newspaper, *The Current*.

Michael Laderman is an Orlando-based award-winning writer and public affairs, marketing, advertising and brand management executive. He serves as the director of public relations and marketing for Orlando Shakes, Central Florida's largest professional theater company. He previously led the public and media relations efforts of the Orlando Museum of Art, Nova Southeastern University and Barry University and directed all academic and executive communications for Clemson University. Throughout his career, Laderman also had the opportunity to represent individuals such as Shaquille O'Neal, world-renowned saxophone player "Mr. Casual" Charlie DeChant and Haiti's Prime Minister Laurent Lamothe, to name just a few of the many celebrities he has worked with and alongside.

Michael North teaches public relations writing and strategic communication concepts as an assistant professor at Middle Georgia State University. He earned his Ph.D. in mass communication at the University of Miami, where he focused his research on how Fortune 500 companies use social media to communicate with stakeholders. North's research focuses on social media with specific attention paid to Twitter. His research interests center on how organizations communicate with stakeholders and what value these organizations can derive from social media.

James Profetto is the social media manager for the Division of Public Relations, Marketing, and Creative Services at Nova Southeastern University. He oversees a team of specialists to produce engaging content, communicate events and help build the culture at NSU. Previously, Profetto served as a social media coordinator for Miami Dade College, where he strategized and created content for the college's district social media accounts. He also managed the social media presence for two of the college's presidents. Prior to his three-year experience at MDC, he worked at WSVN Channel 7 as a web writer after completing his bachelor's degree in broadcast media at Florida International University. Profetto has also been a film/TV critic since 2016 and is the founder of "Reel James," an outlet for entertainment news, reviews and reactions. He currently holds membership with the Southeastern Film Critics Association.

Tasha Yohan is an Industry Marketing Manager at UKG, a leading HR, workforce management and payroll company. With more than 10 years of marketing and public relations experience, she has worked in a range of fields including agency, higher education and now technology. She has been recognized as a Young Professional of the Year by PRSA Fort Lauderdale and an Up & Comer by South Florida Business & Wealth Magazine. Yohan is a graduate of Leadership Broward, Class 38, and previously served in leadership roles in PRSA Fort Lauderdale and the Junior League of Greater Fort Lauderdale. She received her bachelor's degree in public relations from the University of Florida and her MBA from Nova Southeastern University. Tasha lives in downtown Fort Lauderdale with her fiancé and two rescue mutts, Winnie and Waffles.

Introduction

Today, most organizations have a long and varied list of social media channels targeting various publics: an official Facebook page to serve as their social media "store front"; a Twitter account to provide breaking news and customer service; an Instagram account to create visual storytelling; a Snapchat and a TikTok to cater quick, catchy content to Generation Z; a LinkedIn page for professional networking; a blog to serve brand enthusiasts; a YouTube channel to house how-to videos highlighting products; and the list goes on.

The introduction of the World Wide Web and the building of the information "super highway" in the 1990s created an increased need for public relations professionals who could help organizations manage their online presence and, eventually, their social media channels. While these social media lineups often started with the "Big Three" (Facebook, Twitter and Instagram), it wasn't long before the list of options grew as other social media channels launched, organizations scrambled to keep up, and the need for bonafide social media professionals was born.

While today it's not unusual for a brand to have an expansive social media presence, it's also become a non-negotiable component of any organization's communications plan with an estimated 4.5 billion people (more than half of the world's population) using social media and a global pandemic that further increased our dependency on technology (Dean, 2021). As lockdowns and closures of schools, businesses and workplaces ensued, we turned to social media to stay connected, informed and entertained. In 2021, the Pew Research Center reported that seven out of 10 Americans use social media and that 90% of adults said the internet was essential or important for them personally during the coronavirus outbreak (McClain et al., 2022; Pew Research Center, 2022).

The ever-evolving and growing list of available social platforms combined with consumers' increased need to connect with brands digitally has created an urgent and growing need for social media managers who can help companies navigate the social landscape with strategic platforms, engaging, audience-driven content, real-time customer service and authentic brand identity.

In 2017, CNN named social media management as one of its "Top 100 Careers with Big Growth," and in 2018, for the first time, social media sites surpassed print newspapers as a news source for Americans (Schaeffer, 2019; Social Media Manager, 2017). From 2019 to 2029 the U.S. Bureau of Labor Statistics predicts that the overall employment for marketing managers will grow faster than the average for all occupations (U.S. Bureau of Labor Statistics, 2020).

Recognizing the need for students and emerging professionals to possess these coveted social media skill sets, higher education has followed suit and increased offerings in social media courses, programs and certificates. "In the age of Twitter, Facebook and Instagram, social media degrees are #For-Real as colleges and universities aim to educate students about getting the most from online platforms" (Somers, 2016, para. 3).

These social media-specific courses and degree programs are typically housed within a university's department, school or college of communications or business. For example, the University of Florida's College of Journalism and Communications offers a master's degree in social media, the University of Southern California's School of Communication and Journalism offers a master's degree in digital social media, and the Rutgers Business School offers a "Mini-MBA" in social media marketing.

While social media is certainly a valuable tool for reaching business goals, its impact is far beyond the business realm, as our reasons for using social media are as varied as the plethora of social channels themselves. We use social media to meet significant others, list and sell goods and services, research reviews, curate content, create identity, communicate during a crisis, network with professionals, connect with customer service, and the list goes on.

In 2020, and the years surrounding it, we've watched social movements born via social media (#metoo, #blacklivesmatter), #canceled celebrities and public figures, created trends (#milkcratechallenge), copied choreographed dances, witnessed a sitting U.S. president get banned from social platforms, and commended a whistleblower for standing up to a social media giant.

We've experienced social media harnessed for good—for example, the #icebucketchallenge raising awareness for ALS, Facebook's safety check connecting us with friends and family during a crisis, and TikTokers popularizing a distress signal leading to real-life rescues—and sadly have become well aware of its dangers, such as stolen personal data, identity theft, cyberbullying and negative effects on mental health, particularly with teens.

The boom of the social media job market and increased offerings by colleges and universities coupled with the recent focus on social media's impact on our lives and well-being have resulted in the publication of numerous popular and scholarly texts centered around social media. Many are practical in nature with an applied, hands-on focus, such as "Likeable Social

Media: How to Delight Your Customers, Create an Irresistible Brand, & Be Generally Amazing on All Social Channels That Matter," while others, like "Social Media: Enduring Principles," approach the subject matter through a theoretical lens, examining the role of social media in culture and society.

What appears to be missing from the long lineup of social media publications is a book that does both—combining theory with practice, the academic with the applied—to truly give students, scholars and working professionals a well-rounded understanding and appreciation for social media. This book seeks to fill the gap with an integrated text combining theory and practice. We can't—and shouldn't—separate the practice of social media from the ongoing research and conversations about how social media impacts us as individuals and as a society.

Whether you're an aspiring social media student, scholar, educator, strategist or simply just a user of social media, this book aims to offer you a comprehensive crash course into the field by combining the two often separate perspectives to provide you with foundational concepts for navigating social media in your work and everyday lives.

References

Dean, B. (2021, October 10). How many people use social media in 2022? (65+ statistics). *Backlinko*. Retrieved May 28, 2022, from https://backlinko.com/social-media-users

McClain, C., Vogels, E. A., Perrin, A., Sechopoulos, S., & Rainie, L. (2022, April 28). The internet and the pandemic. *Pew Research Center: Internet, Science & Tech*. Retrieved May 28, 2022, from www.pewresearch.org/internet/2021/09/01/the-internet-and-the-pandemic/

Pew Research Center. (2022, January 11). Social media fact sheet. *Pew Research Center: Internet, Science & Tech*. Retrieved May 28, 2022, from www.pewresearch.org/internet/fact-sheet/social-media/

Schaeffer, K. (2019, December 20). U.S. has changed in key ways in the past decade, from tech use to demographics. *Pew Research Center*. www.pewresearch.org/fact-tank/2019/12/20/key-ways-us-changed-in-past-decade/

Social Media Manager. (2017). *CNN money*. https://money.cnn.com/gallery/pf/2017/01/05/best-jobs-2017/42.html

Somers, D. (2016, June 30). You can major in social media? *U.S. News & World Report*. www.usnews.com/education/best-colleges/articles/2016-06-30/you-can-major-in-social-media

U.S. Bureau of Labor Statistics. (2020, September 1). *Advertising, promotions, and marketing managers: Occupational outlook handbook*. www.bls.gov/ooh/management/advertising-promotions-and-marketing-managers.htm

Part 1

What Is Social Media?

1 Defining Social Media

Where were you the first time you used social media? Maybe it was in the mid-2000s creating a Facebook profile from your dorm room. Perhaps it was pinning ideas on a Pinterest board for a home renovation project, following your favorite celebrity on Twitter, or posting a rave review or scathing complaint on Yelp. Or maybe these channels sound like ancient history and your first introduction to social media was re-creating a dance challenge on TikTok, using a funny filter on Snapchat, or jumping on Instagram Live to share something special in real time.

We all have different introductions to social media. We all have different reasons for using social media (see Chapter 6 for more on Uses and Gratifications). We all have different backgrounds, cultures, communities and identities that influence our experiences with social media.

In this chapter, we'll look at how scholars, industry professionals and users themselves define the term "social media," from the most basic and broad ("the practice of using media socially" and "the world's largest cocktail party") to the more complex and narrow ("a group of internet-based applications that build on the ideological and technological foundations of Web 2.0, and that allow the creation and exchange of user-generated content"). We'll also examine social media's purpose across different areas of communications, such as public relations, journalism, advertising and marketing.

What you can expect to learn in this chapter:

- Different definitions of social media offered by academics, industry leaders and everyday users
- Social media as a form of "old media" versus "new media"
- Key concepts associated with social media
- Ways we can describe/further define social media: By category/type, user and region
- Social media as a function of journalism, public relations, advertising and marketing

DOI: 10.4324/9781003255734-2

What Is "Social Media"?

Depending on whom you ask, you'll get a different answer to the question, "What is social media?" Responses range from simple and straight to the point while others are wordy and complex. Some are narrow in nature with specific criteria for what constitutes social media while others are broad and open to interpretation. Since the inception of social media, we've attempted to reach a consensus in the way we define it and describe it, and while many established definitions do find some common ground, the truth is we will probably never have one definition that is agreed upon and accepted by all, because we have all different histories and experiences with social media that affect our perceptions of it, evidenced by the hundreds of edits to the Wikipedia entry of social media since it first appeared in July 2006.

> The concept of Social Media is top of the agenda for many business executives today. Decision makers, as well as consultants, try to identify ways in which firms can make profitable use of applications such as Wikipedia, YouTube, Facebook, Second Life, and Twitter. Yet despite this interest, there seems to be very limited understanding of what the term "Social Media" exactly means . . . the idea behind Social Media is far from groundbreaking. Nevertheless, there seems to be confusion among managers and academic researchers alike as to what exactly should be included under this term.
>
> (Kaplan & Haenlein, 2010, pp. 59–60)

New Media Versus Old Media

Let's begin by reviewing some definitions that align with traditional views of social media—the internet-enabled, accessed through an app on your phone or your desktop kind of social media.

Merriam-Webster (2022, para. 1) defines social media as "forms of electronic communication (such as websites for social networking and microblogging) through which users create online communities to share information, ideas, personal messages, and other content (such as videos)."

According to Cambridge Dictionary (n.d.), social media are "websites and computer programs that allow people to communicate and share information on the internet using a computer or cell phone" (para. 1).

Wikipedia states, "Social media are interactive digital channels that facilitate the creating and sharing of information, ideas, interests, and other forms of expression through virtual communities and networks" (n.d., para. 1).

The "social media" entry in The Associated Press (2022) Stylebook states that social media is "an umbrella term for online services that people use to share posts, photos and videos with small or large groups of people, privately or publicly" (p. 272).

These definitions provide a snapshot of how social media is defined by reference works, such as dictionaries and stylebooks, and suggest that social media is what we call "new media"—media delivered digitally using computer technology and the internet—and not "old media" or "traditional media," such as television, print and radio.

When examining how scholars, academic institutions, industry pros and professional organizations define the term, this trend of describing social media as "new media" continues, with an emphasis on words and phrases such as "internet-based," "online," "Web 2.0," "websites," "electronic communication," and "virtual communities," among others. O'Reilly (2005), who coined the term "Web 2.0" in 2005, describes Web 2.0 as participation instead of publishing and users as contributors in contrast to the read-only static web pages of Web 1.0.

- "Social media can be thought of as forms of electronic communication through which users create online communities to share information, ideas, personal messages, and other content via the social sphere" (Luttrell & Wallace, 2021, p. 5).
- "Social media involves the use of social networks as marketing communications media. These websites often have users actively participate to determine what is popular . . . encouraging users to adopt and pass along widgets or other content modules created by a brand, or to add a brand to the user's social circle of friends" (American Marketing Association, n.d., para. 1).
- "Social media refers to the means of interactions among people in which they create, share, and/or exchange information and ideas in virtual communities and networks" (Tufts University Relations, n.d., para. 1).
- "Social media is, quite simply, anything that uses the Internet to facilitate conversations" (Solis & Breakenridge, 2009, p. xvii).

While many—if not most—definitions define social media as taking place online, it's worth noting and important to explore other perspectives suggesting that "old media" can be social and that we need to place the focus on the motive rather than the type of medium.

In the book "Social Media: Enduring Principles," associate professor Ashlee Humphreys says social media is "a practice, or set of practices, for using media socially" (Humphreys, 2016, p. 1). Social media, she says, is "not dependent on digital communication," meaning that it doesn't solely take place online and can take place via "old media," such as radio and print (p. 7). For example, radio listeners calling into a radio station to report an accident on the highway or readers of early newspapers writing in their own news reports on blank back pages that were then circulated to other readers. "It is not the medium that matters, but the use of it" (p. 1).

Author and marketing strategist Dave Kerpen says, "Social media is like the world's largest cocktail party, where people can listen to others talking and join the conversations with other people about any topic of their choice" (2019, p. 6).

He expands upon this analogy and writes:

> Just as in real-life cocktail parties, in the giant social media cocktail party, there are some participants who are a lot more influential than others (so-called "influencers"). There are two main distinctions, though, between a real cocktail party and an online one: First, there's no drinking online, of course. Second, but more important, whereas at an actual, in-person cocktail party, you can only have a few conversations with a handful of people in one night, online, and through social networks, you can have numerous conversations with potentially thousands or millions of people at once.
>
> (pp. 6–7)

Kerpen also makes the argument that while old media, like books, usually involve one-way communication, they also have the possibility to be "social."

> I write a lot in this book about the two-way interactive nature of social media and the importance of leveraging that potential. Of course, a book is typically as one-directional as a medium can be: author writes, and reader reads and digests. As a social media author, I simply won't allow that to be the case. So here's my promise to you: as you read this book, if you need clarification, you are uncertain about content, or you want to challenge me on the points or strategies within, please do let me know, using social media.
>
> (10)

Like Humphreys, Kerpen challenges us to think about the fact that even traditional "old media" like print, radio and broadcast *can* be social with two-way communication.

Key Concepts Associated With Social Media

In addition to most definitions describing social media as internet-based applications, other key terms/concepts associated with social media include:

- **User-generated Content:** Social media content is created and shared by an application's users. "User-generated content is content created by the regular people on social media, rather than brands" (Hootsuite, n.d.-a).

  "Social media is all about creating and sharing information and ideas, whether it's Wikipedia entries or Facebook updates about favorite football teams, fabulous cheesecakes, and what famous people wore to awards show" (Quesenberry, 2021, p. 8).

- **Shared Content:** While the debate of whether social media constitutes old media, new media or both continues, one thing most definitions agree on is that social media involves the sharing of content, whether it be photos, videos, reviews, memes, emojis or anything else.
- **Social Network:** The content, created and shared by users, is shared with a network of connections often referred to as online or virtual communities. "Social networks allow friends, family and strangers around the world to find each other and connect based on similar interests or hobbies. For example, people with rare diseases can offer support through a social network, even if they live far apart and have never met in person. On the other hand, people with similar viewpoints can also connect and block out those with alternative views" (The Associated Press, 2020, pp. 276–277).

  Examples of social networks created by users could be "Friends" on Facebook or Snapchat, "Connections" on LinkedIn, "Followers" on Instagram, Twitter and TikTok, and "Subscribers" on YouTube. Online/virtual communities can also be groups one participates in, for example, a private Facebook Group that a university creates for newly admitted students.
- **Private or Public:** Social media content can be shared privately (e.g., a private story on Snapchat) or publicly (e.g., posting a comment on a news story) with small groups (e.g., using Slack to communicate with co-workers) or large groups of people (e.g., a public post that goes viral with millions of views). User-generated content must be shared with someone in order for it to be deemed "social."
- **Interaction with Content:** Whether it's radio listeners calling in to a morning show to share their thoughts on a hot topic (old media) or hundreds of thousands of followers commenting on Kim Kardashian's Instagram post, social media typically allows for user-generated content to be interacted with or responded to in some way, be it liking a post, sharing a post, commenting on a post etc. Of course, there are exceptions, like features that allow you to block comments.

Social Spotlight

Earlier in this chapter, we looked at many definitions that describe social media as "internet-enabled" and taking place online with content generated by its users, usually via their mobile devices or computers. But what about content generated and shared not by a phone but via other means, like fashion accessories?

In 2021, Ray-Ban partnered with Facebook to introduce its Stories glasses, sunglasses that can take photos or 30-second videos with neatly hidden with cameras, speakers and microphones. The "smart" glasses even allow users to take calls and listen to audio. "The combined technology makes the total package an easy-to-use device that allows you to be in the moment, racing down a hill, and capture it as well" (Hayes, 2021, para. 2).

By connecting the Ray-Ban branded glasses to the Facebook View app, users can sync photo and video content to their Facebook account. While these social sharing glasses may seem innovative in terms of we gather and share content, they aren't the first smart glasses to partner with a social media giant. Snap Inc. was first to launch its Spectacles smart glasses in 2016 that let users take a photo Snap or record a 10-second video Snap.

The product category of smart glasses isn't slowing down anytime soon as it has grown to include Amazon's Echo Frames with speakers and its Alexa voice assistant, Bose's audio frames, and Razer's gaming glasses.

Time will tell whether or not Ray-Ban's Stories catch on in popularity, but what is certain is that the tools we use to gather and share social media content will continue to evolve, along with social media platforms themselves.

Social Media's Function Across Communications

Now that we've spent some time defining social media, we can now examine its place in the field of communications and its function across different disciplines, such as journalism, advertising, public relations and marketing. While this text specifically examines social media as a function of public relations, it's important to understand the distinct goals of these areas of communications and how they come together to support overall organizational goals.

Journalism

According to the American Press Institute, "Journalism is the activity of gathering, assessing, creating, and presenting news and information. It is also the product of these activities" (American Press Institute, n.d., para. 1). While news may be interesting or entertaining, its primary purpose is to serve as a tool to keep us informed. "The purpose of journalism is thus to provide citizens with the information they need to make the best possible decisions about their lives, their communities, their societies, and their governments" (American Press Institute, n.d., para. 3).

Bill Kovach and Tom Rosenstiel echo these sentiments in their book "The Elements of Journalism: What Newspeople Should Know and the Public

Should Expect," writing, "The primary purpose of journalism is to provide citizens with the information they need to be free and self-governing" (2001, p. 12). The Poynter Institute provides a similar purpose for the field stating, "the central purpose of journalism is to provide citizens with accurate and reliable information they need to function in a free society" (Mitchell, 2022, para. 5).

The Society of Professional Journalists Code of Ethics states, "Ethical journalism strives to ensure the free exchange of information that is accurate, fair and thorough" (n.d., para. 1) and that "the highest and primary obligation of ethical journalism is to serve the public" (n.d., para. 4).

So what is social media's role in journalism? The Associated Press (2022) offers insight with its social media and web-based reporting guidelines.

> With its global and cultural reach, social media is embedded in daily life. It is often the first place people go to share photos, videos and their accounts of major events. Public conversations have migrated onto digital forums. And it's a go-to spot for news consumers. In short, journalists need to pay close attention to social media—and use it wisely.
>
> (p. 378)

According to these guidelines, journalists use social media in their work in a variety of ways:

- To track down sources
- To gather user-generated content like photos or videos
- To get a sense of how people are reacting to an event
- To look for news tips or discussion trends that might lead to a story
- To diversity their sources, including "seeking voices of underrepresented people, groups and communities" (p. 378)
- To directly report news developments to the public
- To promote their work
- To produce and distribute original content that's tailored to a specific platform

Marketing

Marketing is transaction-oriented; it focuses on developing, maintaining and improving a product's market share, attracting customers, and causing a transaction in order to build profitability (Zappala & Carden, 2010). Authors have also defined marketing in the following ways:

> The purpose of marketing is to sell goods and services through attractive packaging, competitive pricing, retail and online promotions, and effective distribution systems. (Wilcox et al., 2016, p. 14)

Marketing is the management function that identifies human needs and wants, offers products and services to satisfy those demands, and causes transactions that deliver products and services to users in exchange for something of value to the provider. (Broom & Sha, 2013, p. 5)

At its core, *marketing* means preparing a product that consumers want and helping them to acquire it. The "marketing mix," meaning everything that might persuade consumers, consists of product design packaging, pricing, product demonstrations, ads and more. The marketing mix even includes the product's name. (Marsh et al., 2018, p. 40)

Marsh et al. (2018) refer to the Four P's of marketing:

- Product (including name, design and packaging)
- Price
- Place (including putting the product where the consumer can buy it)
- Promotion (including tactics from advertising, public relations and sales and marketing)

Social media marketing falls within the fourth P, Promotion, and refers to using social media as a channel to promote the product.

Social media marketing is the use of social media by businesses to increase brand awareness, identify key audiences, generate leads, and build meaningful relationships with customers. Social media marketing should be part of a larger social media strategy that also includes social customer service, community management, and social selling activities.

(Hootsuite, n.d.-b, para. 1)

Public Relations

Public relations is defined by various texts and authors in a multitude of ways:

- "Executives increasingly see public relations not as publicity and one-way communication, but as a complex and dynamic process of negotiation and compromise with a number of key audiences, which are often called 'publics'" (Wilcox et al., 2016, p. 67).
- "Public relations is the management function that establishes and maintains mutually beneficial relationships between an organization and the publics on whom its success or failure depends" (Broom & Sha, 2013, p. 5).
- "Public relations builds goodwill and an understanding of organizational goals among various internal and external publics to help the organization operate smoothly and conduct its business in a cooperative, conflict-free environment" (Zappala & Carden, 2010, p. 4).

While marketing seeks to increase market share in order to meet an organization's economic objectives, public relations is concerned with social capital; it seeks "to build relationships with a variety of publics that can enhance the organization's reputation and establish trust in its policies, products and services" (Wilcox et al., 2016, p. 14).

Goals associated with public relations include creating goodwill, support and mutual understanding. Key terms associated with public relations include deliberate, planned, performance, public interest, two-way communication and strategic management function (Wilcox et al., 2016).

The purpose of public relations writing, specifically, is to communicate information that will influence people.

"Public relations writing succeeds when people respond by doing something your organization wants them to do, whether that be learning something you want them to learn, adopting an attitude or position you want them to adopt, taking a positive action you want them to take, or simply thinking good thoughts about the organization. In the public relations world, writing without such a purpose is a waste of time" (Zappala & Carden, 2010, p. 3).

Social media has become a valuable tool for public relations practitioners to use in building and maintaining mutually beneficial relationships between the organizations they represent and their various publics.

> PR 2.0 is the realization that PR now has an unprecedented opportunity to not only work with traditional journalists, but also engage directly with a new set of accidental influencers. We can now talk with customers directly (through social networks, wikis, micromedia communities, online forums, groups, blogs, and so on). . . . We now have the real ability to put the *public* back into public relations.
>
> (Solis & Breakenridge, 2009, pp. 30–31)

Advertising

Similar to marketing, *advertising* also has the goal of attracting customers but through paid promotional messages that can be controlled (Zappala & Carden, 2010).

> Advertising is information placed in the media by an identified sponsor that pays for the time or space. It is a controlled method of placing messages in the media.
>
> (Broom & Sha, 2013, p. 8)

> Broadly defined, advertising is persuasive communication through purchased media to promote a product, service, or idea on behalf of an identified organization or sponsor.
>
> (Smith, 2017, p. 12)

Publicity, one area of public relations, is *earned media*, meaning it wasn't paid for. "Editors, also known as gatekeepers, make the decision to use the material as a news item and the organization doesn't pay for the placement" (Wilcox et al., 2016, p. 14).

Advertising, on the other hand, is *paid media*, which involves a contracted rate with a media outlet to buy space or time. "An organization writes the content, decides the type and graphics, and controls where and when the advertisement will be used" (Wilcox et al., 2016, p. 14).

When advertisers pay for time or space, they have the ability to control the messaging; public relations practitioners, however, are at the mercy of the media. News organizations choose whether or not to use the information sent to them by PR professionals based on the information's news value. "Publicity is an uncontrolled method of placing messages because the source does not pay the media for placement and cannot guarantee if or how the material will be used" (Universal Accreditation Board, 2017, p. 19).

Social media allows advertisers to reach targeted audiences in a quick and inexpensive way.

"Advertising on social is a hyper-direct way to reach the audience you want. You can target brand new customers or returning ones. (New friends! Hooray!)" (Newberry & McLachlan, 2020, para.

All the major social networks offer advertising options from boosting organic content to photo ads to video ads to story ads to carousel ads to messenger ads and more.

Perspective From the Pros

By Whitney Lehmann

Throughout this text, these "Perspective from the Pros" spotlights feature a variety of communications professionals, including academics, content creators, social media strategists and more who weigh in on chapter topics and lend their expertise and experience.

Since this chapter explores evolving definitions of social media, I thought it was only fitting to hear from our future pros—my social media students.

When asking my students what they consider to be social media, these were some of the responses I received:

- "Any platform where users are able to interact with each other and portray themselves in a way other people can see"
- "A space where people are invited to participate in idea/information sharing and creative exploration, which ultimately combine

to further enhance one's identity and relationships with others through a transcension of physical location boundaries."

- "The public or semi-public archiving of materials that are generated with the intent to engage an audience and/or garner a reaction. Social media can be utilized to represent groups, individuals, and ideas, but overall, it is meant to be a communal experience."
- "An online platform in which a person constructs an online persona. They then generate and interact with curated content based upon their interests or social circle."

As a social media scholar and practitioner, I also thought I'd offer you my own take on social media based on my own personal and professional experiences with social media:

"Social media is a storytelling tool that we can use to connect, curate content, and create identity and culture."

In my opinion, storytelling is and will always be the heart of social media. It's a tool that we use to share stories about ourselves and others, whether that be friends and family, public figures and celebrities, brands and organizations, animals and the environment, our towns, cities, countries, our planet and even other galaxies. Our motives for using social media are varied—from promoting a business, to dating, to connecting with classmates, to creating awareness around a cause, to educating public on a topic, to crowdsourcing for recommendations, to checking in during a crisis, and so much more. While there's no question that why and how we use social media will continue to evolve, I do think the common thread that runs through all types of social media—storytelling—will, and should, always remain.

Chapter Summary

- There is no "correct" or agreed-upon way to define social media. Students, scholars, practitioners and users of social media all define social media differently.
- Most traditional definitions of social media define social media as being "internet-enabled" or a form of "electronic communication" AKA new media.
- Some authors and scholars argue that old media, like print, radio and broadcast, can also constitute social media if they are used socially; for example, radio listeners calling in to give updates to other listeners about an accident on the highway or readers of early newspapers writing in

their own news on a blank back page and then sharing that paper with other households who did the same.

- Popular concepts/key terms associated with definitions and ideas of social media include user-generated content, the sharing of that content either publicly or semi-publicly, with a network of users who have the ability to interact with the content.
- Social media has different functions across different areas of communication. Social media as a function of public relations helps organizations build and maintain mutually beneficial relationships with its publics. Social media as a function of advertising involves using paid spaces to attract customers. Social media as a function of journalism serves as a tool to share information and news. Social media as a function of marketing promotes a product to consumers and helps them acquire it.

Exercise 1.1

Chapter 1 explored various definitions of social media offered by scholars, industry experts, professional organizations and everyday users.

Using peer-reviewed journals, industry sources or news stories quoting, locate a definition of social media that was not introduced in this chapter. Include a citation for the source in APA style.

Compare and contrast the definition you located in Exercise 1.1 with the new media definitions of social media explored in this chapter. How is your definition similar and how is it different?

Exercise 1.2

What is your definition of social media? Does your definition align more with traditional "new media" definitions of social media or with non-traditional definitions, like those offered by Humphreys and Kerpen, that are broader in nature, leaving more room for interpretation? In approximately 250 words, defend your answer.

Discussion Questions

1. Is it possible that definitions of social media will need to change as social media continues to evolve with new platforms and functionalities? Why or why not? If yes, how might our definitions need to adapt?
2. Do you think culture influences our definitions of social media? What types of culture most influence our perceptions of, experiences with and definitions of social media?

References

American Marketing Association. (n.d.). *Social media.* www.ama.org/topics/social-media/

American Press Institute. (n.d.). *What is journalism?* www.americanpressinstitute.org/journalism-essentials/what-is-journalism/

Broom, G. M., & Sha, B.-L. (2013). *Cutlip & Center's effective public relations* (11th ed.). Pearson Education, Inc.

Cambridge Dictionary. (n.d.). *Social media.* https://dictionary.cambridge.org/us/dictionary/english/social-media

Hayes, T. (2021, September 25). Ray-Ban stories: Facebook's camera glasses are the start of smart glasses. *Newsweek.* www.newsweek.com/ray-ban-stories-facebooks-camera-glasses-are-start-smart-glasses-1630818

Hootsuite. (n.d.-a). *User-generated content.* https://blog.hootsuite.com/social-media-definitions/user-generated-content-ugc/

Hootsuite. (n.d.-b). *Social media marketing.* https://blog.hootsuite.com/social-media-definitions/social-media-marketing/#:~:text=Social%20media%20marketing%20is%20the,build%20meaningful%20relationships%20with%20customers

Humphreys, A. (2016). *Social media: Enduring principles.* Oxford University Press.

Kaplan, A. M., & Haenlein, M. (2010). Users of the world, unite! The challenges and opportunities of social media. *Business Horizons, 53*(1), 59–68.

Kerpen, D. (2019). *Likeable social media: How to delight your customers, create and irresistible brand, and be amazing on Facebook, Twitter, LinkedIn, Instagram, Pinterest, and more.* McGraw-Hill.

Kovach, B., & Rosenstiel, T. (2001). *The elements of journalism: What newspeople should know and the public should expect.* Three Rivers Press.

Marsh, C., Guth, D. W., & Poovey Short, B. (2018). *Strategic writing: Multimedia writing for public relations, advertising and more.* Routledge.

Merriam-Webster, Incorporated. (2022). *Social media [Webpage].* www.merriam-webster.com/dictionary/social%20media

Mitchell, B. (2022, August 20). Kovach and Rosenstiel: What is journalism for? *Poynter.* www.poynter.org/archive/2002/kovach-and-rosenstiel-what-is-journalism-for/

Newberry, C., & McLachlan, S. (2020, September 9). Social media advertising 101: How to get the most out of your ad budget. *Hootsuite.* https://blog.hootsuite.com/social-media-advertising/

O'Reilly, T. (2005, September 30). *What is Web 2.0: Design patterns and business models for the next generation of software.* www.oreilly.com/pub/a/web2/archive/what-is-web-20.html

Quesenberry, K. A. (2021). *Social media strategy: Marketing, advertising, and public relations in the consumer revolution.* Rowman & Littlefield.

Smith, R. D. (2017). *Strategic planning for public relations* (5th ed.). Routledge.

Society of Professional Journalists. (n.d.). *SPJ code of ethics.* https://www.spj.org/ethicscode.asp

Solis, B., & Breakenridge, D. (2009). *Putting the public back in public relations: How social media is reinventing the aging business of PR.* FT Press.

The Associated Press. (2020). *The Associated Press stylebook 55th Edition: 2020–2022.* The Associated Press.

The Associated Press. (2022). *The Associated Press stylebook 56th Edition: 2022–2024*. The Associated Press.

Tufts University Relations. (n.d.). *Social media overview*. https://communications.tufts.edu/marketing-and-branding/social-media-overview/

Universal Accreditation Board. (2017). *Study guide for the examination for accreditation in public relations* (4th ed.). Author.

Wikipedia. (n.d.). *Social media*. Retrieved October 15, 2022, from https://en.wikipedia.org/wiki/Social_media

Wilcox, D. L., Cameron, G. T., & Reber, B. H. (2016). *Public relations: Strategies and tactics* (11th ed.). Pearson Education, Inc.

Zappala, J. M., & Carden, A. R. (2010). *Public relations writing worktext: A practical guide for the profession* (3rd ed.). Routledge.

2   Evolution of Social Media

In Chapter 1, we explored the various ways that academics, industry professionals and everyday social media users define social media. While there are certainly commonalities among many definitions, the only true constant in the conversation of defining social media is that there is no one agreed-upon definition. "While brands recognize that social media is a place to share information and to build connections within a community, there often seems to be confusion on what qualifies specifically as *social* media" (Kim, 2021, p. 11).

In addition to reviewing key terms that many definitions have in common, Chapter 1 also pointed out a key distinction—perhaps the largest distinction—that presents itself when comparing and contrasting existing definitions of social media: social media as old media versus new media. Can so-called old media (AKA the media in existence before the introduction of the internet) like newspapers, books, radio, television and movies constitute "social media" or is social media constrained to the more traditional "internet-enabled" definitions that dominate dictionaries, academic journals, social media strategy books and industry publications?

How you choose to answer this question affects the topic of this next chapter—the history and evolution of social media. For those who believe that social media include certain forms of old media, the timeline begins before the invention of the internet but for those who argue that social media are internet-based applications, the starting point begins with the advent of the internet.

In order to fully form an opinion on where you stand on the matter, I think it's important that we examine possible forms of "social media" both pre- and post-internet, along with many other pivotal moments that have influenced the evolution of the field.

What you can expect to learn in this chapter:

- The difference between old and new media
- Examples of social media as old and new media
- Key terms/characteristics shared by most current definitions of social media

DOI: 10.4324/9781003255734-3

- The beginnings of new media with the precursor to the internet called ARPANET
- Early internet milestones such as the first online message, email and webpage
- The creation of the World Wide Web and the evolution from Web 1.0 to Web 2.0
- Participatory culture and early forms of social media

Old Media

So what exactly is *old* media versus *new* media?

> Old media comprise traditional print media—newspapers, magazine and books—and analog broadcast media—TV, radio and films. Starting in the mid 1980s, experts began using the phrase new media to refer to digital media produced using computer-based technologies, distributed via digital platforms and hosted partially or entirely in cyberspace.
>
> (Sterin & Winston, 2018, p. 185)

In the book "Social Media: Enduring Principles," academic Ashlee Humphreys defines social media as "a practice, or set of practices, for using media socially" (Humphreys, 2016, p. 1), putting the emphasis on how we use specific media, rather than the platform itself. Humphreys offers several examples, such as back blank pages of early newspapers that allowed readers to write in their own news and share that news with other households, baseball trading cards, and radio listeners calling in to a live show to give traffic updates to other listeners.

When viewing social media through this lens, the category of what can encompass "social media" broadens from the post-internet age and the applications on our phones and desktops to any form of social media—old *or* new—that allows us to be social. Bulletin boards with job postings, billboards that spark conversation or a call to action, the classified section of newspapers, book clubs, letters to the editor, advice columns and even forms of media that we might never consider—like art and music—could be labeled social media according to this definition. My son's preschool class recently completed a collaborative art project as an orientation activity during the first week of school. Each child was asked to create a personalized apple with their name and information (favorite colors, songs and toys, nicknames, siblings etc.). The teacher added each child's apple to the class tree and then during their morning meeting time, invited the children to learn about one another.

The *New York Times* recently asked readers to submit suggestions for a summer playlist. Melissa Kirsch, an assistant editor for Culture and Lifestyle at The *New York Times*, wrote, "It's an art project with limitless contributors, a way to easily gather the enthusiasms and inspirations from people all over the world. More than just a soundtrack, the collaborative playlist is an engine for discovery" (Kirsch, 2022, para. 3).

Can something as simple as a preschool art project or a collaborative playlist be social media? In theory, or at least according to Humphreys' definition, yes. They are media that are being used socially. In these scenarios, being internet-enabled is no longer a criterion for a medium to be considered social media; the primary consideration is whether or not a medium allows its users to be social.

New Media

Most traditional definitions of social media share a few key criteria: content is user-generated, user-controlled and user-shared, and this exchange takes place via a platform on an internet site (Kim, 2021, p. 11). If these are the core assumptions to consider when defining social media as new media, it's only fitting to begin our conversation with the birth of the internet and the first forms of content that users created and shared using it.

The internet originated in the late 1960s as a U.S. Department of Defense project called ARPANET (Advanced Research Projects Agency Network), nicknamed the "Net," that enabled military and academic researchers to communicate on a distributed network system (Campbell et al., 2019, p. 37). Researchers at major universities around the United States used ARPANET to share their work on defense-related research projects (Sterin & Winston, 2018, p. 187). The experimental computer network linked computers at Pentagon-funded research institutions over telephone lines and became the "forerunner of the internet" (Featherly & Gregersen, 2016, para. 1).

"ARPANET arose from a desire to share information over great distances without the need for dedicated phone connections between each computer on a network" (Featherly & Gregersen, 2016, para. 13). ARPANET created a network system that allowed users from multiple locations to log into a computer whenever they needed to, and it used a system called packet switching to break down messages into smaller components to more easily route them through multiple paths on the network before delivering them (Campbell et al., 2019).

In 1969, a professor of computer science at UCLA and his graduate student sent the first online message from UCLA's computer to another computer at Stanford Research Institute through ARPANET. The message was intended to be "login," however, the system crashed after the second letter was typed. "It took an hour to send the whole word, but by then, "lo" cemented its place in the internet's history" (Bote, 2019, para. 5).

That sparked a revolution in computer networking. New networks formed, connecting universities and research centers across the globe.

But for the next 20 years, the internet wasn't accessible to the public. It was restricted to university and government researchers, students, and private corporations.

(Mozilla, n.d., para. 4)

In 1971, computer engineer Ray Tomlinson developed software to send electronic mail messages to any computer on ARPANET. Tomlinson used the @ symbol to signify the location of the computer user, allowing messages to be targeted at certain users on certain machines. From 1973 to 1977, the Department of Defense under its Advanced Research Projects Agency (ARPA now DAPRA) developed email standards such as to and from fields and the ability to forward an email to others who were not originally recipients (Gibbs, 2016).

From Web 1.0 to Web 2.0

While ARPANET wasn't available to the general public, it wouldn't be long before the network of researchers and universities expanded to everyday users with the creation of the World Wide Web (WWW). In 1989, British scientist Tim Berners-Lee invented the World Wide Web while working at CERN, the European Organization for Nuclear Research, headquartered in Switzerland. Berners-Lee created the World Wide Web as a means of connecting CERN's system to other research institutions like the Massachusetts Institute of Technology (MIT) and Stanford University, which had developed systems for internally sharing information (History.com editors, 2020). The system used hypertext to connect documents on separate computers connected to the internet, and for the first time ever, text documents were linked together over a public network (Fischels, 2021; Mozilla, n.d.). "The web was originally conceived and developed to meet the demand for automated information-sharing between scientists in universities and institutes around the world" (CERN, n.d., para. 1).

In 1991, Berners-Lee published the first web page, which contained information about the World Wide Web Project, (Fischels, 2021; History.com editors, 2020). According to Fischels (2021):

And while perhaps not as exciting or immersive as some of the nearly 1.9 billion websites that exist today, it makes sense that the first web page launched on the good ol' W3 was, well, instructions about how to use it.

(para. 2)

In 1993, CERN put the World Wide Web software in the public domain. Originally called Mesh, the World Wide Web became the first royalty-free, user-friendly browser for navigating the information network that developed into the internet (History.com editors, 2020). "Berners-Lee essentially opened up access to the project to anyone in the world, making it free and (relatively) easy to explore the nascent internet" (History.com editors, para. 3).

"By 1993, the web exploded. Universities, governments, and private corporations all saw opportunity in the open internet" (Mozilla, n.d., para. 7). That same year, American-born software engineer Marc Andreessen created Mosaic, the first web browser to achieve popularity among the general public (Mozilla, n.d.). In 1994, he released Netscape Navigator to the public and officially launched the "browser wars."

> By 1995, Netscape Navigator wasn't the only way to get online. Computer software giant Microsoft licensed the old Mosaic code and built its own window to the web, Internet Explorer. The release sparked a war. Netscape and Microsoft worked feverishly to make new versions of their programs, each attempting to outdo the other with faster, better products.
>
> (Mozilla, n.d., para. 9)

Berners-Lee's development of HTML, HTTP and URLs—the building blocks for creating websites—made it possible for websites to flourish. There were 3,000 websites by 1994 following the WWW entering the public domain and two million websites by the time Google launched as a search engine in 1996 (Fischels, 2021).

> Within a matter of years, Berners-Lee's invention had revolutionized information-sharing and, in doing so, had dramatically altered the way that human beings communicated. The creation and globalization of the web is widely considered one of the most transformational events in human history.
>
> (History.com editors, 2020, para. 4)

The late 1990s and early 2000s introduced new web browsers, including Opera, Safari and Google Chrome (Mozilla, n.d.). This time period also marked the shift of Web 1.0—the first generation of the internet that involved read-only web content—to Web 2.0 with dynamic and user-generated content. From static webpages to now wikis, blogs, Bulletin Board Systems (BBS) and social media, a new era of the internet was born.

Social Media

The participatory culture created by Web 2.0 made social media possible.

> Internet technology experts such as Tim O'Reilly predicted that a more useful Web would emerge, one that would not only be more pervasive in our daily lives, but that would also be driven by us, "we the people." This was the beginning of what eventually became known as Web 2.0.
>
> (Solis & Breakenridge, 2009, p. 29)

Early forms of social media included BBS, blogs, wikis, citizen journalism, Web-based communities such as Yahoo! Groups and other forums, review sites such as Epinions.com, e-commerce like Amazon, and chat services like AOL Instant Messenger. Most traditional timelines examining the history of social media begin with social networking sites (SNS), a specific category of social media with a unique focus on allowing people to "friend" others and share content with them.

> Social networking sites are online communities where people can interact with friends, family, coworkers, acquaintances and others with similar interests. Most social networking sites are Web-based and provide many ways for their users to interact, such as chat, messaging, email, video, voice chat, file-sharing, blogging and discussion groups. . . . Social networking sites provide an immediate and personal way to deliver programs, products and information to individuals or friends within your personal network.
>
> (Centers for Disease Control and Prevention, 2017, para. 1)

Early social networking sites included Classmates.com (1995), SixDegrees.com (1997), Friendster (2002), Myspace (2003), LinkedIn (2003) and Facebook (2004). Other forms of social media gained popularity following social networking sites, including photo-sharing sites like Photobucket and Flickr, social bookmarking sites like del.ici.ous and Pinterest, content-management systems (CMS) like WordPress and Blogger, content-sharing sites like YouTube and Instagram, microblogs like Twitter and Tumblr, location-sharing sites like FourSquare, e-commerce sites like Etsy and Polyvore, dating platforms like Match.com and eHarmony, streaming apps like Meerkat and Periscope, and invitation-only platforms like Google+ among others.

Today, the types of social media we use have evolved to include payment platforms (e.g, Venmo), neighborhood networks (e.g., Nextdoor), politically driven platforms (e.g., Parler and Truth Social), and audio-only apps (e.g., Clubhouse), among others. Chapter 3: Categories of Social Media will explore different types, or categories, of social in more detail.

Perspective From the Pros

By Michael Laderman

So it's the mid-2000s—figure 2005 or 2006—and, at this point in time of my career, I'm overseeing the communications and marketing teams for Barry University in Miami Shores. I have a vacant communications coordinator position on my team that I am trying to fill, and so I lined up in-person interviews with a few candidates and then, of the ones that I liked, asked them to take a simple typing test. Literally one of those free tests that you can still find online, one that measures your accuracy and speed.

Now, for the vacant position, knowing how to type well was a crucial part of the job. And, quite frankly, a few years earlier, I had learned my lesson as a supervisor when I filled another communications position with someone who I had just assumed could type—only to find out that they could not.

Needless to say, as leader of the department, I felt the test was necessary.

However, not everybody felt the same way.

See, one of the candidates made it a point of telling me—politely, while in-person—that she found such a test insulting . . . just before she scored poorly on it. Very poorly on it.

The kicker, though, that truly eliminated her from contention was what she posted publicly on her Facebook page—while she was still a candidate, mind you. She spoke harshly of both me and the university for insulting her by taking a test that she felt she should not have had to take, and for not just trusting her and her word.

Not that it went viral, but her post was public—and was seen by many colleagues.

Even though those were the early days of social media, I expected better from someone applying for a position on my public relations and marketing team. A lapse into misguided judgment on social media led her into missing, at least, one early opportunity in her life. And in airing her grievances publicly on her social media pages, in a complete lack of professionalism and decency, this candidate cost herself a chance at a job that she had initially wanted. [A job that, coincidentally, went to another candidate, one named Whitney Sessa.]

I do truly hope she learned something. And as social media has evolved from those early years of Facebook and MySpace, I hope she, too, evolved with it—as a person, as a candidate and as an entry-level employee entering the communications field.

But in looking at my Twitter feed just a few moments ago, and seeing the nastiness that permeates its walls coming from the likes of your average working-class professional, all under the false protection of believing we are invincible behind our own keyboards, I wonder:

While social media has evolved since the mid-2000s, have *we*?

—30-

The Future of the Internet and Social Media

In the last 30 years, we've witnessed Web 1.0 and the early days of the internet evolve from static webpages, the read-only web and a mostly passive experience to Web 2.0 with participatory culture, user-created content, interactive webpages and more than five billion regular users, more than half of the world's population (Ashmore, 2022). Web 2.0 introduced, and continues to introduce, different forms of social media from online Bulletin Board Systems (BBS), Wikis, blogs and social networking sites to microblogs, content-sharing sites, streaming sites, payment platforms, dating apps, review sites, bookmarking sites, audio apps and more. Smartphones soon followed the emergence of social media, and the first iPhone was released in 2007.

In order to predict where social media may head next, it makes most sense to start with the future of the web, since the internet is where social media started. The internet of the future, some say, is Web 3.0, also known as Web3. If Web 1.0 represented the static read-only Web, and Web 2.0 represents the dynamic read/write Web, then Web 3.0 could represent the "read/write/own" upgrade (Ashmore, 2022, para. 11).

While there isn't a precise, agreed-upon definition of Web 3.0, the core principles of this internet upgrade focus on decentralization, token-based economies and blockchain. The tech giants like Google, Amazon, Facebook and Twitter that amassed power with Web 2.0 would relinquish some of that power to the everyday user with new social networks, search engines and marketplaces that have no big companies or central authorities controlling them. It eliminates the middlemen on the internet.

> This vision of Web3 tends to be a more democratic version of today's online world. It's centered around the idea of ownership, removing control from the dominant big data companies and other central authorities and handing it to the masses. This is what's meant by decentralization. Decentralization means internet users can transact business peer-to-peer, cutting out intermediaries and removing power from controlling entities. There is a greater focus on user privacy, transparency and ownership.
>
> (Ashmore, 2022, para. 13)

W3 is built upon a system called the blockchain, a digital record-keeping system that records transactions. Instead of being operated by a corporation, it's operated by users collectively, who are given "tokens" for participating. "In a Web3 world, people control their own data and bounce around from social media to email to shopping using a single personalized account, creating a public record on the blockchain of all of that activity" (Allyn, 2021 para. 9).

While W3 is creating conversation with its decentralization and ownership-for-all model, it still has its critics, especially among members of the current tech elite.

> Last week on Twitter, Jack Dorsey trashed the buzzy tech trend known as Web3, telling consumers to be wary and dismissing it as a tool for venture capitalists hyping cryptocurrency. Tim O'Reilly, the author who coined the phrase Web 2.0 back in 2004, also warned this month it was too early to get excited about Web3. Time Magazine's Person of the Year, Elon Musk, trolled simply, 'Web3 sounds like bs.'"
>
> (Patterson, 2022, para. 1)

Some experts argue that if W3 does take off, it will operate alongside Web 2.0—not replace it. "In other words, blockchain-based social networks, transactions and businesses can and will grow and thrive in the coming years. Yet knocking out Facebook, Twitter or Google completely is not likely on the horizon, according to technology scholars" (Allyn, 2021, para. 22).

While it's unclear just yet whether or not W3 will become our new norm, what is clear is that this next iteration of the internet would affect the trajectory and future of social media, just like the current iteration that created it.

Social Spotlight

So what does the future of social media look like? According to Meta, the parent company of Facebook, Instagram and What's App, it's AR and VR, or Augmented Reality and Virtual Reality. The company has spent billions on the construction of the metaverse, an "immersive digital world of virtual and augmented reality" (Mac, 2022, para. 4).

In 2021, CEO Mark Zuckerberg announced that Facebook was changing its name to Meta, reflecting the company's growing aspirations beyond social media. In an announcement posted to its newsroom, the newly rebranded company reported:

> The metaverse will feel like a hybrid of today's online social experiences, sometimes expanded into three dimensions or projected into the physical world. It will let you share immersive experiences with other people even when you can't be together—and do things together you couldn't do in the physical world. It's the next evolution in a long line of social technologies, and it's ushering in a new chapter for our company.
>
> (Meta, 2021, para. 2)

The name change interestingly came in the wake of a historic crisis for the company when whistleblower Frances Haugen, a former data scientist at Facebook, testified before a Senate subcommittee and said that Facebook harms children and allows hates speech, misinformation and other threats to the public in its pursuit of growth and profits.

In her opening testimony, Haugen said:

> I'm here today because I believe Facebook's products harm children, stoke division and weaken our democracy. The company's leadership knows how to make Facebook and Instagram safer but won't make the necessary changes because they have put their astronomical profits before people.
>
> (Milmo & Paul, 2021, para. 6)

While Meta has dedicated billions of dollars to its Reality Labs Division and assigned thousands of employees to the project, Zuckerberg said that the company's VR and AR efforts represent only 20% of its investment portfolio (Mac, 2022; Mac et al., 2022).

Will Meta's new moniker and investment pay off? It's too early to tell, although critics have pointed out the company's efforts have had a rocky start with the company's flagship virtual-reality game "buggy and unpopular," Meta executives butting heads over the metaverse's strategy and even employees confused and frustrated by the frequent strategy shifts tied to the Zuckerberg's pet project (Mac et al., 2022, para. 3).

According to Microsoft, however, the metaverse could represent the next iteration of the internet.

> The metaverse will not fundamentally replace the internet, but instead, build upon and iteratively transform it. It is a logical evolution of the internet. Just like fixed-line internet ushered in the age of personal computing and mobile internet increased the proliferation of content and access to the internet, the metaverse will place everyone inside a "virtual" version of the internet on a continuous basis. It will enable us to constantly be "within" the internet, creating more immediate experiences.
>
> (Catzel, 2022, para. 9)

Chapter Summary

- A person's accepted definition of social media and whether they consider social media to be a form of old media and/or new media will influence their perception of where the "timeline" of social media begins. For those who believe that social media include certain forms of old media, the timeline begins before the invention of the internet but for those who argue that social media are internet-based applications, the starting point begins with the advent of the internet.

- Old media comprise traditional print media—newspapers, magazines and books—and analog broadcast media—TV, radio and films. New media refers to technologies, distributed via digital platforms and hosted partially or entirely in cyberspace.
- Most timelines of social media begin with the birth of the internet, Web 2.0 and early forms of social media: Wikis, blogs, bulletin board systems, social networking sites and web-based communities.
- Conversations about the future of social media largely focus on Web 3.0, the next predicted phase of the internet that features decentralization, token-based economies and blockchain.

Exercise 1.1

In this chapter, we examined how the timeline of social media has different starting points depending upon what one considers to be social media (e.g., old media vs. new media). We also examined how our interpretation of social media can affect whether we include certain milestones when tracing the history of social media (e.g., social networking sites vs. other categories of social media).

Select four to six social media milestones that you feel best represent the timeline/journey of social media. Using an infographic maker of your choice (e.g., Canva, Adobe templates and PowerPoint), create an infographic to showcase the milestones you've selected by creating your own timeline of social media.

Exercise 1.2

Meta, the parent company of Facebook and Instagram, is investing in AR/VR, because it believes it's the future of social media. What are other social media giants investing in as the future of social media? Do you agree? Why or why not? In approximately 250 words, defend your answer. Cite your sources in APA style both in-text and with a Reference list.

Discussion Questions

1. Some scholars, such as Ashlee Humphries, make the argument that certain forms of old media can be considered social media, because they involve the practice of using media socially. Do you agree? Why or why not?
2. In your opinion, which moment on the timeline of social media was most impactful in the evolution of social media and why?

References

Allyn, B. (2021, November 21). People are talking about Web3. Is it the internet of the future or just a buzzword? *NPR.* www.npr.org/2021/11/21/1056988346/web3-internet-jargon-or-future-vision

Ashmore, D. (2022, August 26). A brief history of Web 3.0. *Forbes.* www.forbes.com/advisor/investing/cryptocurrency/what-is-web-3-0/

Bote, J. (2019, October 29). The internet is now 50 years old. The first online message? It was a typo. *USA Today.* www.usatoday.com/story/tech/2019/10/29/first-internet-message-sent-50-years-ago-ucla-using-darpa/4062337002/

Campbell, R., Martin, C. R., & Fabos, B. (2019). *Media & culture: Mass communication in a digital age.* Bedford/St. Martins.

Catzel, D. (2022, November 29). The metaverse: An evolution in transportation, travel and hospitality. *Microsoft Industry Blogs.* https://cloudblogs.microsoft.com/industry-blog/automotive/2022/11/29/the-metaverse-an-evolution-in-transportation-travel-and-hospitality/

Centers for Disease Control and Prevention. (2017, April 3). *Social networking.* www.cdc.gov/socialmedia/tools/SocialNetworking.html

CERN. (n.d.). *The birth of the web.* https://home.cern/science/computing/birth-web

Featherly, K., & Gregersen, E. (2016, May 11). ARPANET: United States defense program. *Britannica.* www.britannica.com/topic/ARPANET/additional-info#history

Fischels, J. (2021, August 6). A look back at the very first website ever launched, 30 years later. *NPR.* www.npr.org/2021/08/06/1025554426/a-look-back-at-the-very-first-website-ever-launched-30-years-later

Gibbs, S. (2016, March 7). How did email grow from messages between academics to a global epidemic? *The Guardian.* www.theguardian.com/technology/2016/mar/07/email-ray-tomlinson-history

History.com Editors. (2020, March 30). World Wide Web (WWW) launches into public domain. *History.* www.history.com/this-day-in-history/world-wide-web-launches-in-public-domain

Humphreys, A. (2016). *Social media: Enduring principles.* Oxford University Press.

Kim, C. M. (2021). *Social media campaigns: Strategies for public relations and marketing.* Routledge, Taylor & Francis Group.

Kirsch, M. (2022, August 20). The morning: The ultimate summer playlist. *The New York Times.* www.nytimes.com/2022/08/20/briefing/the-ultimate-summer-playlist.html

Mac, R. (2022, November 30). Mark Zuckerberg defends company's push into the metaverse, where he appeared with a bout of hiccups. *The New York Times.* www.nytimes.com/2022/11/30/business/dealbook/zuckerberg-metaverse-hiccups.html

Mac, R., Frankel, S., & Roose, K. (2022, October 9). Skepticism, confusion, frustration: Inside Mark Zuckerberg's Metaverse Struggles. *The New York Times.* www.nytimes.com/2022/10/09/technology/meta-zuckerberg-metaverse.html

Meta. (2021, October 28). *Introducing meta: A social technology company.* https://about.fb.com/news/2021/10/facebook-company-is-now-meta/

Milmo, D., & Paul, K. (2021, October 5). Facebook harms children and is damaging democracy, claims whistleblower. *The Guardian.* www.theguardian.com/technology/2021/oct/05/facebook-harms-children-damaging-democracy-claims-whistleblower

Mozilla. (n.d.). *The history of web browsers.* www.mozilla.org/en-US/firefox/browsers/browser-history/

Patterson, D. (2022, January 3). Explaining Web3: From the blockchain and crypto to NFTs and the metaverse. *CBS News.* www.cbsnews.com/news/web3-blockchain-crypto-nft-metaverse-explainer/

Solis, B., & Breakenridge, D. (2009). *Putting the public back in public relations: How social media is reinventing the aging business of PR.* FT Press.

Sterin, J. C., & Winston, T. (2018). *Mass media revolution.* Routledge.

3 Categories of Social Media

In Chapter 1, we explored a multitude of ways that academics, industry professionals and everyday social media users define social media. In this chapter, we'll explore an additional way to define and describe social media—by category or type.

Is Instagram a content-sharing site or a photo-sharing app? Or is it now considered a disappearing content-app now that it has Stories? Does the ability to "slide into someone's DMs" make it a social networking site? Or what about Instagram Live? Isn't that streaming? Maybe it's all of the above or none of the above now that it has Reels and short-form video content?

The copycatting trend among the social media giants where they compete with one another to add endless features and functionalities has us all scratching our heads.

> Companies are always eyeing their competitors to see what works; that's just market research. But copycatting on social media has led to platforms that look suspiciously similar, with fewer things that set them apart. It's harder to know what any given platform is *for* when they all do the same thing. Which major platform has a news feed, disappearing posts, private messaging, and a live broadcasting feature? That would be . . . all of them. This sickening homogeny of social media even extends to design: every Stories replicant uses those little circles; every TikTok clone uses the swipe-up-to-scroll. The biggest differentiator is that they all call their Xeroxed features by different names, leading to the maddening vocabulary of social media.
>
> (Padres, 2020, para. 3)

Establishing set, agreed-upon social media categories is one dilemma; deciding where to then place a platform is another. Let's examine how social media pros navigate the name game.

What you can expect to learn in this chapter:

- The purpose of a social media type/category/genre
- Why social media types/categories matter

DOI: 10.4324/9781003255734-4

- Social media types/categories offered by authors, academics and industry leaders
- Definition of the most widely accepted social media categories and examples of social platforms that fall within those categories
- Social media platforms with the most global active monthly users
- What is considered a "hybrid" category
- How to assign a social media platform to a social media category
- Why we should challenge ourselves to keep evolving the categories we use to describe and classify social media

What Is a Social Media Type or Category?

Before we can jump into how we can assign a social media platform to a specific category, let's start by establishing what is meant by a social media *type* or *category*. The terms are often used interchangeably when describing ways that we can classify, or group together, social media based on a common characteristic. We'll take more about one specific characteristic—inherent purpose—later in this chapter when we discuss *how* to assign social media platforms to specific categories.

Social media scholar Ashlee Humphreys (2016) uses the term "genre" to describe categories or types of social media, writing, "A genre is a particular set of conventions within a form," "a form is the type of media that results from a particular technology" and "a technology is a material configuration that allows for the production or reception of media" (pp. 31–32).

Using these definitions, the technology would be the internet; the form would be social media; and genres would be the categories or types of social media that exist.

Why Do We Need Social Media Categories?

In the early days of the internet, social media was limited to wikis, blogs, Bulletin Board Systems (BBS) and nascent social networking sites like SixDegrees.com, and it was relatively easy to navigate the social media landscape before we ever even used the term "social media." As Web 2.0 evolved with interactive content, new social networking sites and eventually new types of social media, brands began creating a presence online, and the need for social media strategists and managers was born.

Today, there are countless options for how organizations can connect with their publics online and create conversation with them via social media; therefore, it's crucial that we, as social media and public relations practitioners, are as strategic as possible when it comes to curating a social media lineup for the organizations we represent, so that we can cut through the clutter to meet them online where they already are with content that creates value for them.

> Should you focus on photos? Videos? Blogs? What about forums? And, once you have your content, how do you want to roll it out? You could post on community review sites or live-stream it to the masses. Understanding these different types of social media will help you develop a better content strategy and know where to focus your time and energy.
>
> (Teves, 2022, para. 2)

Established Types/Categories of Social Media

Just as how there's no single agreed-upon definition for social media, there's also no agreed-upon set of categories. Depending upon the author, expert or user you ask, you'll hear different categories for how we can classify different types of social media.

Let's begin by examining how some social media scholars curate lists of categories. Humphreys (2016) lists genres of social media as Social Network Sites, blogs, message boards or forums, chatrooms, feeds, content sharing and hybrid forms. Fuchs (2014) categorizes social media into social networking sites, video-sharing sites, blogs, wikis and microblogs. Kaplan and Haenlein (2010) list collaborative projects, blogs, content communities, social networking sites, virtual game worlds and virtual social worlds. Luttrell and Wallace (2021) cite the Social Media Pyramid, developed by academic and author Randy Hlavac, which ranks six types of social media, including social networking sites, news aggregators, passion connections, video connections, thought leaders and virtual communities.

Industry leaders are also on different pages when it comes to curating a list of category names. Sprout Social, for example, says there are "14 types of social media every marketer should know," with its must-know categories, including social networking sites, photo and image sharing sites, video sharing sites, audio sharing, live streaming apps, social messaging apps, disappearing content apps, social shopping networks, interactive social media apps, discussion forums, microblogging platforms, community blogging sites, social review sites, and social curation and bookmarking sites (Teves, 2022). Another industry resource, Hootsuite, promotes "9 Types of Social Media and How Each Can Benefit Your Business" with social audio platforms and formats, video social media platforms and formats, disappearing content formats, discussion forms, shoppable social media platforms and features, social media live streams, business social media platforms, closed/private community social media platforms and inspirational social media platforms (Wong, 2021).

Indeed.com, the No. 1 job site in the world, leads with the headline "What are the Different Types of Social Media? 10 Key Types" and lists social networking sites, discussion forums, image-sharing networks, book-marking networks, blogging and publishing networks, consumer review networks, interest-based networks, sharing economy networks, social shopping networks and video hosting platforms (Indeed Editorial Team, 2022b).

While no two lists are the same, there are commonalities that we can use to examine, define and describe some of the most accepted categories:

Social Networking Sites

Social Networking Sites (SNS) are created for the purpose of making social connections, whether those connections be friendly (e.g., Facebook "Friends"), romantic/sexual (e.g., "Matches" on dating sites/apps) and/or professional in nature (e.g., LinkedIn "Connections").

Popular definitions offered for SNS include:

- "Web-based services that allow users to (1) construct a public or semi-public profile within a bounded system, (2) articulate a list of other users with whom they share a connection, and (3) view and traverse their list of connections and those made by others within the system" (Boyd & Ellison, 2007, p. 211).
- "An online platform allowing people to build social networks or social relationships with other people who share similar interests" (Luttrell & Wallace, 2021, p. 197).
- "Any website where one connects with those sharing personal or professional interests" (Quesenberry, 2021, p. 462).
- "Applications that enable users to connect by creating personal information profiles, inviting friends and colleagues to have access to those profiles, and sending e-mails and instant messages between each other" (Kaplan & Haenlein, 2010, p. 63).
- "Social networking sites allow people to connect with each other through a shared online space. Users can like, share, comment on posts and follow other users and businesses" (Teves, 2022, para. 4).

Examples of social networking sites include Classmates.com (1995), SixDegrees.com (1996), Ryze (2001), Friendster (2002), LinkedIn (2003), hi5 (2003), MySpace (2003), Orkut (2004), Facebook (2004), Yahoo! 360 Degrees (2005), Bebo (2005) and Google + (2011) (Ngak, 2011).

Facebook and LinkedIn continue to dominate the SNS category. In 2022, Facebook had roughly three billion monthly active users, making it the world's largest social media site (Lua, n.d.). In 2021, Facebook was also the platform that U.S. users spent the most time on per day (Dixon, 2022). LinkedIn is the world's largest professional network with more than 875 million members in more than 200 countries and territories worldwide (Linked, n.d.).

Content-Sharing Sites

Content-sharing sites were created for the primary purpose of sharing content, originally photo and video content, and now a relatively new category of content called disappearing content. Video content is further delineated by short-form video content and long-form video. In addition to photo and video content, Kaplan and Haenlein (2010) include text and PowerPoint presentations as forms of media and offer the term "content communities," writing:

> The main objective of content communities is the sharing of media content between users. Content communities exist for a wide range of different media types, including text (e.g., BookCrossing, via which 750,000+ people from over 130 countries share books), photos (e.g., Flickr), videos (e.g., YouTube), and PowerPoint presentations (e.g., Slideshare).
>
> (p. 63)

With the different forms of photo and video media that now comprise content, some authors, experts and industry resources suggest creating separate social media categories to cater to each type. Sprout Social, for example, refers to these categories as photo- and image-sharing sites, video-sharing sites, and disappearing content apps (Teves, 2022).

Indeed refers to photo and image-sharing sites as "image-sharing networks" and says, "These social media sites let people share photos and related content. They offer a platform to start conversations, inspire creativity, make products seem more appealing and encourage customers to talk about your brand" (Indeed Editorial Team, 2022b, para. 11). Examples of photo-sharing sites are Instagram, Flickr and Photobucket. In terms of monthly active users, Instagram is the world's fourth-largest social platform with two billion monthly active users (Lua, n.d.).

For video-related content, Sprout Social (Teves, 2022) and Fuchs (2014) refer to "video-sharing sites," while Hootsuite (Wong, 2021) uses the term "video social media platforms and formats" and Luttrell and Wallace (2021) say "video connection sites." Indeed wrote:

> Video sharing sites are websites that allow people and companies to upload or live stream their videos. Users can then search for videos by keyword or topic. The content on these sites can be available to the public or to private or invited audiences. Many video sharing sites use income from advertisements to support their platforms. They might also offer revenue sharing to users whose videos get lots of views.
>
> (Indeed Editorial Team, 2022a)

Popular video-sharing sites include YouTube, TikTok and Vimeo. YouTube is the world's second-largest social media site, not far behind Facebook, with 2.2 billion active users. YouTube users can upload videos that are up to 15 minutes long, and verified accounts can upload videos longer than 15 minutes (YouTube Help, n.d.). YouTube rolled out its Shorts feature globally in 2021, an option that allows content creators to convert segments of their existing long-form content into Shorts variations that are up to 60 seconds long (Ceci, 2022).

Launched in 2016, TikTok quickly became one of the most popular social platforms and video apps among global users and recently surpassed Google as the most visited internet site (Lua, n.d.; Statista, 2022). In 2022, TikTok had one billion monthly active users.

According to LinkedIn, short-form video content refers to any video content that is under 10 minutes in duration, and long-form video content refers to videos that are over 10 minutes in duration (Bolton, 2022). Short-form video first became popular with the Twitter-owned short-form video app Vine and its six-second looping videos in 2012. TikTok, which started as Musical.ly in 2014, followed in Vine's footsteps with its short-form video content, and other platforms added features catering to the short-form video trend like Reels on Facebook and Instagram and Shorts on Tube. In 2020, former Vine co-founder Dom Hofman launched the TikTok competitor Byte, a short-form video app that allows users to create looping six-second video content (Amore, 2020; Hootsuite, n.d.-b). In the Forbes article "Five Insights Into The Popularity of Short-Form Video Content," author Victor Potrel wrote (2022):

> Now, short-form content's popularity is rapidly rising. Many people, especially younger generations, are watching videos that are less than one minute long. Major social media platforms are now offering opportunities to create short content. This can make video content more accessible for viewers and content creators.
>
> (para. 3)

Short-form video content isn't getting all the love, however. YouTube's numbers clearly don't lie, and other platforms want a piece of the pie. In 2021, Instagram video replaced IGTV, allowing users to upload content up to 60 minutes long, and in 2022, TikTok announced an update that users would be able to post videos up to 10 minutes long.

> At that time, TikTok's product manager Drew Kirchhoff said that while creators were skilled in tying multi-part stories together, they often shared that they desired more time to show cooking demos, beauty tutorials, educational lessons and the like on the platform.
>
> (Golob, 2022)

Disappearing content, also known as ephemeral content, first became popular with the launch of Snapchat in 2011, but now other platforms like Instagram, Facebook, WhatsApp and Twitter offer similar features (Teves, 2022). Known as Snaps (Snapchat) and/or Stories (Facebook, Instagram, LinkedIn, Pinterest, Snapchat and YouTube), disappearing content refers to "a social post that vanishes after a set amount of time, usually 24 hours" (Hootsuite, n.d.-c).

Social Spotlight

Social media have come a long way since the early days of the internet that brought us blogs, wikis, online Bulletin Board Systems (BBS) and the very first social networking sites. As we advance through this millennium, there's no question that social media will continue to evolve and that *we*, as people, will continue to evolve along with our motivations for using social media.

As the social media landscape changes, we may need to re-think not only the way we define social media but also the categories we use to classify them.

TikTok, for example, is traditionally considered a video-sharing platform, however, it's also gaining widespread popularity as a search engine. Yes, that's right: a search engine. Watch out, Google. There's a new search engine in town.

TikTok has had an interesting evolution in itself, originally launching as Musical.ly in 2014 as an app for people to share their short-lip sync videos. In 2018, TikTok absorbed Musical.ly, and Musical.ly accounts were automatically migrated to TikTok. The short-form video app originally allowed users to post videos up to one minute in duration and then eventually three minutes, before increasing the time limit again in early 2022 to 10 minutes (Rosenblatt, 2022).

By the fall of 2022, it became clear that the popular video-sharing app once known for its dance videos and pop music was being used for an additional reason: to search. In August 2022, Adweek published a news story titled "Move Over Google. TikTok is the Go-To Search Engine for Gen Z" and a month later the *New York Times* posted an article titled "For Gen Z, TikTok is the New Search Engine" (Huang, 2022; Pogue, 2022).

Adweek reported that 40% of Gen Zers said they preferred using TikTok and Instagram for searching over Google. For nearly two decades, Google has dominated consumer search behavior. Google has even become a verb. So this shift in behavior is indicative of a much larger shift happening across the internet (Pogue, 2022, para. 2).

Gen Z uses the app to search for everything from restaurant reviews to how-to videos to fashion trends and in everything between. What's the appeal? Gen Z prioritizes authentic content, and they prefer visual content over the written word, making TikTok a search slam dunk. Another appealing feature among this digital native generation? Unlike Google, TikTok doesn't provide exact search matches.

> For example, the search results for "feta cheese" on TikTok are very different from the results for "feta cheese" on Google, which is why this audience is attracted to TikTok and finds it more useful. A hashtag or search on TikTok will also generate culturally relevant elements like music, people and live events and can be filtered based on likes and views. This, in turn, yields a different set of videos that consumers can continue to relate to.
>
> (Pogue, 2022, para. 8)

Searching on TikTok is also a more interactive experience than the text-based experience with Google. According to Huang (2022):

> Instead of just slogging through walls of text, Gen Z-ers crowd-source recommendations from TikTok videos to pinpoint what they are looking for, watching video after video to cull the content. Then they verify the veracity of a suggestion based on comments posted in response to the videos.
>
> (para. 12)

TikTok's growing popularity as a search engine represents a larger shift in digital search, Huang (2022) wrote, noting that while Google remains the world's dominant search engine, people are increasingly using social media, in addition to TikTok, to search: Amazon to search for products, Instagram to stay updated on trends, and Snapchat Maps to find local businesses.

As more and more users turn to social media to search, do we need now need to add "search engine" to accepted lists of social media categories?

Live Streaming Sites

Live-streaming apps, also called social media live streams, allow users to share real-time video with their followers. Luttrell (2019) defines live streaming as "streaming of video or audio so that users can experience an event together live via the web" (p. 223). Meerkat was the first app to kick off the streaming craze in 2015 and was followed by Twitter's Periscope, which shut down in 2021.

> Periscope became everyone's favorite, easy-to-use app for streaming and watching live events. Getting showered with "hearts" anytime you hit the record button was pretty much all the incentive anyone needed to try it out. It was so popular that Apple awarded the app the iOS app of the year in 2015.
>
> (Samur, 2018, para. 65)

Twitch launched as the newest streaming-based app in 2011. Facebook, Instagram, LinkedIn, Twitter, YouTube and TikTok eventually added features to "go live."

> From *Saturday Night Live* and the Super Bowl to celebrity slaps at the Oscars, there's no denying the thrill of watching events unfold in real time. You just never know what could happen. That's why social media live streaming is so appealing to viewers and why content creators should be getting in on the action.
>
> (Kutuchief, 2022, para. 1)

Livestreaming surged in popularity during the COVID pandemic when people were stuck at home amid lockdowns, closures and quarantines and seeking out more authentic, less polished and perfect content that reflected the times.

> Disappearing posts like those pioneered by Snapchat have been particularly useful, since they lower the bar for how good or polished content had to be. Similarly, many people took to live-streaming on various platforms, where their unedited, real-time posts felt immediate and more authentic.
>
> (Molla, 2021, para. 42)

Audio-Sharing Sites

The pandemic also introduced audio-sharing sites as people sought out easier ways to consume content. Clubhouse kicked off the audio craze in March 2020 as an invite-only social audio app. Users enter "Rooms," where they can listen to and participate in conversations about different topics.

> Every now and then, a new social media app comes along that changes the way we create and consume content. Snapchat did it with disappearing content, then TikTok did it with short-form videos. In 2020, Clubhouse did it with social audio.
>
> (Cyca, 2022, para. 1)

Clubhouse's popularity spurred other social media platforms to develop their own versions, such as Twitter Spaces, Facebook Live Audio Rooms, Spotify Greenroom, and Amazon's Project Mic, which was announced in 2021 but not released as of 2022.

Blogs

Blogs are one of the earliest forms of social media that originated with Web 2.0. Hootsuite (n.d.-a) defines a blog as the following:

> Originally a contraction of the phrase "web log," a blog is a type of digital publication in which one or more authors regularly post content, generally on a specific topic. Many brands use a blog as a way to share engaging content with their audience and establish their industry expertise.
>
> (para. 1)

Blogs are updated and organized in reverse, chronological order, with the most recent entry appearing first. They are typically written by a single author, although multi-author blogs are also popular that feature a variety of authors publishing different entries around a common theme, for example, a curated group of experts and professionals who can share their ideas on social media (Humphreys, 2016).

Blogs can be used as a form of personal expression or for more formal organizational communication. For example, the blog published by Hootsuite, a global leader in social media management, shares valuable content about social media marketing and how to use social tools.

Forbes named the "Best Blogging Platforms in 2022" as WordPress, Wix, Weebly, Drupal, Squarespace, CMS Hub and Medium (Haan & Main, 2022). Sprout Social also lists Community Blogging Platforms among its list of "14 Types of Social Media" and differentiates community blogs from traditional blogs (Teves, 2022):

> Community blogging sites are platforms where people can come together to write articles, share ideas and collaborate on projects. Most community blogging sites focus on a specific niche or topic, which makes them a great resource for finding new content ideas and connecting with other like-minded individuals. They also tend to have very engaged users, which can be beneficial for promoting your brand or product.
>
> (para. 37)

Sprout Social lists Medium, GrowthHackers, BlogEngage and DoSplash as examples of community blogging sites.

Microblogs

Quesenberry (2021) defines microblogging as "a form of traditional blogging where the content is smaller in both file size and length of content" (p. 455). Similarly, Hootsuite defines microblogging as "the practice of publishing short content updates to platforms such as Twitter and Tumblr" (Hootsuite, n.d.-d).

Twttr—eventually renamed Twitter—was released to the general public in 2006 and created the microblogging category by allowing users to tweet in 140 characters or less and, later, up to 280 characters. Tumblr followed in 2007 and allowed users to curate pictures, videos and text and "reblog" their friends on their "tumblelogs" (Samur, 2018). "Soon after, the term microblogging became widely used to describe both Twitter and Tumblr, which both allowed users to 'exchange small elements of content such as short sentences, individual images, or video links'" (Samur, 2018, para. 28).

While Twitter dominates the microblog category, amassing over 400 million monthly active users in 2022, Tumblr, Pinterest and LinkedIn have also become popular choices for microblogging (Teves, 2022).

Following Elon Musk's purchase of Twitter, which was finalized in October 2022, more than one million users migrated to another microblog called Mastodon, which launched in 2016 (Snider, 2022). Mastodon is an open-source platform that looks similar to Twitter but has been described as more complex.

> Similar to Twitter, it offers microblogging capabilities, but while you can easily pinpoint some similarities to Twitter's web and mobile applications, they're not quite the same. A better (but still incomplete) analogy is Mastodon is what you get if you were to combine Twitter and Tumblr. Instead of tweeting, you *post*, and if you share someone else's post, you've *reblogged* or *boosted* it. There are hashtags and lists, and you have up to 5,000 words to express yourself—as well as the ability to add GIFs, videos, and images.
>
> (Oladipo, 2022, para. 6–7)

As of November 2022, Mastodon had nearly two million users (Snider, 2022).

In 2009, the Chinese technology company Sina Corporation launched its version of Twitter called Weibo. "If you want to go viral on social media or gain a mass audience in China, get on Weibo, China's Twitter and now the country's most popular microblogging site" (Ren, 2018, para. 1).

Bookmarking Sites

Bookmarking sites allow users to discover, save, comment on and share different types of web content (articles, posts, links, ideas, etc.).

> There was a time, many, many years ago, when people got their information from flipping through printed papers, commonly known as

books, and they'd mark their spot with something called a 'bookmark'. . . . No, but seriously—in the age of the internet, it's tough to keep track of all your social media posts, windows, tabs and apps, and tougher still to remember where you left that article you were saving for later. And readers of your site likely have the same problem. That's where social bookmarking comes in.

(Hughes, 2022, para. 1–2)

Social bookmarking gained widespread popularity as a type of social media following the launch of the pinboard-esque social network Pinterest in 2010. The bookmarking site, which has the mission to "connect everyone in the world through the things they find interesting," experienced a surge in use in 2012 and became the fourth-largest social network in the United States (Kerpen, 2019, p. 273). Thanks to Pinterest, "pinning" became a verb and part of our everyday vernacular.

While there are hundreds of social bookmarking sites for users to choose from, Hootsuite listed these seven as its "top social bookmarking sites" in 2022: Digg, Mix, Hootsuite Streams, Scoop.it, Pinterest, Slashdot and Reddit (Hughes, 2022).

Messaging Apps

Social messaging apps are a type of social media that allows users to communicate in real time. "The social messaging phenomenon has completely transformed the way people interact with brands—and ever since the pandemic pushed people toward digital channels for all their social and business interactions, the messaging trend has only accelerated" (Eerdekens, 2021, para. 3).

Since 2016, the number of people using the top social messaging apps—WhatsApp, Facebook Messenger and WeChat/Wexin—has consistently surpassed people using the top social networks, according to Hootsuite (Eerdekens, 2021). With two billion monthly active users in over 180 countries, WhatsApp is the most popular mobile messenger app in the world and the third most-used social media network in the world (Lua, n.d.; Olafson, 2021). WhatsApp started as an independent messenger company when it launched in 2009 before it was acquired by Facebook in 2014 (Olafson, 2021). While it was originally used as a way for friends and family to text each other, it now has also become widely used by businesses as a customer service tool (Lua, n.d.).

By 2023, it's estimated that more than 60% of all customer service interactions will be delivered via digital and self-serve channels like social messaging, chat apps and live chat (Eerdekens, 2021).

People will no longer settle for one-way communication or outdated 1–800 numbers when dealing with a customer service issue. They expect brands to use the most convenient channels for them, including social messaging apps. If you're not available to support your customers with social messaging, you will leave gaps in the customer experience.

(Smith, 2022, para. 8–9)

In 2022, Sprout Social listed the "11 most popular social messaging apps" as WhatsApp, Instagram Direct Messages, Facebook Messenger, TikTok Direct Messages, WeChat, Snapchat, Telegram, Discord, Viber, Twitter Direct Messages and Zendesk.

Message Boards/Forums

Early online forms of asynchronous communication were called BBS, Bulletin Board Systems, because they were developed based on the idea of a bulletin board (Humphreys, 2016).

BBSes once numbered in the tens of thousands in North America. These mostly text-based, hobbyist-run services played a huge part in the online landscape of the 1980s and '90s. Anyone with a modem and a home computer could dial-in, often for free, and interact with other callers in their area code. Then the internet came along in the mid-1990s. Like a comet to the dinosaurs, it upended the natural order of things and wiped BBSes out.

(Edwards, 2016, para. 3–4)

Bulletin Board Systems evolved into the social platforms used today called message boards or forums, which people use to ask questions, give answers and start discussions about different topics (Humphreys, 2016).

Discussion forums encourage people to answer each other's questions and share ideas and news. Many of these social media sites focus on posing questions to solicit the best answer. Answering them correctly and honestly can increase your credibility on the forum.

(Indeed Editorial Team, 2022b)

Message boards and discussion forums can also be used by organizations to engage in social listening to learn what people are saying about their brands and crowdsource product ideas. Examples of discussion forums include Reddit, Quora and Stack Overflow. In 2023, Reddit had 430 million active users, just shy of Twitter's 436 million, and Quora had 300 million (Lua, n.d.).

Social Review Sites

Social review sites, also referred to as consumer review networks, allow users to curate, collect and engage with online reviews. "These sites display customers' reviews of businesses, giving users a full perspective of the type of services and products offered and the overall satisfaction rate" (Indeed Editorial Team, 2022b). Most review sites are catered to specific industries. For example, Yelp for restaurants and other local service providers; TripAdvisor for hotels, vacation rentals and other travel-based accommodations and experiences; and Angi, formerly Angie's List, for home-related service professionals. While it's not a traditional social review site, Google ranks as consumers' favorite social review site, with nearly 65% of consumers reporting that they're likely to use Google reviews to research a business (Hill, 2022).

Organizations use social review sites to monitor and respond to reviews in a timely manner, encourage satisfied customers to share their experiences and improve upon negative feedback.

Shopping Platforms

According to Hootsuite, "Social shopping refers to the selling and buying of products directly on social media. With social shopping, complete transactions take place without leaving the social network app" (Christison, 2022, para. 4). In 2022, social commerce generated more than $700 billion in revenue (Chevalier, 2022).

Another important characteristic of social shopping sites is that they integrate word-of-mouth communications like reviews into the purchase infrastructure itself, which attracts more shoppers to the site. According to Humphreys (2016):

> Imagine that you need a new hairdryer. Whose opinion would you take more seriously—a spokesperson on a television advertisement, your best friend, or the reviews on Amazon.com? If you are like most people, the recommendation of others, either your friend or your friends on Amazon, has an impact on your ultimate purchase.
>
> (p. 196)

Certain platforms, like Etsy and Poshmark, were created as social shopping platforms, whereas some existing platforms have added social shopping elements like Pinterest Product Pins, Instagram Shops and TikTok's in-app shopping.

Assigning Platforms to Categories

Now that we've covered some of the widely accepted categories of social media, how do we go about actually assigning specific social media platforms to their respective categories? No surprise here that's there also no agreed-upon methodology for how we classify social media sites.

> Within this general definition, there are various types of Social Media that need to be distinguished further. However, although most people would probably agree that Wikipedia, YouTube, Facebook, and Second Life are all part of this large group, there is no systematic way in which

different Social Media applications can be categorized. Also, new sites appear in cyberspace every day, so it is important that any classification scheme takes into account applications which may be forthcoming.

(Kaplan & Haenlein, 2010, p. 61)

This task becomes especially tricky, with platforms constantly competing with one another when it comes to functions and features. That said, perhaps the easiest and most popular way of placing platforms in categories is by examining the original intention the platform was created for—in other words, its inherent purpose. For example, while Facebook now has Stories, live features, Pages for businesses, Messenger and a marketplace (among other added features), it was originally created for the purpose of connecting classmates, which would classify it as a social networking site. You can now shop on Instagram or connect with customer service through Direct Message, but the platform was first launched as a photo-sharing app, which would classify it as a content or photo-sharing app. "Fleets" introduced disappearing content to Twitter, but the original app that centered on 180-character messages makes it a microblog.

Kaplan and Haenlein (2010) created a social media classification system that relies on a set of theories in the field of media research (social presence and media richness) and social processes (self-presentation and self-disclosure), the "two key elements of social media" (p. 61). A first classification can be made based on the richness of the media (the amount of information transmitted) and the degree of social presence (the level of acoustic, visual and physical contact) it allows. Social platforms are classified as "low," "medium" or "high" for this dimension titled "social presence/media richness." A second classification can be made based on the degree of self-disclosure (the conscious or unconscious revelation of personal information) it requires and type of self-presentation (any action or behavior intending to influence others' perceptions of us) it allows. Social platforms are rated as "low" or "high" for this second dimension titled "self-presentation/self-disclosure."

Combining both dimensions creates a classification system with six types of social media: collaborative projects, blogs, content communities, social networking sites, virtual game worlds and virtual social worlds. See Table 3.1.

Table 3.1 Classification of social media by social presence/media richness and self-presentation/self-disclosure

Self-Presentation/ *Self-Disclosure*	*Social Presence/Media Richness*		
	Low	*Medium*	*High*
Low	Blogs	Social Networking Sites	Virtual Social Worlds (e.g., Second Life)
High	Collaborative Projects (e.g., Wikipedia)	Content Communities (e.g., YouTube)	Virtual Game Worlds (e.g., World of Warcraft)

Perspective From the Pros

By Whitney Lehmann

It's been nearly 20 years since I had my first experience with social media and created a Facebook profile from my college dorm room. It's been over 10 years since I first used a social media site for work purposes, when the communications team I worked with launched a Facebook page to connect with members of the media. These personal and professional experiences, along with so many others, have helped me truly understand and appreciate the different types of social media that exist.

When I first began working in public relations in 2009, I was hired as a communications coordinator for Barry University in Miami Shores, Florida. Our Office of Communications created an official Facebook page as a way to build and maintain relationships with members of local, regional, national and international media. Facebook, one of the first social networking sites (and certainly one of the most popular, even today), showed me the value of social media when it came to social capital—AKA connections and relationships.

In 2014, as I was planning my wedding, I turned to the popular bookmarking site Pinterest, like many brides do, to curate inspiration for our wedding theme, with ideas for everything from the venue to the cake to the flowers and everything in between. Years later, I would rely on Pinterest yet again when I needed to organize inspiration for my son's nursery.

In 2015, I was hired as the first-ever social media manager for Miami International Airport, and I was introduced to Twitter as a tool for customer service. MIA uses the microblog to provide excellent customer service and important updates. During my time at the airport, we used Twitter to reply to customers about overflowing bathrooms, to direct them to coffee shops and bars, to live tweet special events like inaugural flights, and even to communicate minute-by-minute updates during bomb scares.

Twitter proved to be particularly valuable during one specific interaction with airport customers when the Skytrain that transports customers from end of the concourse to another stopped operating during a lightning storm. Passengers were stuck inside and they were confused and scared. We used Direct Message (DM) on Twitter to make contact with certain passengers and let them know that help was on the way.

When I decided to shift gears professionally and return to practicing PR, I turned to LinkedIn to connect with potential employers. The social networking platform was invaluable in terms of making professional connections that helped me stand out among a pile of resumes and cover letters. I even landed a few job interviews simply by reaching out to job contacts via LinkedIn's messaging feature to follow up after I had applied for a position.

During my time as a public relations manager for Seminole Hard Rock Hotel & Casino Hollywood, I realized the power of social review sites when disgruntled guests would complain about their wait time at our restaurants, their dissatisfaction with their hotel room, or the smoke smell in the casino, among many other gripes. We'd work with the appropriate department on property to investigate and address their concerns before carefully crafting a reply. At the same, we'd take the time to thoughtfully respond to and thank guests who gushed about wonderful their experience was.

In my role as communications manager for the Department of Writing and Communication (now the Department of Communication, Media, and the Arts) at Nova Southeastern University, I learned how content-sharing apps like Instagram, YouTube, Snapchat and TikTok can be used to create visual storytelling for academic programs and communicate campus culture to current and prospective students and their parents.

In 2022, my husband and I embarked upon our first major home renovation project and we relied heavily upon online reviews like Google Reviews when researching contractors to hire for the job. In our last eight years as homeowners, we've also turned to sites like Angi (previously Angie's List) to find reputable and top-rated professionals in area whether it be plumbers, roofers, gutter specialists, landscapers or anything else.

What I have learned through these personal and professional experiences is that while all social media aren't created for the same purpose, they can all be equally valuable depending upon what you're using them for.

Chapter Summary

Exercise 3.1

In this chapter, we examined popular categories or types of social media. Do you agree with these established categories? Why or why not? Make your argument in approximately 250 words and cite your sources (in text and with a Reference List) in APA style.

Exercise 3.2

The social platform Clubhouse helped launch a relatively new category/type of social media called audio-sharing sites or social audio platforms. Based on current or forecasted social media trends, what social categories can we predict to pop up next?

Discussion Questions

1. The Social Spotlight for this chapter highlights how definitions of social media and the categories we use to classify them will need to evolve as the social media landscape evolves. In your opinion, are there any categories of social media that are extinct? If so, which ones and why?
2. One popular method used to classify social media platforms is examining an app's inherent purpose (the original reason it was created). Do you agree with this method? Why or why not?

References

Amore, S. (2020, July 10). What is Byte, the app that just passed TikTok on app store charts. *Yahoo! Entertainment*. www.yahoo.com/entertainment/byte-app-just-passed-tiktok-220456924.html

Bolton, D. (2022, March 9). Short-form versus long-form video content. *LinkedIn*. www.linkedin.com/pulse/short-form-versus-long-form-video-content-darren-bolton/?trk=pulse-article_more-articles_related-content-card

Boyd, D. M., & Ellison, N. B. (2007). Social network sites: Definition, history, and scholarship. *Journal of Computer-Mediated Communication, 13*(1), 210–230.

Ceci, L. (2022, July 5). YouTube Shorts: global user engagement. *Statista*. www.statista.com/statistics/1314183/youtube-shorts-performance-worldwide/

Chevalier, S. (2022, September 16). Social commerce revenue worldwide 2022–2030. *Statista*. www.statista.com/statistics/1231944/social-commerce-global-market-size/

Christison, C. (2022, October 6). Social shopping: How to sell products directly on social media. *Hootsuite*. https://blog.hootsuite.com/social-shopping/

Cyca, M. (2022, May 5). What is clubhouse? Everything you need to know about the audio app. *Hootsuite*. https://blog.hootsuite.com/clubhouse-app/

Dixon, S. (2022, October 27). *Facebook quarterly number of MAU (monthly active users) worldwide 2008–2022*. www.statista.com/statistics/264810/number-of-monthly-active-facebook-users-worldwide/

Edwards, B. (2016, November 4). The lost civilization of dial-up bulletin board systems. *The Atlantic*. www.theatlantic.com/technology/archive/2016/11/the-lost-civilization-of-dial-up-bulletin-board-systems/506465/

Eerdekens, L. (2021, May 20). 5 reasons why messaging should be part of your social media strategy. *Hootsuite*. https://blog.hootsuite.com/why-messaging-belongs-in-social-strategy/

Fuchs, C. (2014). *Social media: A critical introduction*. SAGE Publications.

Golob, L. (2022, February 28). TikTok expands into long-form content. *Hootsuite*. https://blog.hootsuite.com/social-media-updates/tiktok/tiktok-long-form-content/

Haan, K., & Main, K. (2022, December 6). Best blogging platforms of 2022. *Forbes Advisor.* www.forbes.com/advisor/business/software/best-blogging-platforms/

Hill, C. (2022, August 11). 15+ social media platforms your brand should use in 2022. *Sprout Social.* https://sproutsocial.com/insights/social-media-platforms/

Hootsuite. (n.d.-a). *Blog.* https://blog.hootsuite.com/social-media-definitions/blog/

Hootsuite. (n.d.-b). *Byte.* https://blog.hootsuite.com/social-media-definitions/byte/

Hootsuite. (n.d.-c). *Disappearing content.* https://blog.hootsuite.com/social-media-definitions/disappearing-content/

Hootsuite. (n.d.-d). *Microblogging.* https://blog.hootsuite.com/social-media-definitions/microblogging/

Huang, K. (2022, September 16). For Gen Z, TikTok is the new search engine. *The New York Times.* www.nytimes.com/2022/09/16/technology/gen-z-tiktok-search-engine.html

Hughes, J. (2022, August 17). How social bookmarking works [plus 7 tools to help you do it]. *Hootsuite.* https://blog.hootsuite.com/social-bookmarking/#The_top_7_social_bookmarking_sites

Humphreys, A. (2016). *Social media: Enduring principles.* Oxford University Press.

Indeed Editorial Team. (2022a, January 3). 10 video sharing sites and their benefits. *Indeed.* www.indeed.com/career-advice/career-development/video-sharing-sites

Indeed Editorial Team. (2022b, November 22). What are the different types of social media? 10 key types. *Indeed.* www.indeed.com/career-advice/career-development/types-of-social-media

Kaplan, A. M., & Haenlein, M. (2010). Users of the world unite! The challenges and opportunities of social media. *Business Horizons, 53*(1), 59–68.

Kerpen, D. (2019). *Likeable social media: How to delight your customers, create and irresistible brand, and be amazing on Facebook, Twitter, LinkedIn, Instagram, Pinterest, and more.* McGraw-Hill.

Kutuchief, B. (2022, September 29). Social media live streaming: How to go live on every network. *Hootsuite.* https://blog.hootsuite.com/social-media-live-streaming/

LinkedIn. (n.d.). *About LinkedIn.* https://about.linkedin.com/

Lua, A. (n.d.). 20 top social media sites to consider for your brand in 2023. *Buffer.* https://buffer.com/library/social-media-sites/

Luttrell, R. (2019). *Social media: How to engage, share, and connect.* Rowman & Littlefield.

Luttrell, R., & Wallace, A. A. (2021). *Social media and society: An introduction to the mass media landscape.* The Rowman & Littlefield Publishing Group, Inc.

Molla, R. (2021, March 1). Posting less, posting more, and tired of it all: How the pandemic has changed social media. *Vox.* www.vox.com/recode/22295131/social-media-use-pandemic-covid-19-instagram-tiktok

Ngak, C. (2011, July 6). Then and now: a history of social networking sites. *CBS News.* www.cbsnews.com/pictures/then-and-now-a-history-of-social-networking-sites/

Oladipo, T. (2022, November 16). A beginner's guide to Mastodon. *Buffer.* https://buffer.com/resources/mastodon-social/

Olafson, K. (2021, April 14). How to use WhatsApp for business: Tips and tools. *Hootsuite.* https://blog.hootsuite.com/whatsapp-marketing/

Padres, A. (2020, November 30). All the social media giants are becoming the same. *Wired.* www.wired.com/story/social-media-giants-look-the-same-tiktok-twitter-instagram/

Pogue, W. (2022, August 4). Move over Google. TikTok is the go-to search engine for Gen Z. *Adweek.* www.adweek.com/social-marketing/move-over-google-tiktok-is-the-go-to-search-engine-for-gen-z/

Potrel, V. (2022, September 6). Five insights into the popularity of short-form video content. *Forbes*. www.forbes.com/sites/forbescommunicationscouncil/2022/09/06/five-insights-into-the-popularity-of-short-form-video-content/

Quesenberry, K. A. (2021). *Social media strategy: Marketing, advertising, and public relations in the consumer revolution*. Rowman & Littlefield.

Ren, Y. (2018, November 19). Know your Chinese social media. *The New York Times*. www.nytimes.com/2018/11/19/fashion/china-social-media-weibo-wechat.html

Rosenblatt, K. (2022, February 28). TikTok will now let users post videos up to 10 minutes long. *NBC News*. www.nbcnews.com/pop-culture/pop-culture-news/tiktok-will-now-let-users-post-videos-10-minutes-long-rcna17965

Samur, A. (2018, November 22). The history of social media: 29+ key moments. *Hootsuite*. https://blog.hootsuite.com/history-social-media/

Smith, A. (2022, May 10). 11 social messaging apps every marketer should know in 2022. *Sprout Social*. https://sproutsocial.com/insights/social-messaging-apps/

Snider, M. (2022, November 16). What is Mastodon? What to know about the decentralized site some see as a Twitter alternative. *USA Today*. www.usatoday.com/story/tech/2022/11/16/twitter-alternative-mastodon-social-network/8303119001/

Statista. (2022). *Most popular social networks worldwide as of January 2022, ranked by number of monthly active users*. www.statista.com/statistics/272014/global-social-networks-ranked-by-number-of-users/

Teves, C. (2022, July 21). 14 types of social media every marketer should know. *Sprout Social*. https://sproutsocial.com/insights/types-of-social-media/#video-sharing

Wong, L. (2021, September 2). 9 types of social media and how each can benefit your business. *Hootsuite*. https://blog.hootsuite.com/types-of-social-media/

YouTube Help. (n.d.). *Upload videos longer than 15 minutes*. https://support.google.com/youtube/answer/71673?hl=EN

4   Social Media by Demographics, Psychographics and Location

In Chapter 3, we talked about the different categories or types of social media. In this chapter, we'll explore two additional ways we can describe social media: by user characteristics (demographics and psychographics) and location.

What you can expect to learn in this chapter:

- How to define demographics and psychographics
- Examples of demographics and psychographics
- How social media is used differently by established generations
- How other demographics, such as race, gender, ethnicity, education level and community type, can influence social media usage
- How psychographics such as lifestyle, interests, personality, values, attitudes/beliefs/opinions and social status can influence social media usage
- How access to and usage of social media differs across various regions of the world

Social Media by Demographics

One way that we can describe or further distinguish social media is by the demographics of its users. Demographics typically group individuals by characteristics over which they have little or no control, for example, age, race, gender and ethnicity (Bobbitt & Sullivan, 2014). Other popular pieces of demographic data that instead focus on characteristics that don't often change about individuals include marital status, parental status, education, occupation, health, income level and education level. "Demographic data is a key building block in defining your target audiences on social media. Generational nuances have a huge impact on how people interact with your brand, from the awareness stage all the way on to advocacy" (Sprout Social, n.d., para. 1).

Age

Let's begin by examining age. The Pew Research Center (2018b) identifies five generations: the Silent Generation (born 1928–1945), the Baby

DOI: 10.4324/9781003255734-5

Boomers (born 1946–1964), Generation X (Born 1965–1980, Millennials (born 1981–1996) and Generation Z (born after 1996) (Parker & Igielnik, 2020). These generations have been shaped, in part, by their access to and experiences with technology. Dimock (2019) wrote:

> Technology, in particular the rapid evolution of how people communicate and interact, is another generation-shaping consideration. Baby Boomers grew up as television expanded dramatically, changing their lifestyles and connection to the world in fundamental ways. Generation X grew up as the computer revolution was taking hold, and Millennials came of age during the internet explosion.
>
> In this progression, what is unique for Generation Z is that all of the above have been part of their lives from the start. The iPhone launched in 2007, when the oldest Gen Zers were 10. By the time they were in their teens, the primary means by which young Americans connected with the web was through mobile devices, WiFi and high-bandwidth cellular service. Social media, constant connectivity and on-demand entertainment and communication are innovations Millennials adapted to as they came of age. For those born after 1996, these are largely assumed.
>
> (para. 11–12)

While social media was once considered a tool for the youth, that is not the case anymore. According to Sprout Social (n.d.):

> Social media is no longer a young person's game. People of all ages are participating in the billions of conversations that take place online. As adoption continues to rise, brands need to be even more intentional about who they're trying to reach and how.
>
> (para. 62)

A closer look shows that communication preferences, including social media activity, differ widely across these age groups.

Silent Generation (1928–1945)

The Silent Generation refers to children of the Great Depression and World War II. In 2022, its youngest members were 77 years old and its oldest members were 94 years old. The "Silent" label refers to the generation's image as "conformist and civic-minded" (Pew Research Center, 2015b, para. 11). *TIME* magazine coined the term "Silent" in a 1951 article describing the emerging generation and describing its members as "working fairly hard and saying almost nothing" (Pew Research Center, 2015a, para. 18). According to Sugarman (2018):

> One thing to know about the Silent Generation is how reserved and traditional they are. Right in line with history, this generation experienced

one of the greatest financial hardships the US has ever known during the Great Depression of the 1930s. They believe in hard work and saving every dollar earned. The Silent Gen tends to stick to what they do best. When you communicate with the Silent Generation, be willing to show that you respect hard work and earning every dollar.

(para. 2)

In 2021, Statista reported that there were approximately 19 million members of the Silent Generation in the United States, accounting for about 6% of the population (2022b, 2022c). Strategies for communicating with members of this generation include listening with your ears and paying close attention to body language (Sugarman, 2018).

In 2019, the Pew Research Center reported that 28% of the Silent Generation uses social media (Vogels, 2019). The majority of seniors use social media to gather information rather than to share information about themselves; for example, they use Facebook to keep in touch with their families, especially their grandchildren (Yassky, 2021). From 2015 to 2019, usage of Facebook by the Silent Generation nearly doubled, increasing from 22% to 37% (Vogels, 2019). The Silent Generation is embracing digital life in other ways with 40% of members reporting they own a smartphone and 33% reporting they own a tablet computer in 2019 (Vogels, 2019).

Baby Boomers (1946–1964)

The Baby Boomer name originated from spike in fertility that began shortly after World War II and continued through the early 1960s. In 2021, Statista (2022b) reported that members of the Baby Boomer generation accounted for approximately 21% of the U.S. population. In 2022, its youngest members were 58 years old and its oldest members were 76 years old. According to the Pew Research Center (2015b):

> The Baby Boom generation is an example of a generation that is largely delineated by demography. Its oldest members were part of the spike in fertility that began in 1946, right after the end of World War II. Its youngest members were born in 1964, shortly before a significant decline in fertility that occurred after the birth control pill first went on the market.

(para. 7)

Boomers lived through many significant political and historical moments in history, including the 1962 Cuban Missile Crisis, the 1963 March on Washington led by Martin Luther King Jr., and the 1969 first moon landing. When communicating with Boomers, it's important to remain open to creative ideas (Sugarman, 2018). "Speak with Boomers about the importance of values, empowering the individual, as well as respecting the individual's uniqueness. By doing so, you'll be aligning language with Boomers' entrepreneurial strengths" (Sugarman, 2018, para. 4).

In 2019, the Pew Research Center reported that 59% of Boomers use social media, 68% own a smartphone and 52% own a tablet computer (Vogels, 2019). Sprout Social (n.d.) reported that 40% of Baby Boomers consider social media as an essential part of their lives with 73% using social media to stay connected with friends and family, 35% using social media to discover new brands, and 48% reporting that social media enables them to interact with brand and companies online. Baby Boomers have a preference for more established platforms, specifically Facebook, with the number of Boomers using Facebook increasing from 43% in 2012 to 60% in 2019 (Vogels, 2019). Statista (2022a) reported that in 2022, about one-fourth of the users on YouTube, LinkedIn and Pinterest were Baby Boomers.

Generation X (1965–1980)

The Generation X label was popularized by a Canadian journalist and novelist named Douglas Coupland, who used the term in a 1987 article he wrote for Vancouver Magazine and further popularized it with his 1991 novel "Generation X: Tales for an Accelerated Culture." Coupland said the term "X" referred to a group of people who did not want to concern themselves with societal pressures, money and status (Britannica, n.d.-a). Sometimes called the "middle child" generation, because it follows the Baby Boomer generation and precedes the Millennial Generation, this generation has fewer members than Boomers and Millennials, "which is one of the reasons that Generation X is considered to be forgotten or overlooked when the generations are discussed" (Britannica, n.d.-a, para. 1). This generation is defined, in part, by the relatively low birth rates during these years compared with the years associated with Boomers and Millennials (Pew Research Center, 2015b).

In 2021, Statista (2022b) reported that members of Generation X accounted for about 20% of the U.S. population. In 2022, its youngest members were 42 years old and its oldest members were 57 years old. As children and young adults in the 1980s and 1990s, they lived through turbulent economic times and grew up in a time when there were more dual-income families, single-parent households and children of divorce (Britannica, n.d.-a). "Many Gen Xers were latchkey kids, spending part of the day without adult supervision, as when they got home from school while their parents were still away at work" (Britannica, n.d.-a, para. 2). As a generation, they are described as being resourceful and self-starters and place importance on their independence and maintaining a work-life balance. According to Gorman (2019):

> Growing up as Gen Xers, it was not uncommon to come home from school to an empty home. Our parents were working and many of us

were growing up in single parent homes. The image in pop culture was that of a child getting off the school bus with their front door key hanging around their neck, who had to manage their afternoon schedule without parental supervision. Even if you weren't an actual 'latch key kid,' you were expected to be independent.

(para. 6)

GenXers are the first generation to grow up with personal computers, making them more tech-savvy than previous generations (Britannica, n.d.-a). In 2019, the Pew Research Center reported that 76% of Gen Xers used social media and 90% owned a smartphone (Vogels, 2019). Seventy-four percent of Gen X say social media is an essential part of their life, with most members preferring YouTube and Facebook (Sprout Social, n.d.). Members of this generation have been described as some of the most loyal consumers, with 37% reporting they've used social media for customer service (Sprout Social, n.d.).

"As Gen X moves toward social for questions, complaints and everything in between, brands will need to bridge the gap between their social and customer support teams" (Sprout Social, n.d., para. 48).

Millennials (Generation Y) (1981–1996)

The Millennial Generation—also referred to as Generation Y because it follows Gen X—is largely made up of children of the Baby Boomer Generation. They are the first generation to come of age in the new millennium. In 2020, they surpassed Baby Boomers as America's largest generation with immigration adding more numbers to this group than other generations (Fry, 2020). In 2021, they accounted for about 22% of the U.S. population (Statista, 2022b). In 2022, its youngest members were 26 years old and its oldest members were 41 old.

Born into a technological world, they are considered more progressive, creative and far-thinking than earlier generations. Many also identify as being more concerned with intrinsic and moral values versus extrinsic and material ideologies (Indeed Editorial Team, 2020). Millennials grew up during the 9/11 terrorist attacks and during the wars in Afghanistan and Iraq. Many were old enough to vote during the 2008 election that elected the first black president. Politically, Millennials are the most liberal and Democratic of the older generations (Pew Research Center, 2018a).

Many entered the workforce during the Great Recession. Dimock (2019) wrote:

As is well documented, many of Millennials' life choices, future earnings and entrance to adulthood have been shaped by this recession in a way that may not be the case for their younger counterparts. The long-term effects of this "slow start" for Millennials will be a factor in American society for decades.

(para. 10)

In addition to surpassing Baby Boomer's as the largest generation in the United States, Millennials have also led older generations in their adoption and use of technology, coming of age during the internet explosion (Dimock, 2019; Vogels, 2019). Most of their online minutes are via mobile and are dedicated to social media or online shopping (Statista Research Department, 2022). In 2019, nearly 100% said they used the internet, 86% used social media, 93% owned a smartphone and 53% owned a tablet computer (Vogels, 2019). "Social media, constant connectivity and on-demand entertainment and communication are innovations Millennials adapted to as they came of age" (Dimock, 2019, para. 12). While they are digitally inclined, their generation is also the most distrustful of ads on social media, and a large share of Millennials are concerned about the vulnerability of their personal data and digital privacy.

According to Sprout Social (n.d.), 72% of Millennials state that social media is an essential part of their lives, the highest of all age groups. Millennials report using social media to connect with brands and companies (75%), communicate with family, friends and acquaintances (61%), kill time (51%), learn about new trends (47%) and get breaking news (43%). Millennials have high customer service expectations but are also the most likely of any age group to express love for a product or service (Sprout Social, n.d.). The most popular social media platforms among Millennials are Facebook, YouTube and Instagram (Statista Research Department, 2022).

Generation Z (1997–2012)

Generation Z—also called Gen Z, zoomers, the iGeneration, centennials, post-Millennials and Homelanders—encompasses those born from 1997 to 2012 (Britannica, n.d.-b; Hect, 2022). The generation comprised roughly 21% of the U.S. population in 2021 (Statista, 2022b). In 2022, its youngest members were 10 years old and its oldest members were 25 years old.

They are the country's most ethnically and racially diverse generation—a title they stole from Millennials—with nearly half identifying as racial or ethnic minorities in 2018 and one in four identifying as Hispanic (Britannica, n.d.-b; Parker & Igielnik, 2020; Wang, 2018). They have grown up in more diverse settings than previous generations with higher percentages of single-parent families, mixed-race families, and LGBTQ+ parents in legally recognized partnerships. They are also more likely to have at least one foreign-born parent, although immigrants make up a smaller percentage of Gen Z compared to Millennials (Britannica, n.d.-b).

Sixteen percent of Gen Zers identify as belonging to the LGBTQ+ community, more than any previous generation. They also shun gender norms more than any other generation with more than half of its members saying that forms and profiles should have gender or sex options other than "man" or "woman" (Britannica, n.d.-b). More than one-third say they know someone who prefers that others use gender-neutral pronouns when referring to them (Parker et al., 2019).

Generation Z is on its way to becoming the best-educated generation yet with its members more likely to graduate high school and pursue college (Britannica, n.d.-b; Parker & Igielnik, 2020; Wang, 2018). Its members are more likely than Millennials to live with a college-educated parent (Wang, 2018). Its oldest members are delaying or foregoing marriage altogether, perhaps because more are going to college (Britannica, n.d.-b). Gen Zers are less likely to work as teens and young adults than other generations, again, perhaps due to their commitment to educational endeavors (Parker & Igielnik, 2020). Politically, Gen Z is similar in its views to the Millennial Generation and also tends to be more liberal than older generations (Parker et al., 2019).

Growing up in the era of the iPhone, Gen Z is considered the "first true digital native generation" (Britannica, n.d.-b, para. 5). Sprout Social (n.d.) describes their generation as "extremely online," with most members having some form of a social media presence for more than half of their lives (para. 5).

> As opposed to millennials, the generation that lived through the rise of the Internet while still growing up with cable television and landline phones, Gen Zers have lived their lives fully connected digitally. Most of them do not remember life before smartphones, and all have grown up during a time of ubiquitous access to streaming content and social media.
>
> (Britannica, n.d.-b, para. 5)

Fifty percent of Gen Z reported using social media daily compared to 44% of Millennials (Watson, 2022). Gen Zers are also unique in how they interact with the internet, compared to previous generations. As opposed to their Millennial predecessors who posted "deeply personal and public posts" on Facebook, Twitter or blogs, Gen Z prefers more anonymous forms of social media like Snapchat with content that disappears after a recipient views it (Britannica, n.d.-b).

Their motivations for using social media are also different. According to Sprout Social (n.d.):

> This social-savvy generation represents a changing tide in social media usage. Sixty-six percent of Gen Z consumers state that social media is an essential part of their lives, but their reasoning is unique. The most common reason Gen Z uses social media is to kill time, making them the only generation to rank that above connecting with family and friends.
>
> (para. 6)

Forty-three percent of Gen Zers reported making a purchase directly from a social media platform, making them the second-fastest adopters of social commerce, behind Millennials (Sprout Social, n.d.). Nearly 90% of teens ages 13 to 17 report being online almost constantly or several times a day, either on a computer or on a smartphone. A 2018 survey conducted by the Pew Research Center reported the most popular social media sites among this age group were YouTube, Instagram and Snapchat, with 85%, 72% and 69% of teens saying they use these social sites, respectively. Facebook and Twitter were less popular with only 51% reporting they use them (Parker & Igielnik, 2020).

In 2020, Forbes reported that 60% of TikTok users were comprised of Gen Z (Muliadi, 2020). That same year, CNBC reported that TikTok had surpassed Instagram as the second-most popular social app for U.S. teens, with 34% saying Snapchat was their favorite social app, followed by 29% picking TikTok and 25% picking Instagram (Rodriguez, 2020).

Gen Z prefers to consume content in rich video formats and prioritizes engaging with authentic content, which makes TikTok's dynamic content with lip-syncs, skits and dance challenges more popular among members of this generation than the more polished videos that are characteristic of Instagram. According to Muliadi (2020):

> Just as millennials fueled the rise of earlier social media platforms, like Facebook and Instagram, Generation Z is fueling the rise of TikTok, and understanding the relationship between people and platforms is very telling of what to expect of this rising generation.
>
> (para. 5)

Social Spotlight

We all know that TikTok is the social media playground for Gen Z, but the over-65 set is getting in on the fun, too. Dubbed the "Grand-fluencers," these senior influencers are proving that they can be successful content creators in their own right. Accounts like The Old Gays and the Retirement House have amassed millions of followers and views on videos with content combatting the notion that life is winding down for senior citizens. According to Locke (2022):

> So, what do you get when you give six elders and two young producers a ring light and a platform on TikTok? The Retirement House's videos are more silly than shocking: lip-syncing trending songs, playing practical jokes on each other."
>
> (para. 23)

While there's no question that content produced by the Grandflu-encers is unique and entertaining with a shock value, there's another quality that makes it wildly popular—it has heart. The Old Gays are four survivors of the AIDS epidemic who consider each other their chosen family. They use social media to showcase their playful take on TikTok dance challenges and trends—while clad in risqué outfits and costumes—that often inspire a new conversation around aging. "The Old Gays said they are often stopped by young gay fans who thank them for showing what their own golden years could look like" (Locke, 2022, para. 39).

In the United States, over one million seniors live in nursing homes, and some of these seniors are going viral, too. Lou Scott, 78, who lives at Burr Ridge Senior Living in Burr Ridge, Illinois, is a regular guest on the Spectrum Retirement TikTok account that has over 100,000 followers and millions of views on its videos. The account is produced by a company called Spectrum Retirement Communities and features residents from its senior living facilities across the country. Locke (2022) wrote:

> Mr. Scott recorded his first video right after a month alone in his apartment, and the response astounded him: thousands of likes and comments from viewers asking him to be their grandfather and hoping to be like him when they're older. "It's brought people to me," he said. "When you get inquisitive, it keeps your mind working, your body working."
>
> (para. 35)

Race, Gender, Ethnicity, Education Level and Community Type

In addition to the age of its users, social media can be described by examining other user demographics, such as race, gender, ethnicity, education level and community type. Some sites stand out for their demographic differences (Auxier & Anderson, 2021):

- Instagram: Larger percentages of Hispanic Americans (52%) and Black Americans (49%) report using the app compared to White Americans (35%).
- WhatsApp: Hispanic Americans are far more likely to use the app (46%) than Black (23%) or White Americans (16%).
- LinkedIn: Users with higher levels of education are more likely than those with lower levels of education to report being LinkedIn users. Fifty-one percent of adults with a bachelor's degree or advanced degree used LinkedIn compared to 28% of adults with some college experience and 10% of adults with a high school diploma or less.

- Pinterest: Women are far more likely than men to use the social platform (46% compared to 16%).
- Nextdoor: More adults living in urban (17%) or suburban communities (14%) use the platform than adults living in rural areas (2%).

Social Media by Psychographics

While demographics focus on characteristics that are usually fixed about an individual, psychographics, on the other hand, focus on characteristics that individuals can usually control, such as values, interests, attitudes, lifestyles, wants, needs, concerns, spending habits and hobbies (Indeed Editorial Team, 2021a).

> When used in marketing campaigns, psychographics attempts to understand the values and emotions that drive a potential customer to purchase a certain good or service. It does so by using data to analyze a consumer's spending habits, passions, ethics and any other personal element that may explain why they make the decision to purchase a certain product.
>
> (Indeed Editorial Team, 2021b, para. 2)

Research organizations like the Pew Research Center conduct national surveys and report psychographic data across many topics. Other popular ways to obtain psychographics include interviews, surveys, social media analytics and website analytics. For example, Google Analytics collects website data that analyzes users by demographics, such as age and gender, but also by psychographics like interest categories.

The Indeed Editorial Team (2021b) lists six examples of psychographic characteristics that can be assessed:

1. Lifestyle: This refers to everyday activities and can include the area where they live, the people they associate themselves with, hobbies/ interests, and other characteristics relating to how a person spends his/ her/their time.
2. Interests: Interests include any activities that a person pursues in their spare time, including hobbies, media consumption habits, pastimes and passions.
3. Personality: Personality as a psychographic involves assessing common personality traits/dimensions such as agreeableness, openness, extraversion, conscientiousness and neuroticism.
4. Values: Values refer to a person's view of what is right and what is wrong, also sometimes referred to as morals.
5. Attitudes, beliefs, opinions: Attitudes, beliefs and opinions form a person's general worldview and can be analyzed together or as separate

psychographics. They describe an individual's overall attitude and view on the events happening around them and are influenced by education, personality and upbringing.

6. Social status: "A person's social status and desired social status are two very important factors that influence their buying habits and they can be categorized with the help of psychographics."

(para. 11)

Some social media are specifically tailored to psychographics. An example of a social media app targeting a person's "lifestyle" could be Grindr, the world's largest social networking app for gay, bi, trans and queer people. Facebook Groups focusing on certain hobbies would be an example of social media catered to interests. For example, the Facebook Group "House Plant Lovers" has nearly 150,000 members. Parler, the alternative social network popular with conservatives, could be considered a social media platform targeting attitudes, beliefs and opinions while Raya, the invite-only, membership-based dating app popular among influencers and celebrities, could be considered a social media app targeting social status.

Perspective From the Pros

By Michael North

Teach enough social media courses and you'll learn that roughly four-out-of-five Pinterest users are women; three-out-of-five LinkedIn users are men; two-out-of-five Instagram users are white; one-out-of-five TikTok users are 17 or younger; and just about everyone watches YouTube videos.

But this demographic information is too broad. Demographic information relates to the structure of populations and commonly includes age, race and sex. While demographic information provides a sketch, psychographic information is needed to paint the picture.

Psychographic information organizes people by attitudes, interests, beliefs, opinions and values. In short, psychographic information reveals personality. What people believe, where they spend their time, what they purchase, or how they consume media reveals a lot about a person.

Combining demographics with psychographics provides you with a complete view of the person you're targeting. David Meerman Scott—author of "The New Rules of Marketing and PR"—said an overly broad audience will lead to bland writing that targets everyone but appeals to nobody. Instead, get granular with your data and put the person you are targeting across the table. Visualizing the person you're targeting shows you the clothes they wear, helps you understand their slang, reveals how they spend their time online, and more.

One psychographic attribute to monitor is political ideology. Politics in the United States is becoming more polarized and we're seeing that in social media. I envision entire social media platforms adopting the owner's political ideology or aligning with a political party to become its digital communication apparatus.

Twitter banned President Donald Trump soon after Jan. 6, 2021, so Trump launched Truth Social about a year later (Bhuiyan, 2022). Then Elon Musk bought Twitter, which was followed by Ye's—formerly known as Kanye West—near acquisition of Parler, which became the social media platform of choice for those angry about Twitter banning Trump. Cult-like personalities need a following and social media platforms provide this.

It's not surprising then that these platform's posts tend to align with the platforms' owners. Truth Social and Parler are far right (Newhouse, 2021). And Twitter has become libertarian reflecting Musk's goal of live and let live by giving everyone a voice (Milmo, 2022).

President Joe Biden's White House recruited the most popular TikTokers to promote COVID-19 vaccine updates (Sprunt, 2022), and to disseminate information about the war in Ukraine (Lorenz, 2022). TikTok is loved by Generation Z, so the Biden White House used TikTok to reach America's youth. And it's no wonder that Generation Z voted for Democrats by 28 points in the 2022 midterms (Frey, 2022).

TikTok doesn't have an owner with a cult-like following. But TikTok has bypassed parents in American households, and the Biden White House capitalized.

Watch Mastodon as well. Mastodon is similar to Twitter and has seen its usage rate increase dramatically in a left-leaning response to Musk's libertarian vision for Twitter (Chan, 2022).

The point? Intense social media segmentation is coming. And you'll need more than just demographics to meet and communicate effectively with the person you're targeting on social media.

Social Media by Region/Location

In addition to describing social media by the people who use them through demographics and psychographics, we can also describe social media in terms of how it's used by location or region. For example, while the social media is a daily activity for *most* Americans, that isn't the case for everyone—or everywhere.

In 2017, the Pew Research Center reported differences in social media usage across 14 countries with advanced economies and found that many people in Europe, the United States, Canada, Australia and Japan do not regularly visit social media sites, although the majority did report that they use the internet (Poushter, 2017). Social media use was relatively common among people in Sweden, the Netherlands, Australia and the United States, with seven-in-10 people saying they used social sites like Facebook and Twitter; however, "that still leaves a significant minority of the population in those countries (around 30%) who are non-users" (Poushter, 2017, para. 2). In France (48%), Greece (46%), Japan (43%) and Germany (37%), less than half of internet users said they use social media.

The difference in usage is due in large part to whether or not people have access to the internet, since low rates of internet access limit access to social media. Poushter (2017) points out, though, that internet access doesn't guarantee social media usage.

> In Germany, for example, 85% of adults are online, but less than half of this group report using Facebook, Twitter or Xing. A similar pattern is seen in some of the other developed economies polled, including Japan and France, where social media use is low relative to overall internet penetration.
>
> (para. 5)

Internet access can also be a matter of government control. Before Facebook and Twitter were banned in North Korea in 2016, few North Koreans had access to the internet with most only having access to a government-controlled intranet. "The official blocking of social media websites mostly affected foreigners from posting information from North Korea to the wider world" (Barry, 2022, para. 13).

While internet access can certainly influence whether or not one uses social media, another important factor is access to social media period. For example, China, the world's most populous country, has some restrictions when it comes to the web, and some social media sites are blocked entirely. Meta-owned Facebook and Twitter have been blocked in China since 2009 following deadly riots by activists in the Xinjiang province, and Meta's messaging platform WhatsApp and photo- and video-sharing app Instagram were also blocked.

"Rather than Facebook or Twitter, Chinese netizens are more likely to be on networks created by Chinese businesses" (Washenko, 2015, para. 7). Meltwater reported that the top eight Chinese social media apps, sites and platforms in 2022 were Sina Weibo, WeChat, TikTok (aka Douyin), Tencent QQ, Baidu Tieba, Tencent Video, Zhihu and Little Red Book (Kiely, 2022). In general, there's a strong interest in messaging apps compared to social networks that broadcast status updates (Washenko, 2015). Since WhatsApp is blocked in China, the widely used alternative is WeChat, a multi-purpose messaging system developed by Tencent (Barry, 2022).

Despite the fact that the video-sharing app TikTok was developed by the Chinese company Bytedance, it is not available in China. A twin app called Douyin, also developed by Bytedance, is available for download but has restrictions on international content and limits on children's usage. "China's restriction of foreign media platforms and censorship of non-governmental material has been dubbed the Great Firewall of China" (Barry, 2022, para. 5).

In 2020, Iran announced it was working on a national Iranian internet that has been compared to the Great Firewall of China. Facebook and Twitter have been blocked in the country since 2009 following disputed elections and mass protests in an attempt to limit government opposition.

According to *TIME* magazine, 30% of TikTok's downloads in April 2020 came from India. India became one of Bytedance's largest markets outside of China with TikTok supporting multiple regional languages and becoming accessible to many people in the country. Two months later, the Indian government banned 58 other mobile apps, including the Chinese app WeChat. The bans were viewed as retaliation by the Indian government for clashes that took place between Indian and Chinese forces at the Himalayan border (Barry, 2022).

In 2022, Nigeria lifted a seven-month ban on Twitter, which was blocked in June 2021 after Twitter removed a tweet by President Muhammadu Buhari that it said incited ethnic violence and breached its "abuse behavior policy." The ban was viewed as a form of retaliation against the microblog, popular among journalists and activists in the country, with the Nigerian administration criticizing the platform for "activities that are capable of undermining Nigeria's corporate existence" (Barry, 2022, para. 2).

In addition to access to the internet and/or access to certain social media sites, cultural norms are another factor affecting social media usage in certain parts of the world, for example, in Japan. "The cultural mores of Asia Pacific countries has also impacted the adoption of social media networks. For instance, Japanese culture discourages boasting and self-promotion" (Washenko, 2015, para. 9).

The ex-Soviet Central Asian state Turkmenistan, which is largely Muslim, blocks Facebook and Twitter. Citizens are asked to swear on the Quran when signing up for a home internet connection that they will not access VPNs, and students are asked to sign statements pledging not to use the internet to access banned sites (Barry, 2022).

Chapter Summary

- In addition to categorizing social media by type/category, we can also describe social media by their users through demographics like age, sex, gender, race, ethnicity, income level, education level and community type.

- Twenty-eight percent of the Silent Generation reported using social media in 2019. The majority use social media to gather information rather than to share information about themselves; for example, using Facebook to keep in touch with their families, especially their grandchildren.
- More than half of Baby Boomers reported using social media in 2019. Members of this generation have a preference for more established platforms such as Facebook, with 60% of Boomers reporting they used Facebook in 2019.
- Generation X is the first generation to grow up with personal computers, making them more tech-savvy than previous generations. Seventy-six percent reported using social media in 2019. Members of this generation have a preference for Facebook and YouTube.
- Millennials came of age during the internet boom with nearly 100 percent reporting they used the internet in 2019 and 86% saying they use social media. The most popular social media platforms among Millennials are Facebook, YouTube and Instagram.
- Generation Z is described as "extremely online" with most members having some form of a social media presence for more than half of their lives. They grew up in the era of the iPhone and are considered the first true digital natives. Fifty percent reported using social media daily, with Snapchat, TikTok and Instagram as their "favorite" platforms.
- While social media sites/apps can be described using the demographics of their users, certain social media are also catered to users by psychographics, such as lifestyle, interests, personality, values, attitudes/beliefs/opinions, and social status.
- Social media usage differs across the world and is influenced by access to the internet and access to certain social media sites, for example, in China. Cultural mores, rules that cultures/societies develop to govern how to behave in social settings, also affect social media usage, for example, in Japan.

Exercise 4.1

In this chapter, we examined key characteristics of each generation, along with their respective communication preferences. Let's imagine you are the social media manager for a luxury vacation concierge company, and you've been charged with targeting Baby Boomers with an upcoming social campaign.

Based on what we know about Baby Boomers as a generation coupled with their communications and social media preferences, what social media channels do you recommend we incorporate into the campaign and what themes/messaging should the content emphasize?

Exercise 4.2

This chapter examined differences in social media usage in different regions of the world due to internet access, social media access, government controls and/or cultural norms. Select a country and examine differences in social media usage within the different regions of that particular country. For example, in the United States, what does social media usage look like in the Northeast, Southwest, West, Southeast and Midwest? What similarities exist, and what notable differences exist?

Discussion Questions

1. According to the Pew Research Center, a generation typically refers to groups of people born over a 15- to 20-year span. If Gen Z refers to those born after 1996, the next generation would begin with those born after 2012. Some sources are referring to this next generation as Generation Alpha. Based on technology and social media trends that have taken place in the past 10 years, how can we expect Generation Alpha to be different from the generation that precedes it in terms of how it communicates and uses social media?

2. Despite their affinity for all things digital, a large share of Millennials in the United States are concerned about the vulnerability of their personal data and digital privacy. Are data rights becoming the new human rights? What events led to these concerns?

References

Auxier, B., & Anderson, M. (2021, April 7). Social media use in 2021. *Pew Research Center*. www.pewresearch.org/internet/2021/04/07/social-media-use-in-2021/

Barry, E. (2022, January 18). These are the countries where Twitter, Facebook and TikTok are banned. *Time*. https://time.com/6139988/countries-where-twitter-facebook-tiktok-banned/

Bhuiyan, J. (2022, February 21). Donald Trump's social media app launches on Apple Store. *The Guardian*. Retrieved November 27, 2022, from https://www.theguardian.com/us-news/2022/feb/21/donald-trumps-social-media-app-truth-social-launches-on-apple-store

Bobbitt, R., & Sullivan, R. (2014). *Developing the public relations campaign: A team-based approach*. Pearson.

Britannica. (n.d.-a). Generation X. *Britannica.com Encyclopedia*. Retrieved December 4, 2022, from www.britannica.com/topic/Generation-X

Britannica. (n.d.-b). Generation Z. *Britannica.com Encyclopedia*. Retrieved December 4, 2022, from www.britannica.com/topic/Generation-Z

Chan, W. (2022, November 2). Mastodon gained 70,000 users after Musk's Twitter takeover. I joined them. *The Guardian*. Retrieved November 27, 2022, from https://www.theguardian.com/media/2022/nov/01/mastodon-twitter-elon-musk-takeover

Dimock, M. (2019, January 17). Defining generations: Where Millennials end and Generation Z begins. *Pew Research Center*. www.pewresearch.org/fact-tank/2019/01/17/where-millennials-end-and-generation-z-begins/

Frey, W. H. (2022, November 18). Midterm exit polls show that young voters drove Democratic resistance to the 'red wave'. *The Brookings Institution.* Retrieved November 27, 2022, from https://www.brookings.edu/research/midterm-exit-polls-show-that-young-voters-drove-democratic-resistance-to-the-red-wave/

Fry, R. (2020, April 28). *Millennials overtake Baby Boomers as America's largest generation.*

Gorman, M. (2019, April 19). How Gen X's 'latch key kid' mentally propels their financial success. *Forbes.* www.forbes.com/sites/megangorman/2019/04/19/how-gen-xs-latch-key-kid-mentality-propels-their-financial-success/?sh=4d9671ca31b4

Hect, E. (2022, September 2). What years are Gen X? What about Baby Boomers? When each generation was born. *USA Today.* www.usatoday.com/story/news/2022/09/02/what-years-gen-x-millennials-baby-boomers-gen-z/10303085002/

Indeed Editorial Team. (2020, June 7). 10 common characteristics of the Millennial generation. *Indeed.* www.indeed.com/career-advice/interviewing/10-millennial-generation-characteristics

Indeed Editorial Team. (2021a, April 26). Demographics vs. psychographics in audience segmentation. *Indeed.* www.indeed.com/career-advice/career-development/demographics-vs-psychographics

Indeed Editorial Team. (2021b, May 17). 6 psychographics examples for effective marketing segmentation. *Indeed.* www.indeed.com/career-advice/career-development/psychographics-examples

Kiely, T. J. (2022, June 23). The top 8 Chinese social media apps, sites & platforms 2022. *Meltwater.* www.meltwater.com/en/blog/top-chinese-social-media-apps-sites

Locke, C. (2022, May 25). 'Grandfluencers' are sharing a new vision of old age: On Tik-Tok, the over-65 set is thriving. *The New York Times.* www.nytimes.com/2022/05/25/style/tiktok-old-gays-retirement.html

Lorenz, T. (2022, March 13). The White House is briefing TikTok stars about the war in Ukraine. *The Washington Post.* Retrieved November 25, 2022, from https://www.washingtonpost.com/technology/2022/03/11/tik-tok-ukraine-white-house/

Milmo, D. (2022, April 14). How 'free speech absolutist' Elon Musk would transform Twitter. *The Guardian.* Retrieved November 27, 2022, from https://www.theguardian.com/technology/2022/apr/14/how-free-speech-absolutist-elon-musk-would-transform-twitter

Muliadi, B. (2020, July 7). What the rise of TikTok says about Generation Z. *Forbes.* www.forbes.com/sites/forbestechcouncil/2020/07/07/what-the-rise-of-tiktok-says-about-generation-z/?sh=7f4760f65490

Newhouse, A. (2021, January 12). Big Tech's rejection of Parler shuts down a site favored by Trump supporters – and used by participants in the US Capitol insurrection. *The Conversation.* Retrieved November 27, 2022, from https://theconversation.com/big-techs-rejection-of-parler-shuts-down-a-site-favored-by-trump-supporters-and-used-by-participants-in-the-us-capitol-insurrection-153070

Parker, K., Graf, N., & Igielnik, R. (2019, January 17). Generation Z looks a lot like Millennials on key social and political issues. *Pew Research Center.* www.pewresearch.org/social-trends/2019/01/17/generation-z-looks-a-lot-like-millennials-on-key-social-and-political-issues/

Parker, K., & Igielnik, R. (2020, May 14). On the cusp of adulthood and facing an uncertain future: What we know about Gen Z so far. *Pew Research Center.* www.pewresearch.org/social-trends/2020/05/14/on-the-cusp-of-adulthood-and-facing-an-uncertain-future-what-we-know-about-gen-z-so-far-2/

Pew Research Center. (2015a, September 3). *Most Millennials resist the "Millennial" label.* www.pewresearch.org/politics/2015/09/03/most-millennials-resist-the-millennial-label

Pew Research Center. (2015b, September 3). *The whys and hows of generations research.* www.pewresearch.org/politics/2015/09/03/the-whys-and-hows-of-generations-research/

Pew Research Center. (2018a, March 1). *The generation gap in American politics.* www.pewresearch.org/politics/2018/03/01/the-generation-gap-in-american-politics/

Pew Research Center. (2018b, March 1). *The generations defined.* www.pewresearch.org/st_18-02-27_generations_defined/

Poushter, J. (2017, April 20). Not everyone in advanced economies is using social media. *Pew Research Center.* www.pewresearch.org/fact-tank/2017/04/20/not-everyone-in-advanced-economies-is-using-social-media/

Rodriguez, S. (2020, October 6). TikTok passes Instagram as second-most popular social app for U.S. teens. *CNBC.* www.cnbc.com/2020/10/06/tiktok-passes-instagram-as-second-most-popular-social-app-for-us-teens.html

Sprout Social. (n.d.). *How different generations use social media—and what this means for your business.* https://sproutsocial.com/insights/guides/social-media-use-by-generation/

Sprunt, B. (2022, October 9). The White House is turning to TikTok stars to take its message to a younger audience. *NPR.* Retrieved November 26, 2022, from https://www.npr.org/2022/10/09/1127211983/the-white-house-is-turning-to-tiktok-stars-to-take-its-message-to-a-younger-audi

Statista. (2022a). Distribution of leading social media platform users in the United States as of August 2022, by age group. *Statista.com.* https://www-statista-com.ezproxylocal.library.nova.edu/statistics/1337525/us-distribution-leading-social-media-platforms-by-age-group/

Statista. (2022b). Population distribution in the United States in 2021, by generation [Infographic]. *Statista.com.* www.statista.com/statistics/296974/us-population-share-by-generation/

Statista. (2022c). Resident population in the United States in 2021, by generation [Infographic]. *Statista.com.* www.statista.com/statistics/797321/us-population-by-generation/

Statista Research Department. (2022, July 6). *Internet usage of Millennials in the United States—Statistics and Facts.* www.statista.com/topics/2576/us-millennials-internet-usage-and-online-shopping/#topicHeader__wrapper

Sugarman, J. (2018, June 28). Four key communication strategies each generation uses: How to become a "Generational Whisperer." *LinkedIn.* www.linkedin.com/pulse/four-key-communication-strategies-each-generation-uses-jim-sugarman

Vogels, E. A. (2019, September 9). Millennials stand out for their technology use, but older generations also embrace digital life. *Pew Research Center.* www.pewresearch.org/fact-tank/2019/09/09/us-generations-technology-use/

Wang, H. L. (2018, November 15). Generation Z is the most racially and ethnically diverse yet. *NPR.* www.npr.org/2018/11/15/668106376/generation-z-is-the-most-racially-and-ethnically-diverse-yet

Washenko, A. (2015, January 21). How social media behaviors differ across Asia Pacific. *Sprout Social.* https://sproutsocial.com/insights/social-media-by-country/

Watson, A. (2022, August 18). Consumption frequency of news from social media in the U.S. 2022, by generation. *Statista.* www.statista.com/statistics/1124159/us-generational-social-media-news/

Yassky, B. (2021, November 2). How social media can give the Silent Generation a voice. *Wired.* www.wired.com/story/social-media-silent-generation/

Part 2

Social Media and Theory

5 Theory and Communications Research

In Part 1 of this book, we explored definitions of media, the evolution of social media, various categories of social media and social media usage by different demographics and across different regions of the world. In Part 2, we'll continue the conversation of social media through a theoretical lens with an overview of how social media academics, educators, and practitioners are applying communication theories to the ever-evolving field of social media with grounded and applied research.

What you can expect to learn in this chapter:

- How to define the terms "theory" and "research"
- Different assumptions/worldviews about the nature of human communication
- The difference between quantitative and qualitative methods in research
- The difference between basic and applied research
- Major approaches to communication research, including the social science approach, the interpretive approach, and the critical approach
- Categories of communication research
- Social media's place in communication research
- An introduction to the scientific method
- An overview of past and present models of communication
- How social media scholars and practitioners can apply theories, models and concepts from communication and related fields in their research and work

What Is Theory and Research?

Theory

To put it simply, theory is an explanation for how the world works. Some formal definitions of theory include:

- "General statements that summarize our understandings of the way the world works" (Severin & Tankard, 2001, p. 11)
- "The rationale we extend to understand the world around us" (Stacks & Salwen, 2009, p. 3)

DOI: 10.4324/9781003255734-7

- "Proposed explanation for how a set of natural phenomena will occur, capable of making predictions about the phenomena for the future, and capable of being falsified through empirical observation" (Wrench et al., 2008, p. 515)
- "A set of statements that explains a particular phenomenon" (Alberts et al., 2019, p. 26)
- "A plausible or scientifically acceptable general principle or body of principles offered to explain phenomena" (Merriam-Webster, n.d.)

Theory is the ultimate goal of science. "The scientist believes that the greatest faith should be placed in those statements about the way things work that have been tested and verified that have some greater generality and predictive power" (Severin & Tankard, 2001, pp. 11–12). According to Wrench et al. (2008):

> The term "theory" is used for many purposes and in many ways. There are theories that are meaningless (chicken or egg?) and there are theories that are important (the theory that a certain medication will kill cancer). . . . People typically are not highly committed to their speculations or guesses. However, people are likely to be very committed theories that they and others believe to be strong, solid theories supported by empirical research (anyone want to jump off a skyscraper and test the theory of gravity?).
>
> (p. 21)

Assumptions

The research process begins with a question that may later develop into a hypothesis, and research advances the theory behind the question/hypothesis. In the field of human communication, researchers have different assumptions about the nature of human communication and can use different approaches in the quest to "know" something. According to Treadwell (2017):

> The next step after finding questions of interest is deciding how to best get an answer to these questions. You will find from scholarly literature that this can be a hotly contested issue. Choosing a research method or methods unavoidably requires making assumptions and decisions about the nature of human behavior, such as whether are basically all alike or are unique individuals. These assumptions and decisions will help you prefer some methods over, but you may well find that for every researcher going down your road, there is another researcher opting for a different route to answering essentially the same question.
>
> (p. 2)

As assumption, or worldview, asks,

> What do we really believe about human communication?" and whether or not people are fundamentally all alike or different and, whether they're predictable or unpredictable, and whether reality is objective or subjective. "As evidence supports any and all such views, ultimately we are obliged to decide which basic beliefs will inform our research, and to live with them, based on our own best judgement.
>
> (Treadwell, 2017, p. 29)

Treadwell (2017) introduces two worldviews or belief systems. Worldview I assumes that human behavior is predictable, objectively measurable and generalizable. Researchers with these basic beliefs aim to make generalizations about human communication. Advertising and audience research, for example, subscribe to Worldview I. According to Treadwell (2017):

> Researchers seek to find rules that will predict the success of interpersonal relationships, direct-marketing or broadcast content, or cat videos on social media, or the ability of group members to work together or how to increase sales or hold a broadcast audience. Television infomercials, for example, are presumably based on research indicating that using a particular type of spokesperson plus showing the product plus repeated exposure of the 1–800 phone number will maximize the number of consumer call-ins. In principle, such as a generalization would apply to most products and most television audiences.
>
> (p. 29)

By contrast, Worldview II assumes human behavior is individualistic, unpredictable, and subjective and that knowledge is subjective. "Research based on these assumptions attempts to describe and assess the subjectivity and individuality of human communication, rather the aiming to discover universal laws" (Treadwell, 2017, p. 29). The goal is to understand rather than to predict or generalize. Whereas Worldview I emphasizes the researchers' perspectives, Worldview II emphasizes participants' perspectives.

The research methods—the specific ways that scholars collect and analyze data—chosen should reflect the basic assumptions and belief systems the researcher has about human communication.

> The first question for researchers, then, is not whether to prefer qualitative over quantitative methods. Rather, it is 'What are my basic assumptions about human communication?' It is the answer to this question that will drive the decisions about the nature of the research data to be gathered and therefore the research methods to be employed.

Quantitative and qualitative studies ask different questions and collect data differently. Quantitative studies ask "how many?" or "what proportion?" Data collected from quantitative studies is expressed as numbers. Researchers analyze these numbers using statistics to establish relationships among concepts. Quantitative research attempts to be objective "or to create knowledge by examining facts through the scientific method without distorting the findings by personal feelings, prejudices, and interpretations" (Wrench et al., 2008, p. 12). It generally relies on large samples of people, so that we can generalize findings to the population.

Qualitative research, on the other hand, asks questions like "What is it like?" or "How does it feel?" and seeks to understand people's beliefs, experiences, attitudes, behavior and interactions using non-numerical data, such as language, and, therefore, is usually subjective and based on very small sample sizes that cannot be used to generalize to larger groups of people.

"Every research question has assumptions behind it that reflect the researcher's view of communication and how to study it" (Treadwell, 2017, p. 2). Popular methods of quantitative research include surveys, content analysis and experiments, whereas widely used methods of qualitative research include in-depth interviews, focus groups, ethnography and observational studies.

Approaches and Goals

The study of social media is interdisciplinary with knowledge and theories coming from communication, sociology, anthropology, psychology, marketing, cultural studies, informatics and more. This book focuses on social media through a communication lens.

Alberts et al. (2019) introduce three major approaches in the communication discipline: the social science, interpretive and critical approaches.

> Each of these approaches to understanding the situation is actually represented by contemporary scholars conducting real research. Each approach also reflects different assumptions about the nature of human behavior and the best way to obtain insights and build knowledge about human behavior. And each represents a particular historical tradition, some hundreds of years in the making.
>
> (p. 25)

The social science approach has origins in the fields of psychology and sociology with roots in behaviorism, a branch of psychology focusing on observable behavior. This approach seeks to predict human behavior, emphasizes universal theories, and typically uses quantitative methods. "Therefore, social scientists believe knowledge can best be acquired through observing the behavior of a group of individuals and generalizing from that group to other groups of people" (Alberts et al., 2019, p. 25).

The interpretive approach was influenced by the ancient Greek tradition of rhetoric, the art of persuasion, and by humanism, a branch of philosophy that celebrates human nature. This approach seeks an in-depth understanding of communication in specific situations and typically uses qualitative methods. According to Alberts et al. (2019):

> Originating with the ancient Greek rhetoricians, and then later with humanists (during the Renaissance), the interpretive approach has emphasized the creativity, instead of predictability, of human behavior. Interpretive researchers assume that humans construct their own reality and that researchers must tap into these constructions for a full understanding of human communication.
>
> (p. 32)

Whereas the social science and interpretive approaches focus on individual behavior, the critical approach is concerned with how societal forces influence and interact with individual forces. It examines the roles that power and hierarchy play in these interactions and ultimately seeks to change society. "Critical scholars believe that by examining such interactions and writing about how power functions in them, people gain the awareness they need to resist societal forces of power and oppression" (Alberts et al., 2019, p. 37). Critical researchers generally use qualitative methods, such as conducting textual analyses on media such as TV, movies, blogs, speeches and social media.

All three approaches have been used in the study of social media and have contributed to knowledge of the field. According to Humphreys (2016):

> There are a number of ways to approach the emerging topic of social media. Computer scientists and engineers have methods for understanding the flows of data and content between networked computers. . . . Critical studies in the humanities can enlighten us to the importance of social media in political and cultural life and sensitize us to the continuing power imbalances that these discourses reproduce. . . . Sociologists can enable us to see how dynamics emerge between groups of people as they communicate. Psychologists can tell us how people pursue goals online. Communication scholars can help us understand power relationships between audience and producer in historical context and enlighten us to the rhetoric and genres of social media as well as the interpersonal dynamics and human communication. Ethnography from anthropology can give us a grounded perspective on changing cultural practices.
>
> (p. 3)

In addition to different assumptions and approaches, research has different goals. Basic research seeks to expand knowledge while applied research seeks to solve real-world knowledge. Basic research often serves as the foundation for applied studies.

> Basic research, or fundamental research, is a type of investigation focused on improving the understanding of a particular phenomenon, study or law of nature. This type of research examines data to find the unknown and fulfill a sense of curiosity. Usually, these involve "how," "what" and "why" questions to explain occurrences. Basic research looks at how processes or concepts work. Information obtained from basic research often creates a foundation for applied studies.
>
> (Indeed Editorial Team, 2022, para. 2)

While basic research is driven by curiosity, applied research is driven by solutions. Applied research aims to solve practical problems of the modern world, rather than to acquire knowledge for knowledge's sake. "In applied research, researchers often work to help a client and are driven by the client's desires. Basic research tends to be self-initiated and caused by an individual's motivation to learn more about an area" (Indeed Editorial Team, 2022, para. 9).

Finally, communication research is also organized by various areas of communication study. This book follows the classification system offered by Stacks and Salwen (2009), which categorizes the various theoretical approaches into mass communication, human communication and integrated approaches—"those that crossed the traditional divide between mass and human communication" (p. x).

Social Spotlight

Social media scholars and industry professionals might approach the field differently—and publish their work in different places—but their theoretical and practical insights are equally valuable. In order to stay up-to-date and knowledgeable on important social media findings and trends, social strategists can consult the following sources and professional organizations:

Academic Journals

- *Convergence: The International Journal of Research into New Media Technologies*
- *Cyberpsychology, Behavior, and Social Networking*
- *Journal of Computer-Mediated Communication*
- *Journal of Magazine and New Media Research*
- *New Media and Society*

Industry Publications and Websites

- Hootsuite Blog: https://blog.hootsuite.com/
- PR Daily: www.prdaily.com/category/social-media/
- Sprout Social Blog: https://sproutsocial.com/insights/
- Social Media Examiner: www.socialmediaexaminer.com/
- Social Media Today: www.socialmediatoday.com/
- Strategies & Tactics: www.prsa.org/publications-and-news/strategies-tactics
- The Associated Press Stylebook: www.apstylebook.com

Professional Organizations

- National Communication Association (NCA)
- International Communication Association (ICA)
- Canadian Communication Association (CCA)
- Public Relations Society of America (PRSA)
- International Public Relations Association (IPRA)
- American Marketing Association (AMA)
- Society of Professional Journalists (SPJ)
- Association for Education in Journalism and Mass Communication (AEJMC)

The Scientific Method

Research is the use of the scientific method to answer questions. The scientific method is a systematic way of pursuing knowledge, meaning it follows a set process. This process involves observing some phenomenon that needs to be explained, developing research questions and/or hypotheses, collecting data through various means, and accepting, rejecting or modifying the hypotheses based on the outcome of the test. "From that data and the many different scientific investigations undertaken to explore hypotheses, scientists are able to develop broad general explanations, or scientific theories" (Britannica, n.d.). The scientific method, therefore, is a means to developing theory.

Models of Communication

A model suggests relationships and helps to formulate theory; it is a simplified representation of the real world. According to Severin and Tankard, Jr. (2001):

> A model provides a frame within which we can consider a problem, even if in its early versions it does not lead to successful prediction. A model may also point out important gaps in our knowledge that are

not apparent, and it may suggest areas where research is needed (the goal of closure). Failure of a model when it is tested may lead to an improved model.

(p. 47)

Two early models of communication included Laswell's Model and the Shannon-Weaver Model. Laswell's Model from 1948 served as early verbal model in communication and explains the communication process as linear with five basic questions: Who, Says What, In Which Channel, To Who and With What Effect. Shannon and Weaver's 1949 model also explained the communication process as linear. In this model, an information source creates a message; a sender/transmitter converts the message to a signal; the channel transmits the signal from the sender to the receiver; and the receiver sends feedback to the sender. The model also identifies noise as anything and everything that interferes with the transmission of the message (e.g., traffic, internal dialogue and stress).

While not abandoned, these linear models have been criticized by some researchers as unrealistic because they do not accurately represent the dynamic and interactive process of communication. "This is especially true in the Digital Age, as information does not have to be consumed linearly (from beginning to end) and individuals are able to respond and participate in the creation and communication of messages" (Sterin & Winston, 2018, p. 11).

Sterin and Winston (2018), instead, propose a transactional model that "shows how the sender and receiver are constantly encoding and decoding messages, providing feedback to each other, and being affected by noise—all at the same time."

Perspective From the Pros

By Megan Fitzgerald Dunn, Ph.D.

While the mention of theory and the scientific method often elicits yawns from students, communication theory, and the research related to it, is essential to the field. Mass communication research plays a pivotal role in the discovery of how people use, distribute and interact with media. It also allows both scholars and practitioners to understand the benefits and consequences of this media consumption. The impacts of social media is one area of communication research that has received a great deal of attention—from both communication scholars and the popular press.

The book "Social Media Communication: Trends and Theories" by author Bu Zhong, a journalism and communication professor at Penn State, explores all aspects of social media's influence. It examines how social media affects the media industry, interpersonal and group communication, information processing, and even marketing. It provides a close-up examination of how social media is transforming the way people think and behave.

A particularly interesting insight from Zhong's work is how challenging group communication was prior to social media. Social media has made it possible for large groups of people to easily find one another and connect. This, according to Zhong, is particularly evident in both the positive and negative social movements that have gained momentum in recent years. For example, in August 2022, the Associated Press reported that Facebook parent company, Meta, removed a network of accounts linked to the Proud Boys, a far-right extremist group it banned in 2018. Although the group is banned from Facebook and Instagram, the Associated Press reported that the social media sites repeatedly see users attempt to evade the ban. In fact, according to the AP, in just the first six months of 2022, over 750 accounts linked to the Proud Boys were removed. The continuous cropping up of these accounts speaks to Zhong's research on the ease of group communication since the advent of social media. While the Proud Boys may find homes on smaller internet platforms, none comes close to the reach of sites like Facebook and Instagram, where the group can recruit more members.

Without communication theory and research, such as the work by Zhong, social media practitioners would not be able to grasp the scope or the impact of the medium. Communication research allows communication professionals to better understand their field and their clients.

Chapter Summary

- Theories are explanations for how the world works. The development of theory is the ultimate goal of science.
- In the field of human communication, researchers have different assumptions or worldviews about the nature of human communication and can use different approaches in the quest to "know" something.
- The research methods—the specific ways that scholars collect and analyze data—chosen should reflect the basic assumptions and belief systems the researcher has about human communication.

- Quantitative and qualitative methods collect data differently. Quantitative studies rely on numerical or measurable data, whereas qualitative studies rely on non-numerical data, such as personal accounts or documents.
- Three major approaches to studying human communication include the social science approach, the interpretive approach and the critical approach
- Basic research seeks to expand knowledge, while applied research seeks to solve real-world knowledge.
- Communication research is organized by various areas of communication study, such as mass communication, human communication and integrated approaches.
- Research is the use of the scientific method to answer questions. The scientific method is a systematic way of pursuing knowledge, meaning it follows a set process and is a means of developing theory.
- A model suggests relationships and helps to formulate theory; it is a simplified representation of the real world.
- Early models of communication described the communication process as linear. More current models describe communication not as linear but as transactional.

Exercise 5.1

This chapter introduced different definitions for the term "theory." Locate a definition of theory offered by an author, a scholar or a communications expert that was not explored in this chapter. Compare and contrast this definition with the other definitions presented in this chapter. How is the definition similar? How is it different? Include a full APA citation for the source.

Exercise 5.2

The "Social Spotlight" section of this chapter introduces peer-reviewed academic journals that publish social media-related studies. Select a study/article from one of these journals and respond to the following prompts:

1. Which approach (social science, interpretive or critical) does this study take and why?
2. Does the study use quantitative or qualitative methods? How is the data expressed? What specific method is used (e.g., survey, in-depth interview, experiment and focus group)?

Include an APA citation of the journal article.

Discussion Questions

1. An assumption, or worldview, asks, "What do we really believe about human communication?" Do you subscribe more to Worldview I or Worldview II presented in this chapter? Why?
2. Critical studies have the ultimate goal of changing society. What are some social media-specific problems that could serve as the focus of future critical research?

References

Alberts, J. K., Nakayama, T. K., & Martin, J. N. (2019). *Human communication in society*. Pearson Education, Inc.

Britannica. (n.d.). *Scientific method*. www.britannica.com/science/scientific-method

Humphreys, A. (2016). *Social media: Enduring principles*. Oxford University Press.

Indeed Editorial Team. (2022, May 26). Basic research vs. applied research: What's the difference? *Indeed Career Guide*. www.indeed.com/career-advice/career-development/basic-research-vs-applied-research

Merriam-Webster. (n.d.). *Theory*. www.merriam-webster.com/dictionary/theory

Severin, W. J., & Tankard Jr., J. W. (2001). *Communication theories: Origins, methods, and uses in the mass media*. Addison Wesley Longman.

Stacks, D. W., & Salwen, M. B. (2009). Integrating theory and research: Starting with questions. In D. W. Stacks & M. B. Salwen (Eds.), *An integrated approach to communication theory and research* (pp. 3–11). Routledge.

Sterin, J. C., & Winston, T. (2018). *Mass media revolution*. Taylor & Francis.

Treadwell, D. (2017). *Introducing communication research: Paths of inquiry*. SAGE Publications, Inc.

Wrench, J. S., Thomas-Maddox, C., Richmond, V. P., & McCroskey, J. C. (2008). *Quantitative research methods for communication: A hands-on approach*. Oxford University Press.

6 Mass Communication Approaches

Mass media—the media we use to communicate with the masses—can be traced back to oral storytelling, the scribes and the visual arts, such as prehistoric cave paintings, maps, illustrations in early editions of the Bible, and even masterpieces created by some of the greatest artists and musicians during the Renaissance. Gutenberg's invention of the movable-type printing press in 1450 is considered the birth of modern mass media, long before the development of today's mass media (print, radio, broadcast and the internet, among others).

Mass media has been defined in a variety of ways. Sterin and Winston (2018) define the term as "the communication platforms that enable the exchange of information and meanings (content) between individuals and groups" (p. 473). The strength in this particular definition is its connection to the primary purpose of communication—the creation of shared meaning.

Since the 1970s when mass communication was established as an area of study, most researchers have generally studied the field by examining media effects on audiences, although critical research has expanded the lens to also look at societal influences on media production. According to Greenberg and Salwen (2009):

> The quantitative tradition in mass communication has become dominant in the United States today, although there has been a renewed interest in qualitative research and the macro-level social effects. . . . Critical scholarship also has had an impact on mass communication thinking. It has stimulated interest in expanding inquiry beyond media effects on audiences—traditionally the main focus on mass communication—and looking at media production processes as well.
>
> (p. 65)

A large portion of mass communication research has been guided by models such as agenda-setting, cultivation analysis, and uses and gratifications, which this chapter will explore further and in relation to one specific mass media platform—social media.

DOI: 10.4324/9781003255734-8

What you can expect to learn in this chapter:

- An introduction to mass communication research, including an overview of three select theories/models/concepts representing mass communication research: Agenda-Setting, Cultivation Theory, Uses and Gratifications
- The origins of these theories, models and concepts of mass communication
- Methods associated with these theories, models and concepts of mass media
- An application of these theories, models and concepts to the field of social media
- Other theories/models/concepts representing mass communication research

Theories and Models of Mass Communication

Agenda Setting

The agenda-setting hypothesis has been a dominant concept in communication theory since the early 1970s. This function of the media refers to "the media's capability, through repeated news coverage, of raising the importance of an issue in the public's mind" (Severin & Tankard, 2001, p. 219).

Maxwell McCombs and Donald Shaw (1972) conducted the first systematic study of the agenda-setting hypothesis during the U.S. presidential campaign of 1968. McCombs and Shaw, professors at the University of North Carolina Chapel Hill, were interested in whether the issues selected and covered by the news media influenced people's perception of the world and if there was a relationship between the priority issues of the media and priority issues of the public. The scholars focused their study on undecided voters in Chapel Hill, North Carolina, and hypothesized these voters would be most susceptible to the effects of agenda-setting. The researchers interviewed a sample of 100 respondents and simultaneously conducted a content analysis of the mass media serving these voters that included five newspapers, two news magazines and two TV network evening news broadcasts. The findings supported the agenda-setting effect and showed a strong relationship between the campaign issues emphasized by the media and the various campaign topics perceived as important by voters (Severin & Tankard, 2001).

Since the Chapel Hill study, the agenda-setting function of the mass media has been widely studied in election and non-election settings. Most studies use a methodology similar to that of the Chapel Hill study: a quantitative content analysis for examining the media agenda that is compared with results of public opinion polls. Other methods, such as laboratory experiments, have also been used (Valenzuela & McCombs, 2009).

Scholars have applied the ideas of agenda-setting—the transfer of salience from one agenda to another—to other areas such as professional sports, classroom teaching, corporate reputations, and the internet. According to Valenzuela and McCombs (2009):

> Across both the traditional and new domains of agenda setting, the Internet is a major research frontier. For some observers, the availability of many channels and the opportunity for users to seek their own personal agendas challenges a basic tenet of agenda setting that the media tend to share the same set of news priorities. Consequently, the argument goes, the power of the mass media to set the public agenda may be on the wane.
>
> (p. 102)

The study of agenda-setting in a social media setting has examined whether social media coverage leads to an increase of activism. A study by Hassid (2012) suggests the answer often depends on who leads the agenda. Hassid found that when blogs lead the agenda in advance of mainstream media, it can create a "pressure cooker" effect in which mainstream media are forced to cover an issue that may have otherwise been ignored. When mainstream media lead the agenda, however, blogs serve as more of a "safety value" where people can discuss the headlines and recap the media coverage.

Cultivation Theory

Cultivation Theory seeks to explain the effects of television viewing on people's perceptions, attitudes and values. According to Signorielli and Morgan (2009):

> People around the world have been fascinated by television but concerned about its effects almost since the first show was broadcast. In this country, the popular press and politicians keep asking, "What is television doing to us?" "Is television somehow responsible for all the violence in our society?" Parents and teachers wonder whether television makes children more aggressive, or whether television helps or hinders learning. Critics of all political stripes complain about how television portrays men and women, the family, politics, war, nutrition, sexuality, consumption, minorities, substance abuse, and a host of other issues, as well as the massive number of hours we spend watching.
>
> (p. 106)

This approach started with George Gerbner at the Annenberg School of Communication at the University of Pennsylvania in the 1960s (Signorielli & Morgan, 2009). Gerbner attempted to develop a new approach to the study of mass communication that focused on the process of mass communication itself. Gerber framed mass communication as the mass production of messages (Morgan & Shanahan, 2010). The exposure to the same messages produces an effect called cultivation, "or the teaching of a common worldview, common roles, and common values" (Severin & Tankard, 2001, p. 268). In 1967, Gerbner's Cultural Indicators project, funded by the National Commission on the Causes and Prevention of Violence, began conducting annual analyses of prime-time broadcasting with the goal of documenting the extent to which violence dominated dramatic television programming and describing the nature of television violence (Morgan & Shanahan, 2010; Signorielli & Morgan, 2009).

Rather than examining the impact of any specific TV show, genre or episode, cultivation analysis is concerned with a system of messages such as cultural themes, images, lessons and values that are present across many genres and programs (Signorielli & Morgan, 2009). "If cultivation theory is correct, then television could be having important but unnoticeable effects on society. For instance, cultivation theory suggests that heavy television watching makes people feel that the world is an unsafe place" (Severin & Tankard, 2001, p. 268). Identifying and assessing these patterns in television content is accomplished by using content analysis or by examining consistent content studies. According to Signorielli and Morgan (2009):

> Designed primarily for television and focusing on its pervasive and recurrent patterns of representation and viewing, cultivation analysis concentrates on the enduring and common consequences of growing up and living with television: the cultivation of stable, resistant, and widely shared assumptions, images, and conceptions reflecting the institutional characteristics and interests of the medium itself and the larger society.
>
> (p. 118)

Early research using cultivation theory compared heavy and light television viewers. Gerbner and his team found that heavy television viewers often responded to questions in surveys with answers that are closer to the way the world is portrayed on television (Gerbner & Gross, 1976). While the theory originally applied to television viewing, it's also evolved along with technology. For example, the theory has been used to look at the possible effects of cable television and VCR content and even pornography content (Severin & Tankard, 2001).

Morgan and Shanahan (2010) posed the question, "But can we still talk about cultivation in the age of YouTube, Facebook, Hulu, Twitter and Tivo?" (p. 350). They say yes, especially since the age of social media and streaming makes it more convenient for us to watch and, therefore, we spend even more time watching. "As long as there are popular storytelling systems and purveyors of widely shared messages, Gerbner's main ideas are likely to persist" (p. 350).

Uses and Gratifications

Approaches such as agenda-setting approach and cultivation theory examine the effects of media upon an audience and largely assume a passive audience, with "the media 'acting' upon their viewers, listeners and readers" (Severin & Tankard, 2001, p. 293). Uses and gratifications (U&G), however, assumes an active audience and examines how individuals select and use mass media and content to fulfill needs and desires. Instead of asking "What do media do to people?" U&G asks "What do people do with the media?" According to Severin and Tankard (2001):

> The uses and gratifications approach reminds us of one very important point—people use the media for many different purposes. This approach suggests that, to a large extent, the user of mass communication is in control. The uses and gratifications approach can serve as a health antidote to the emphasis on passive audiences and persuasion that has dominated much earlier research.
>
> (p. 302)

Uses and gratifications has its origins in Lasswell's (1948) model that asks who uses which media, how and with what effect. Lasswell identified three primary functions of mass media: surveillance of the environment, correlation of events, and transmission of social heritage, which became the foundation for formulating media needs and expectations with the uses and gratifications model (Papacharissi, 2009).

Early U&G studies examined people's motivations for listening to different radio content, such as quiz shows and soap operas, and found that the media can help fulfill several everyday needs (Herzog, 1940, 1944; Lazarsfeld, 1940). Studies later examined how other media, like cable television, film, the VCR and computers, fulfill various needs. According to Papacharissi (2009):

> The strength of the U&G perspective lies in its applicability to a variety of media contexts. Despite the diversity of context and interests, U&G studies tend to share a common frame of analysis that focuses on motives, social and psychological antecedents, and cognitive, attitudinal, or behavioral outcomes. A typical U&G study will focus on a particular medium or compare uses and gratifications across media.
>
> (p. 139)

So what about the internet and social media? According to Papacharissi (2009), "Considerable attention has also been devoted to the informational and social uses of newer media, like the Internet" (p. 143). For example, Chang (1998) sent an email questionnaire to students asking about their reasons for visiting online news sites and found that the media attributes of immediacy (knowing something right away) and stability (getting news when they want it) were the most important to users of online news sites.

The introduction of social media has offered communication researchers the opportunity to examine media audiences, not just as consumers of media but as producers of media.

> For U&G researchers, this is an opportunity to examine the audience member under a new light and in a different role. . . . A typical U&G study of blogging, therefore, would be focused on understanding how blogs are put to use, which factors mediate that use, and what types of consequences follow this use.
>
> (Papacharissi, 2009, p. 145)

While surveys with scales measuring motives are a popular method used by researchers, studying U&G, textual and content analyses can also be useful, for example, the use of blog text in assessing consequences of media use in addition to those self-reported by bloggers. "The combination of survey and content analysis would thus expand the methodological scope of U&G" (Papacharissi, 2009, p. 146).

Social Spotlight

Uses and Gratifications theory examines how people use media to fulfill certain needs. People use social media for a variety of reasons—to connect, to be entertained, to escape, to create identity, and to learn something. But to adopt?

In 2022, "USA Today" reported that some people were bypassing the traditional route of using an adoption agency to grow their families and turning to social media instead. Families are creating social media pages, promoting their adoption searches, and hoping to reach expectant mothers.

According to Zignal Labs, an online tool for analyzing social media content, mentions of the hashtag #Adoption have increased 92% on Twitter in the last five years, along with a 76% increase for #HopingToAdopt during the same time frame. The hashtag #AdoptionJourney appears in nearly 400,000 Instagram posts and on TikTok videos with more than 400 million views. The hashtags #AdoptionStory, #AdoptionRocks, #AdoptionDay and #AdoptionIsLove have together garnered millions of views, as well. Looker (2022) wrote:

> Social media platforms are a relatively new frontier for those seeking to adopt—particularly now that the demand for newborns

exceeds the supply. Instagram, Facebook, TikTok and Twitter all are taking on the liaison role traditionally played by adoption agencies.

(para. 4)

While social media allows families to cast a wider net in the adoption search, this strategy can lead to letdowns and scams without the oversight and protection of an adoption agency. There's also no professional guidance offered to families during the process. AdoptMatch Co-founder Celeste Liversidge said:

> We hear lots of horror stories from adoptive parents who have been through the wringer and have unfortunately learned the hard way about the importance of working with an ethical adoption attorney or agency. For expectant moms, pursuing adoption using the internet is very confusing. . . . It's very difficult for them to discern between licensed and unlicensed and then, within that orbit, who are the good guys.
>
> (Looker, 2022, para. 19)

There's no question that the ways that people use social media to connect and fulfill other needs will continue to evolve. The question that remains, however, is whether or not these niche needs can be successfully met by social media.

Perspective From the Pros

By Whitney Lehmann, Ph.D., APR

The Uses and Gratifications Model assumes that communication behavior, including media selection, is goal-directed in that we select specific communication channels to fulfill specific needs and desires. While we know that traditional word-of-mouth—the informal conversations that take place between friends, family, co-workers and neighbors—has been found to have a significant impact on consumer choice, including the choice of where to enroll for college, I was interested in learning if electronic word-of-mouth, also known as eWOM, had a similar effect on the college choice process. eWOM exists online and allows consumers, who are typically strangers, to interact with one another and share opinions about various goods and services through review sites, social networking sites, blogs, content-sharing sites and other forms of social media.

I made this research question the topic of my doctoral dissertation in 2015 and decided to focus on the search and choice phases of the college choice process. Hossler and Gallagher (1987) define the search phase as the stage during which a student gathers information and forms a "choice set" of institutions to apply to and the choice phase as the stage in which a student decides where to enroll.

In my review of the literature, I learned that no existing studies had specifically examined eWOM's perceived influence on the college choice process; however, there were limited studies examining the perceived influence of social media on college choice and found that prospective students consider social media to be the least important, least influential and least reliable source of information among college search and enrollment source. Admission counselors, friends, relatives and currents students at the school of interest are all considered more influential than social media in terms of influencing the enrollment decision (Constantinides & Zinck Stagno, 2011; Noel-Levitz, 2014; Parrot & Tipton, 2010).

Based on findings from the literature review, I developed hypotheses and designed an online survey that was administered to first-year, non-transfer undergraduate students at the University of Miami. Two hundred seventy-six students responded to the survey. The results supported previous findings that prospective students place more importance on traditional word-of-mouth than electronic word-of-mouth during the college choice process. These findings should not be taken to mean, however, that social media and eWOM do not play a role in the college choice process or that marketing and recruitment officials should stop creating and maintaining official college social media. A third of students reported that they used eWOM when making an application decision, and a fourth of students reported that they used eWOM when making an enrollment decision.

The findings of this study, which were published in the journal College & University (Lehmann, 2017), suggest that higher education officials can be more strategic in their social media efforts by fostering the creation and exchange of eWOM on their official social media presences, specifically, eWOM pertaining to the college search. Furthermore, because this study suggests that eWOM has the greatest perceived influence on college search and choice when consumed on online review/forums sites, higher education officials should encourage the creation and exchange of eWOM on these sites.

Other Theories/Models of Mass Communication

This chapter provides a snapshot of three models/theories/concepts representative of the mass communication approach to research, including their origins, initial applications and considerations for application to social media. Other widely used theories, concepts and models in this area of research include media gatekeeping, spiral of silence, and the knowledge-gap hypothesis, among others, which can also be examined and applied through a social media lens.

Chapter Summary

- Mass media are defined as "the communication platforms that enable the exchange of information and meanings (content) between individuals and groups" (Sterin & Winston, 2018, p. 473).
- Since the 1970s when mass communication was established as an area of study, most researchers have generally studied the field by examining media effects on audiences, although critical research has expanded the lens to also look at societal influences on media production. In addition, some models, like Uses & Gratifications, assume audiences are active, rather passive, and examine how individuals select and use mass media.
- The agenda-setting hypothesis has been a dominant concept in communication in communication theory since the early 1970s and has been widely studied in election and non-election settings to examine how the media set the agenda for what the public think and talk about. An example of the agenda-setting approach applied in a social media setting is examining whether social media coverage leads to an increase in activism.
- Cultivation Theory seeks to explain the effects of television viewing on people's perceptions, attitudes, and values and was first used in the late 1960s to analyze prime-time broadcasting with the goal of documenting the extent to which violence dominated dramatic television programming. Cultivation theory has been examined in the digital age in terms of how streaming services and social media make it easier to consume content, and, therefore, increase the time people spend viewing content. Just as cultivation theory analyzes a system of messages used across television genres, programs and episodes, it can also evaluate patterns of messages used across types of social media and on specific social media sites.
- The Uses and Gratifications Model assumes that communication behavior, including media selection, is goal-directed in that we select specific communication channels to fulfill specific needs and desires. Uses and gratifications model can be applied in a social media context to examine the reasons people seek out and use social media or the reasons they are motivated to produce social media content.

- Other widely used theories, concepts and models in the area of mass communication research include media gatekeeping, spiral of silence, the hypodermic needle theory, and the knowledge-gap hypothesis, among others, which can also be examined and applied through a social media lens.

Exercise 6.1

Cultivation analysis is concerned with a system of messages such as cultural themes, images, lessons and values that are present across many genres and programs. While the approach has traditionally been used to analyze television content, it's also been used to examine other forms of content, such as DVR content, cable TV content, pornography, streaming content and social media. Locate a study that applies cultivation analysis to social media content and respond to the following prompts:

1. Which approach (social science, interpretive or critical) does this study take and why?
2. What specific method is used (e.g., survey, in-depth interview, experiment and focus group)?
3. What is the "system of messages" that was analyzed?

Include an APA citation of the journal article.

Exercise 6.2

Locate another theory/model/concept of mass communication not explored in this chapter, such as spiral of silence, media gatekeeping or the hypodermic needle. How is this theory/model/concept defined, what are its origins, and which methodology do researchers using this approach typically employ? Has this theory/model/concept been examined in relation to social media? If so, how?

Discussion Questions

1. The "Social Spotlight" section of this chapter examined how some people are turning to social media to fulfill their adoption desires. What are some other, nonconventional ways that people are using social media to satisfy needs or fulfill desires?
2. The agenda-setting approach theorizes that media set the public agenda and influences what we think about and talk about. Using agenda-setting as a framework, do you think social media influencers also influence the public agenda? Why or why not?

References

Chang, Y.-M. (1998). *Audience analyses of online news: Who uses online news and why do people use online news?* Unpublished master's thesis, The University of Texas at Austin.

Constantinides, E., & Zinck Stagno, M. C. (2011). Potential of the social media as instruments of higher education marketing: A segmentation study. *Journal of Marketing for Higher Education, 21*(1), 7–24.

Gerbner, G., & Gross, L. P. (1976). The scary world of TV's heavy viewer. *Psychology Today,* (April), 41–45.

Greenberg, B. S., & Salwen, M. B. (2009). Mass communication theory and research. In D. W. Stacks & M. B. Salwen (Eds.), *An integrated approach to communication theory and research* (pp. 61–74). Routledge.

Hassid, J. (2012). Safety valve or pressure cooker? Blogs in Chinese political life. *Journal of Communication, 62*(2), 212–230.

Herzog, H. (1940). Professor quiz: A gratification study. In P. F. Lazarsfeld (Ed.), *Ratio and the printed page* (pp. 64–93). Duell, Sloan & Pearce.

Herzog, H. (1944). What do we really know about daytime serial listeners? In P. F. Lazarsfeld & F. N. Stanton (Eds.), *Radio research 1942–1943* (pp. 3–33). Duell, Sloan & Pearce.

Hossler, D., & Gallagher, K. (1987). Studying student college choice: A three-phase model and the implications for policymakers. *College and University, 62*(3), 207–221.

Lasswell, H. (1948). The structure and function of communications in society. In L. Bryson (Ed.), *The communication of ideas* (pp. 37–51). Harper & Row.

Lazarsfeld, P. F. (1940). *Radio and the printed page.* Duell, Sloan & Pearce.

Lehmann, W. (2017). The influence of electronic word of mouth on the college search and choice. *College & University, 92*(4), 2–11.

Looker, R. (2022, June 7). *Now trending: Instagram adoptions. How social media has influenced the way people adopt kids.* www.usatoday.com/in-depth/news/investigations/2022/06/07/social-media-influence-instagram-facebook-tiktok-adoptions-of-babies/9734980002/

McCombs, M., & Shaw, D. L. (1972). The agenda-setting function of mass media. *Public Opinion Quarterly, 36*(2), 176–187.

Morgan, M., & Shanahan, J. (2010). The state of cultivation. *Journal of Broadcasting and Electronic Media, 54*(2), 337–355.

Noel-Levitz. (2014). *2014 E-expectations report: The online preferences of college-bound high school seniors and their parents.* www.noellevitz.com/papers-research-higher-education/2014/2014-e-expectations-report

Papacharissi, Z. (2009). Uses and gratifications. In D. W. Stacks & M. B. Salwen (Eds.), *An integrated approach to communication theory and research* (pp. 137–152). Routledge.

Parrot, T. V., & Tipton, S. (2010). Using social media "smartly" in the admissions process. *College & University, 86*(1), 51–53.

Severin, W. J., & Tankard Jr., J. W. (2001). *Communication theories: Origins, methods, and uses in the mass media.* Addison Wesley Longman.

Signorielli, N., & Morgan, M. (2009). Cultivation analysis: Research and practice questions. In D. W. Stacks & M. B. Salwen (Eds.), *An integrated approach to communication theory and research* (pp. 106–121). Routledge.

Sterin, J. C., & Winston, T. (2018). *Mass media revolution.* Taylor & Francis.

Valenzuela, S., & McCombs, M. (2009). The agenda-setting role of the news media. In D. W. Stacks & M. B. Salwen (Eds.), *An integrated approach to communication theory and research* (pp. 90–105). Routledge.

7 Human Communication and Integrated Approaches

The last chapter provided an overview of communication research through a mass media lens and examined how various theories, models and concepts can be used to study media effects on audiences and also how audiences use mass media to fulfill specific needs and desires.

This chapter examines communication research through a different lens—a human communication lens—that explores how, when, where and why humans interact. The study of human communication differs from other fields that study humans like psychology and sociology in that it exclusively focuses on the exchange of messages to create meaning. It also explores an integrated approach that crosses the traditional divide between mass and human communication, taking into consideration new media technologies that don't necessarily fit into categories of mass communication or human communication.

What you can expect to learn in this chapter:

- An introduction to human communication research, including an overview of interpersonal communication, rhetoric/persuasion and political communication
- An introduction to integrated approaches of communication research, such as diffusion of innovation and communication ethics
- The origins of these theories, models and concepts of human communication and integrated communication
- Methods associated with these theories, models and concepts
- An application of these theories, models and concepts to the field of social media
- Other theories/models/concepts representing human communication research and integrated approaches

Theories of Human Communication

Unlike most social sciences, the study of human communication has a long history and can be traced back thousands of years. "We can safely safe that,

DOI: 10.4324/9781003255734-9

since humankind first acquired the ability to communicate through verbal and nonverbal symbols and norms, people have 'studied' communication" (Richmond & McCroskey, 2009, p. 223).

The study of human communication can be divided into two major classifications—relational and rhetorical (Shepherd, 1992). The relational approach examines communication from a transactional or co-orientational perspective, whereas the rhetorical approach focuses on persuasion. These two approaches should not be viewed as polar opposites but rather as representing differences in emphasis. "Both are interested in accomplishing objectives and maintaining good relationships through communication. Each, however, emphasizes one objective over the other" (Richmond & McCroskey, 2009, p. 224).

In the next section, we'll examine the objectives of interpersonal communication and rhetorical study. In addition to these two dominant areas of study, other areas of human communication research widely studied include intercultural communication, intrapersonal communication, nonverbal communication, small group communication and organizational communication.

Interpersonal Communication

Interpersonal communication research examines social interaction between people and seeks to understand how people use verbal and nonverbal messages to achieve different communication goals, such as informing, persuading and providing emotional support to others (Berger, 2009).

The study of interpersonal communication developed during the years following World War II and focused on two distinct areas of social-psychological research: the role that communication plays in persuasion and social influence and social interaction within small groups (known as group dynamics). Today, the study of interpersonal communication can be categorized into six unique yet related areas of study, with each representing a body of theory and research (Berger, 2009):

1. Uncertainty Reduction Theory
    Uncertainty Reduction Theory argues relationship development is facilitated or derailed by participants' efforts to reduce their uncertainty about each other and that assumes that people are uncomfortable with uncertainty about others and seek to reduce it to determine if the other person is "safe, interesting, and desirable—or dangerous, boring, and undesirable" (Alberts et al., 2019, p. 197).
2. Interpersonal Adaptation
    Interpersonal adaptation refers to the strong tendency of individuals to reciprocate each other's verbal and nonverbal behaviors when they converse.

3. Message Production

   Message production focuses on social interaction being used as tool or instrument for attaining everyday goals.

4. Relationship Development

   Relationship development focuses on the idea that interpersonal communication plays an important role in the development, maintenance and breakdown of social and personal relationships. This area of research has examined romantic relationships, as well as communication between friends, spouses and family members.

5. Deceptive Communication

   This area of research examines the role of deception in social interactions. "So called 'white-lies' are commonplace in everyday social commerce. Some have gone as far as to argue that deception is an important lubricant that enables the smooth operation of the social interaction machine" (Berger, 2009, p. 268).

6. Mediated Social Interaction

   Mediated Social Interaction refers to social interactions that take place through communicated technologies such as computers with email and social media and cell phones with text messages and video chat like FaceTime.

In addition to these six dominant areas, other areas of interpersonal communication inquiry include communication competence and communication routines, among others.

By eliminating the need for geographic proximity, social media can influence many aspects of relationships (Luttrell & Wallace, 2021). Interpersonal relationships on social media have been studied by virtual community researchers, organizers, advertisers, marketers and others who are interested in how social media can shape aspects of relationships like trust, participation and influence.

Luttrell & Wallace (2021) identifies two specific areas of interpersonal communication that have been studied in relation to social media. The first is the influence of networking on social connection, social support and social capital. The interpersonal connection behaviors framework states that social networking sites benefit end users when they are used to make connections but harm them when things like isolation and direct social comparisons are experienced. The concept of social support suggests that people visit different social sites based on their need for social support and connection. Social networking provides the social connections and social support that can lead to the development of social capital, an individual's networks and contacts.

The second area of interest is user-generated content (UGC) for influence and decision making. Beveridge (2022) defines user-generated content as "any content—text, videos, images, reviews, etc.—created by people, rather than brands" (para. 1). Studies have examined how UGC builds trust and drives decision making, especially in relation to purchasing decisions.

"More and more frequently, brands are using UGC for direct advertising to all generations" (Luttrell & Wallace, 2021, p. 37).

Rhetoric/Persuasion

Rhetoric, also called the art of persuasion, refers to communication used to influence the attitudes or behaviors of others. "The rhetorical tradition lies at the heart of communication studies. Since the days of Aristotle in ancient Greece, rhetoric has been considered the art of persuasion" (Alberts et al., 2019, p. 286). The study of communication can be traced back over 2,000 years ago when ancient philosophers such as Aristotle in Greece and Confucius in China recognized the relationship between rulers and the people they governed. According to Sterin and Winston (2018):

> Confucius believed that spoken and written words served as forces for social change and could significantly influence how both individuals and even entire societies behaved. Aristotle also recognized the power of spoken and written words, especially when they were expressed persuasively and in the right setting by a well-respected person. He believed that in the right combination, words could shape what people thought and how they.
>
> (p. 8)

Rhetorical communication serves at least three important social functions. First, it's essential to democracy. According to Alberts et al. (2019):

> For people to make informed decisions (and vote) about a range of issues, they must consume rhetorical messages critically and then advocate with care. By advocating for one's perspective and engaging with the perspectives of others, people can make decisions together regarding the common good.
>
> (p. 287)

Second, it helps people seek justice, for example, in a courtroom setting where lawyers and jurors need rhetorical skills not only to argue their case or persuade others of the proper verdict but also to listen critically. Third, rhetoric helps individuals clarify their own beliefs and actions, for example, when experts and national leaders comment in the aftermath of a crisis to help society make sense of it.

Cisneros et al. (2009) outlined four primary areas of scholarship related to rhetorical theory:

1. A more traditional paradigm of rhetorical theory in which rhetoric is viewed as a strategic means to persuasion
2. Rhetoric's influence on sense of self and on larger social realities

3. The shaping of ideological cultures, such as those based on class, gender and ethnicity, by popular discourse
4. An examination of how rhetoric works or what rhetoric does

In choosing their areas of research, rhetorical critics make choices along at least two broad levels. First, they select a unit of analysis, the instances of rhetoric or messages they will study, which are often referred to as "texts," because of the traditional focus on speech texts, although rhetorical studies can examine a variety of messages such as pamphlets, newspapers, or TV and radio content. Second, rhetorical researchers establish goals for their research by asking what the purpose is of their analysis. For example, some scholars study rhetorical texts to learn more about the texts themselves or about the processes of persuasion or to understand the possible role(s) rhetoric can play within society and politics.

One common application of rhetorical study within a social media landscape is examining the influence of electronic word-of-mouth, also known as eWOM, which exists online and allows consumers, who are typically strangers, to interact with one another and share their opinions about various goods and services. An increasing number of consumers make purchasing decisions based on social media referrals (Chu & Choi, 2011). eWOM's influence in relation to consumer decisions has been examined across numerous industries, including tech-electronics (e.g., DVD players and computers), books, high-touch retail (e.g., clothing, appliances and furniture), no-touch services (e.g., travel, vacations and financial services), household staples (e.g., beverages and pet supplies) and online entertainment (e.g., movies, music, games and television content available on the web) and for specific consumer products and services, such as video games, beauty products, box-office movies, music and mortgages.

Another application of rhetorical study on social media is examining the influence of political communication, for example, how social media is used by activists and social movements to increase civic engagement and amplify social issues. Activists have employed different types of social media, such as blogs, microblogs and content-management sites (e.g., WordPress) to spur social media movements like #OccupyWallStreet (OWS), #BlackLivesMatter and the #MeToo movement, among countless others. In recent years, social media, particularly Twitter, have become a popular way for political groups and social movements to organize, even leading to the widespread use of the term "hashtag activism." "Social media activism is an online form of protest or advocacy for a cause. Because hashtags play a central role in mobilizing movements on social media, the term is often used interchangeably with hashtag activism" (Newberry & Reid, 2022, para. 1).

Social media has also been examined as a vehicle for political communication, for example with hashtag activism on Twitter, or on social platforms created for the purpose of political discourse like Parler and Truth Social.

Social Media Spotlight

By Megan Fitzgerald Dunn, Ph.D.

Since the 2016 U.S. presidential election, social media and its role in political persuasion have been a staple of news coverage, heated-family dinner conversations and angry tweets. Much of this discussion focuses on false news—news articles that are intentionally shared on social media to manipulate people's perception of reality.

In a 2018 study published in "Science," MIT scholars Soroush Vosoughi, Deb Roy and Sinan Aral found that Tweets containing false information were 70% more likely to be retweeted than truthful tweets. The research also shows that people, not bots, are primarily responsible for spreading misinformation on social networks. In fact, Tweets with misinformation reach 1,500 people on Twitter six times faster than truthful tweets. The study concluded that lies spread faster than truth, leaning into the concern that false news can influence political opinion. While this research sheds important light on how information spreads on social media, the human element is even more interesting. Why do people share these stories? Vosoughi, Roy and Aral hypothesize that it boils down to people like new things.

In an article for MIT News, Aral said that false news is more novel and that people are more likely to share this kind of information. He also pointed out that on social networks people gain attention by being the first to share information, even if possibly false.

"People who share novel information are seen as being in the know," he said to MIT News.

While the speed with which false news spreads on social media is clear, other communication scholars are dedicated to understanding the societal impact of it. Chrysalis Wright, an expert on fake news and director of the University of Central Florida's Media and Migration Lab, helps identify and develop methods to combat false news. In a 2020 article by Jenna Marina Lee for UCF Today, Wright said, "We tend to think that our opinions, attitudes, and beliefs are our own, but that's not 100 percent correct because we are influenced by what we see. Fake news absolutely influences our attitudes, our beliefs, and we also know that that can influence our actual behavior."

Integrated Approaches to Communication

The advent of the internet and new media technologies has created the need for a new category of communication research that can encompass areas of study that do not neatly fit into the box of mass communication or interpersonal communication. Stacks and Salwen (2009) refer to those that cross the traditional divide between mass and human communication as integrated approaches. Since internet research is still evolving and developing its own theoretical base, it applies existing theories, like those established in the field of communication (Messner & Garrison, 2009).

Next, we'll examine internet and social media research using two existing areas of communication study: diffusion of innovation and communications ethics.

Diffusion of Innovations

Diffusion research examines how innovations (e.g., ideas, practices and objects) become known and spread through a social system (Severin & Tankard, 2001). The study of diffusion of innovations began during World War II and can be traced to Bryce Ryan and Neal C. Gross' classic 1943 study of the diffusion of hybrid seed corn among Iowa farmers (Rogers et al., 2009).

Diffusion research in the field of communication began in the 1960s when Deutschmann, a former newspaper reporter and editor who earned his doctorate in communication at Stanford University, and Danielson, a fellow doctoral student at Stanford who also had professional newspaper experience, published an article on the diffusion of news events (Deutschmann & Danielson, 1960).

Most diffusion studies follow the methodology employed by Ryan and Gross in the hybrid corn study and use quantitative analysis of data gathered by survey interview methods from large samples. "The overall effect of these dominant research methods has been to emphasize an understanding of the diffusion process as the product of individual decisions and actions" (Rogers et al., 2009, p. 426).

The introduction of the internet, social media and new media technologies have increased interest in the study of diffusion. The Pew Research Center, for example, examines the diffusion of new media technologies and social media platforms among different demographics. In 2021, the think-tank reported the use of the most popular social media platforms by age, race, gender, income level, level of education and type of community, including urban, suburban, and rural (Auxier & Anderson, 2021). The Pew Research Center also examines the adoption of new media technology, such as smartphones and tablets, and has tracked social media adoption in the United States since 2005 (Pew Research Center, 2021).

Communications Ethics

In Chapter 13: Social Media Policies, Laws and Ethics, we'll examine communications ethics from an applied social media standpoint and how organizations use different types of social media policies to maintain brand identity and protect themselves from compliance-related issues, such as rules issued by regulatory bodies.

From a theoretical perspective, communication ethics examines "the standards of right and wrong that one applies to messages that are sent and received" (Alberts et al., 2019, p. 378).

> Although truthfulness is one of the most fundamental ethical standards, communicating ethically requires much more than simply being truthful. It also involves deciding what information can and should be disclosed or withheld, and assessing the benefit or harm associated with specific messages.
>
> (Alberts et al., 2019, p. 17)

The study of ethics in the social sciences is centuries old. The contemporary study of ethics in communication research and practice is relatively new in comparison and generally reflects some interpretation or judging of value systems. Most of the research surrounding ethics and communications uses a wide variety of quantitative and qualitative methods tied to the areas of journalism and broadcasting, public relations and speech communication.

Communication ethics should not be confused with communication-related laws, such as media law. According to Wright (2009):

> The central core of what ethics and morality are all about deals with differences between good or bad. Laws focus on questions of what is right or wrong. Although it is possible for a law to be bad something ethically good should always be right. Societies make and change laws, but ethical principles, theoretically at least, remain constant over time.
>
> (p. 530)

In navigating ethical communication situations, communication practitioners and scholars can consult the codes of ethics issued by professional organizations in their respective fields. The Associated Press, for example, has a section of its AP Stylebook dedicated to social media guidelines for journalists and other communications professionals.

Perspective From the Pros

By Megan Fitzgerald Dunn, Ph.D.

For some, social media does not require much thought. Take a pretty picture. Write some nice words. Post. However, those posts can have far-reaching impacts. Social media professionals, like all communication professionals, may encounter ethical dilemmas. The Public

Relations Society of America (PRSA) identifies some of these as a lack of transparency, unreported endorsements, consumer privacy breaches, and misrepresentation of a brand or organization.

Take, for example, an Advent Health first-year medical resident who was fired in 2020 over his social media posts. The Central Florida medical resident came under for a series of posts where he endorsed products, including supplements made by Rave Doctor, a company that sells supplements for people attending raves and electronic music festivals, of which he was an authorized representative.

In addition to the ethical issue of product endorsement, the medical resident was also scrutinized for online posts that were deemed inappropriate and unprofessional. These lapses in ethical judgment often result in termination.

In November 2022, the Marked Tree, Arkansas fire chief was fired after less than 10 months in the position over "inappropriate" use of emojis in a private Facebook message that was later made public. The Mayor of Marked Tree, Danny Johnson, said the use of the offensive emojis violated city policy.

And, let's not forget the 2013 incident that made international news, when senior director of corporate communications, Justine Sacco, at InterActiveCorp, tweeted before boarding a plane to Cape Town, South Africa, "Going to Africa. Hope I don't get AIDS. Just kidding. I'm white!" Sacco only had 200 followers at the time but someone shared it and the tweet went viral from there. All of the major news networks covered the story, including NBC, CNN, the BBC and "The New York Times." InterActive Corp terminated Sacco within days.

Social media professionals, and all those in the public eye, must be mindful of making ethical choices and plan for potential ethical dilemmas. The building of trust and the ability to keep that trust is paramount to their success in the field.

Other Integrated Approaches

In addition to the areas of study examined in this section, internet and social media research has applied many other existing theories and models of communication, for example, changes in gatekeeping theory, intermedia agenda-setting, the concept of credibility, uses and gratifications, health communication, and feminist theory and research, among others.

Chapter Summary

- Unlike most social sciences, the study of human communication has a long history and can be traced back thousands of years. The study of human communication can be divided into two major classifications—relational and rhetorical.

- The study of interpersonal communication developed during the years following World War II. This area of research examines social interaction between people and seeks to understand how people use verbal and nonverbal messages to achieve different communication goals, such as informing, persuading and providing emotional support to others.
- Interpersonal communication has been studied within a social media setting, for example, examining the influence of networking on social connection, social support and social capital and the influence of user-generated content (UGC) on decision making.
- Rhetoric, also called the art of persuasion, refers to communication used to influence the attitudes or behaviors of others and can be traced back over 2,000 years ago to ancient philosophers, such as Aristotle in Greece and Confucius in China.
- One common application of rhetorical study within a social media landscape is examining the influence of electronic word-of-mouth, also known as eWOM, which exists online and allows consumers, who are typically strangers, to interact with one another and share their opinions about various goods and services. Another application of rhetorical study on social media is examining the influence of political communication, for example, how social media is used by activists and social movements to increase civic engagement and amplify social issues.
- In addition to interpersonal communication, rhetoric/persuasion and political communication, other widely studied areas of human communication research include intercultural communication, intrapersonal communication, nonverbal communication, small group communication and organizational communication.
- The advent of the internet and new media technologies has created the need for a new category of communication research that can encompass areas of study that do not neatly fit into the box of mass communication or interpersonal communication. This category has been referred to as integrated approaches.
- Diffusion research began during World War II and examines how innovations (e.g., ideas, practices and objects) become known and spread through a social system. The introduction of the internet, social media and new media technologies have increased interest in the study of diffusion, for example, tracking the adoption of social media over time or by different demographics.
- From a theoretical perspective, communication ethics examines "the standards of right and wrong that one applies to messages that are sent and received." The contemporary study of ethics in communication research and practice is relatively new and generally reflects some interpretation or judging of value systems.

- In navigating ethical communication situations, communication practitioners and scholars can consult the codes of ethics issued by professional organizations in their respective fields.
- Internet and social media research has applied many other existing theories and models of communication, for example, changes in gatekeeping theory, intermedia agenda-setting, the concept of credibility, uses and gratifications, health communication, and feminist theory and research, among others.

Exercise 7.1

The concept of social support suggests that people visit different social sites based on their need for social support and connection. Locate a journal article or an article from an industry publication that examines the interpersonal communication concept of social support in relation to specific social media channels and respond to the following prompts:

1. What social media platforms are the focus of the study?
2. How do people seek out social support and connection on these sites?
3. How do the social connections and social support offered through the platform(s) lead to the development of social capital for individuals?

Include an APA citation of the journal or industry article.

Exercise 7.2

This chapter discussed how communication practitioners and professionals can and should consult professional codes of ethics when navigating ethical dilemmas in the field and offered the social media guidelines published by the AP Stylebook as an example.

Locate a code of ethics issued by a professional organization in the field of communication. Is there content dedicated to navigating ethical situations on social media? If so, what specific topics do the guidelines or best practices address in relation to social media?

Discussion Questions

1. Rhetorical study examines writing or speaking as a means of persuasion. How can the study of rhetoric be applied to the content created by social media influencers?
2. Tracking social media adoption rates is one example of how diffusion of innovations can be examined within a social media setting. What's another way that diffusion of innovations theory can be used to study social media?

References

Alberts, J. K., Nakayama, T. K., & Martin, J. N. (2019). *Human communication in society.* Pearson Education, Inc.

Auxier, B., & Anderson, M. (2021, April 7). Social media use in 2021. *Pew Research Center.* www.pewresearch.org/internet/2021/04/07/social-media-use-in-2021/

Berger, C. R. (2009). Interpersonal communication. In D. W. Stacks & M. B. Salwen (Eds.), *An integrated approach to communication theory and research* (pp. 260–279). Routledge.

Beveridge, C. (2022, January 13). What is user-generated content? And why is it important? *Hootsuite.* https://blog.hootsuite.com/user-generated-content-ugc/

Chu, S., & Choi, S. M. (2011). Electronic word-of-mouth in social networking sites: A cross-cultural study of the United States and China. *Journal of Global Marketing, 24,* 263–281.

Cisneros, J. D., McCauliff, K. L., & Beasley, V. B. (2009). The rhetorical perspective: Doing, being, shaping and seeing. In D. W. Stacks & M. B. Salwen (Eds.), *An integrated approach to communication theory and research* (pp. 223–231). Routledge.

Deutschmann, P. J., & Danielson, W. A. (1960). Diffusion of knowledge of the major news story. *Journalism Quarterly, 37,* 345–355.

Luttrell, R., & Wallace, A. A. (2021). *Social media and society: An introduction to the mass media landscape.* The Rowman & Littlefield Publishing Group, Inc.

Messner, M., & Garrison, B. (2009). Internet communication. In D. W. Stacks & M. B. Salwen (Eds.), *An integrated approach to communication theory and research* (pp. 389–405). Routledge.

Newberry, C., & Reid, A. (2022, September 26). Social media activism in 2023: How to Go Beyond the Hashtag. *Hootsuite.* https://blog.hootsuite.com/social-media-activism/

Pew Research Center. (2021, April 7). *Social media fact sheet.* www.pewresearch.org/internet/fact-sheet/social-media/

Richmond, V. P., & McCroskey, J. C. (2009). Human communication theory and research: Tradition and models. In D. W. Stacks & M. B. Salwen (Eds.), *An integrated approach to communication theory and research* (pp. 223–231). Routledge.

Rogers, E. M., Singhal, A., & Quinlan, M. M. (2009). Diffusion of innovations. In D. W. Stacks & M. B. Salwen (Eds.), *An integrated approach to communication theory and research* (pp. 418–434). Routledge.

Severin, W. J., & Tankard Jr., J. W. (2001). *Communication theories: Origins, methods, and uses in the mass media.* Addison Wesley Longman.

Shepherd, G. J. (1992). Communication as influence: Definitional exclusion. *Communication Studies, 43,* 203–219.

Stacks, D. W., & Salwen, M. B. (2009). Integrating theory and research: Starting with questions. In D. W. Stacks & M. B. Salwen (Eds.), *An integrated approach to communication theory and research* (pp. 3–11). Routledge.

Sterin, J. C., & Winston, T. (2018). *Mass media revolution.* Taylor & Francis.

Wright, D. K. (2009). Communication ethics. In D. W. Stacks & M. B. Salwen (Eds.), *An integrated approach to communication theory and research* (pp. 389–405). Routledge.

8 Developing a Strategic Social Media Presence

In the early 2000s, brands eager to explore social media for business purposes were quick to jump on the "big three": Facebook, Twitter and Instagram. Most organizations couldn't tell you *why* they needed a presence on these three social media sites; they just knew they were missing a marketing opportunity if they weren't jumping on the bandwagon.

Today, it's not quite as simple as creating accounts on the "Big Three." There are countless social platforms and, as we learned in Chapter 3, various categories of social media to consider for marketing purposes from content-sharing sites to review sites to social networking sites to e-commerce sites and much more. Today, we also know that a social media presence should be strategic and tied to specific business goals.

In this chapter, we'll explore how organizations, brands and even individuals can create a social media presence that is goal-oriented and tied to specific goals and priority audiences while also tracking success.

What you can expect to learn in this chapter:

- Social media's place in public relations
- How to identify business goals for an organization
- How to define social media goals that align with business goals
- How to tie priority publics to specific social channels
- How to define priority publics using demographics and psychographics
- How to use social media to best tell your organization's story
- How to measure success across your channels using Key Performance Indicators (KPIs)

Social Media's Place in Public Relations

As mentioned in Chapter 1, social media can serve as a function of various communications disciplines, including journalism, public relations, advertising and marketing. This text, specifically, examines social media as a function of public relations. If the goal of public relations is to build and maintain mutually beneficial relationships between an organization and its various publics, where does social media fit into the picture?

DOI: 10.4324/9781003255734-10

Let's imagine for a minute that you are the public relations manager for a university. Who are the priority publics that you help manage for the university? Internal publics may include students, faculty and stuff. External publics most likely include prospective students, their parents, alumni, donors, the media, government, accrediting bodies and more. How does a public relations professional communicate with these publics? He or she uses various types of public relations writing, such as memos (for communicating with internal audiences); news releases, media advisories, and media pitches (for communicating with the media); website content like bio sketches, fact sheets and backgrounders (for communicating with current students and prospective students); newsletters (for communicating with employees and alumni); letters (for communicating with potential donors) and more.

Social media serves as another form of public relations writing that we can use when communicating with priority publics. For example, a Facebook page for providing parents with timely information like admission and scholarship deadlines, a Twitter page for connecting with members of local and national media or for scheduling Twitter chats with admission reps and prospective students, an Instagram and TikTok for showcasing campus culture through visual content like photos and short-form video, a LinkedIn account for recruiting faculty and staff, a YouTube channel for attracting potential donors with curated long-form video, and the list goes on. In the next chapter, we'll learn about social media projects, programs and campaigns and how public relations professionals incorporate social media into these efforts to strategically connect with their organization's publics.

Since social media is often described as "marketing," it's also worth mentioning social media's place in the "marketing mix." As we reviewed in Chapter 1, public relations focuses on "social capital" (AKA people and relationships) while marketing focuses on developing, maintaining and improving a product's market share using the four P's also known as the "marketing mix": Product, Price, Place and Promotion.

> At its core, *marketing* means preparing a product that consumers want and helping them to acquire it. The 'marketing mix,' meaning everything that might persuade consumers, consists of product design, packaging, pricing, product demonstrations, ads and more. The marketing mix even includes the product's name.
>
> (Marsh et al., 2018, p. 40)

Promotion focuses on the channels we use to promote a product. Brands rely on a variety of channels to promote their products, including print, radio, broadcast, websites, email marketing, outdoor advertising and more. Social media is another tool that marketers incorporate into their toolbox of marketing channels.

Defining Goals

The first step in creating a strategic social media presence is identifying your goals for having a social presence.

> The word *strategy* itself comes to English from Greek. In Greek, *strategos* means *military leader* or *general*. As a strategic writer, you're like a general: With each document, you direct your ideas, words and other multimedia elements on a specific mission.
>
> (Marsh et al., 2018, p. 9)

According to Chen (2021):

> It seems like every month, there's a new social media channel that pops up. Should you create a TikTok account? Clubhouse? Would Twitter Spaces work for your business? It can be tempting to be active on all the available social channels but is that the right course of action? Instead, it's best to strategically choose the right social media channels.
>
> (para. 1)

Where do social media goals come from? Start by examining your business goals for your organization. You might be thinking, "But where do business goals come from?" Business goals originate from an organization's mission statement.

> Many organizations have a values statement, a brief set of core values that ideally guide their actions. Those general values often lead to a mission statement that more precisely describes the organization's purpose. In order to fulfill that mission, organizations usually create annual business goals.
>
> (Marsh et al., 2018, p. 9)

Business goals for a college or university, for example, would include increasing enrollment, increasing donations, improving retention rates, earning national media hits and attracting accomplished faculty, among others. Business goals for another industry, like technology, may be completely different. Goals for a new Apple product, for example, might include creating awareness for a new product, creating understanding of the product, and increasing sales for a product. Business goals in hospitality or a service industry, on the other hand, might include providing excellent customer service or gaining a certain amount of positive reviews/ratings.

Business goals can also originate from an organization's vision statement, which is closely related to an organization's mission.

> It distills your company's vision for the future in a way that outlines your company's long-term goals and, similar to a mission statement, reflects

your company's core values. A well-crafted vision statement should serve as a guide or a mantra that inspires your employees to work toward the greater goal of your organization.

(MasterClass, 2021, para. 4)

A mission statement is focused on the present, whereas a vision statement is focused on the future and where or what the organization is working toward. For example, a university's vision statement might state that it aims to be ranked among the best national universities, to increase its endowment, to be recognized for its research or to be a leader in student retention and graduation rates.

The biggest difference between mission and vision statements is in the time frame. A mission statement outlines all the things your company is doing in the present to reach your goal, while a vision statement describes what your company is building toward in the future.

(MasterClass, 2021, para. 8)

Another difference between mission statements and vision statements are their audiences. In general, mission statements are "public-facing statements primarily geared toward consumers," while vision statements are "more focused on employees of the company (and other existing stakeholders or interested investors) to help drive their work in the best direction for the future" (MasterClass, 2021, para. 9).

Once you've identified business goals, identify which goals, specifically, you want to support with your social media presence. "Different platforms offer different advantages. Oftentimes, social media goals align with your overall business goals. So, when you're setting your social media goals, a few platforms will stand out as the best ones to reach those goals" (Chen, 2021, para. 9). Using the higher education example provided earlier, let's say you want to focus on increasing enrollment, earning national media hits and attracting accomplished faculty. Your social media goals, then, might include attracting and engaging prospective students and their parents, connecting with members of the media and creating awareness for job opportunities at your institution.

Identifying Publics

The next step in creating a strategic, AKA goal-oriented, social media presence is to tie your identified goals to specific publics. For example, who are the priority publics associated with increasing enrollment? For this particular business goal, you'd want to focus on prospective students and their parents. What about earning national media hits? In this case, you'd want to hone in on reporters, writers, editors and producers working for national media outlets. Finally, for attracting accomplished faculty, you'd want to target job seekers in academia.

We now need to describe these publics using demographics and psychographics, different ways that we categorize individuals. Demographics typically group individuals by characteristics over which they have little or no control, for example, age, gender, race and ethnicity (Bobbitt & Sullivan, 2014). Other popular pieces of demographic data, that instead focus on characteristics that don't often change about individuals, include marital status, parental status, education, occupation, health and income level.

The U.S. Census, which takes place every 10 years, reports demographics such as age, sex, race, Hispanic origin, education, health and income, among others. The U.S. Bureau of Labor Statistics reports information on the employment and unemployment of the population classified by age, sex, race, ethnic origin, educational attainment and veteran status. An organization can also collect demographic data through social media and website analytics, among other methods. For example, Facebook Insights allows businesses to see the percentage of people who like their Facebook page by age, gender, country, city and language.

While demographics focus on characteristics that are usually fixed about an individual, psychographics, on the other hand, focus on characteristics that individuals can usually control, such as values, interests, attitudes, lifestyles, wants, needs, concerns, spending habits and hobbies (Indeed Editorial Team, 2021). Research organizations like the Pew Research Center conduct national surveys and report psychographic data across many topics. For example, "How Americans' attitudes about climate change differ by generation, party and other factors." Other popular ways to obtain psychographics include interviews, surveys, social media analytics and website analytics. For example, Google Analytics collects website data that analyzes users by demographics, such as age and gender, but also by psychographics like interest categories.

Let's focus on prospective college students for a moment. Beginning with demographic data, traditionally aged college applicants are 17 or 18 years old, juniors or seniors in high school, making them members of Generation Z. They are more racially and ethnically diverse than any previous generation, and they are on track to be the most educated generation yet, less likely to drop out of high school and more likely to be enrolled in college (Parker & Igielnik, 2020).

What are some psychographics for Generation Z? They are digital natives, meaning they were born into technology and the era of the internet and "have little or no memory of the world as it existed before smartphones" (Parker & Igielnik, 2020, para. 4). Nearly all (95%) have access to a smartphone and nearly half (45%) say they are "almost constantly" on the internet (Schaeffer, 2019). Similar to Millennials, members of Gen Z are progressive and pro-government and are more likely to look to government, rather than businesses or individuals, to solve problems. Millennials and members of Gen Z are also less likely than members of Gen X, the Boomer generation or Silent generation to say the United States is better than all other countries. They are also more active when it comes to addressing climate change than older generations (Tyson et al., 2021), and they outvoted older generations during the 2018 midterms (Cilluffo & Fry, 2019). In terms of how they spend their time, Gen Zers are less likely to be working than previous generations when they are teens and young adults, perhaps because they spend more time dedicated to educational activities than previous generations. The way U.S. teens spend their summer hours is changing, with more of their time in the summer engaged in homework or classwork and less time dedicated to leisure (Livingston & Barroso, 2019).

Once you've identified demographics and psychographics for one public (in this case, prospective college students), do the same for the other publics you're targeting (e.g., parents of prospective students, members of the media and job-seeking faculty).

Meeting Your Publics Where They Are

An important psychographic to know about your priority publics is their communication preferences, or in other words, how they prefer to be communicated with. According to the Pew Research Center, nearly all teens (97%) say they use the internet daily, with 46% of teens saying they use the internet almost constantly and 36% saying they spend too much time on social media (Vogels et al., 2022).

When creating a social media strategy, it's particularly important to know what social media channels are most widely used by your priority publics. According to a 2022 survey by the Pew Research Center, YouTube, TikTok, Instagram and Snapchat are the most popular social media sites and apps used by Gen Zers ages 13 to 17. YouTube is the most widely used social site by teens with 95% of 13- to 17-year-olds reporting using it, followed by TikTok (67%), Instagram (62%), and Snapchat (59%). The share of teens using Facebook has dropped drastically in the past decade, with 71% of teens reporting they used Facebook in 2014–2015 compared to 32% in 2022. Twitter usage has also dropped from 33% in 2014–2015 to 23% in 2022 (Vogels et al., 2022).

For a college or university wanting to target prospective undergraduate students, a strategic social media lineup would want to take into consideration the most valuable players for this public: YouTube, TikTok, Instagram and Snapchat. What about the other priority publics?

While Facebook may not be as popular among today's teens, the platform is still widely used by adults, which is important to know when creating a social strategy to target parents of prospective students. "Parents use a variety of social network sites, with Facebook being the most popular" (Duggan et al., 2015, para. 1). Members of the media, meanwhile, are on Twitter. Twitter is the go-to social media site for U.S. journalists, with around seven-in-ten journalists reporting it's the social media site they use most or second most for their job (Jurkowitz & Gottfried, 2022). What about job seekers?

Are they on social media? According to a 2021 survey by Live Career, Facebook and LinkedIn are the most popular social networks for professional networking, with 18.4 million applicants reporting they'd found their jobs on Facebook and 10.2 million finding their jobs on LinkedIn. "Social media in the workplace has been a subject of heated discussion for some time. What's undeniable however is that social networking sites are gaining popularity when it comes to searching for jobs and job candidates" (Cekala, 2021, para. 26).

See Chapter 4: Social Media by Demographics, Psychographics and Region for more information about tying social media to specific audiences.

Social Spotlight

Kylie Jenner is known for being the youngest sister of the Kardashian clan and, more recently, for her success in the beauty industry with her powerhouse beauty brand Kyle Cosmetics, which earned her the title of the world's youngest billionaire at the age of 21 (Robehmed, 2019). When she launched her brand in 2015, which marketing channels did she turn to? Her own social media, where she has amassed nearly 500 million loyal followers across TikTok, Snapchat, YouTube, Instagram and Twitter. Today Jenner continues to use her social presence to announce product launches, preview new items and showcase the shades of Kyle Cosmetics she's wearing.

What's the secret to her social media success? She knows where to find her target audience on social media and the content needed to connect with them.

"As a global influencer and youngest member of one of the most famous families, Kylie has cornered the fashion and beauty market. She's tapped into the demographic of millennials and Gen Z'ers who are passionate about new trends and have grown up with reality tv and social media. Because of this, she speaks to her followers similarly how she'd talk to her own friends and family" (Talbot, 2018, para. 3).

In 2018, Forbes reported that Jenner focused her content distribution across Snapchat, Instagram and YouTube, with each channel creating unique value for her target demographic: Instagram for brand discoverability, YouTube for shopping recommendations and Snapchat for documenting shopping experiences. In addition to understanding her audience, Jenner's social strategy includes a mix of personal and promotional content, authentic engagement with fans through replies and reposts of their content, partnerships with a variety of influencers, and educational posts that teach consumers how to use her products (Talbot, 2018).

Since joining TikTok, the beauty mogul has already achieved record numbers on the video-driven platform.

"Whatever happens next, one thing is certain. Jenner will share it all on social media, much to the delight of her tens of millions of fans" (Robehmed, 2019, para. 12).

Using Social Media for Storytelling

Knowing where your priority publics spend time on social media is a good starting point for selecting a channel lineup for your social media presence. In addition to considering communication preferences for your publics, a social strategist also needs to consider which types of content and which social channels can best communicate an organization's mission, vision, product or service. "There are five main types of social media content: video, images, text, stories and live video. The content that you create and curate will directly influence your social media channel decision" (Chen, 2021, para. 17).

For example, does a product or service involve a how-to element? Video content or blog content might be useful storytelling tools for creating understanding. TikTok caters to short-form video content, YouTube now caters to both short-form and long-form video content, and Wix, WordPress and Blogger are popular choices for launching a blog. According to Sons (2022):

The content you use to promote your products and services will also determine the social networks you can turn to. For example, if you promote your products using videos, YouTube might be a great choice. Conversely, if you use images, then Instagram is a good pick. The point here is that choosing a social network that suits your business and what you're promoting is essential.

(para. 8)

For a college or university wanting to communicate campus culture, photo and video content are strategic choices, lending themselves to platforms like Instagram, TikTok, YouTube and Snapchat.

Visual storytelling is a strategy for using visual content to communicate a narrative. An effective piece of visual storytelling inspires an emotional response, educates the audience, and/or guides them to a particular conclusion. Visual storytelling can take place in a single piece of content— such as a motion graphic, infographic, or social media post—or it can be achieved over the course of several connected and complementary pieces of content.

(McCoy, 2020, para. 5)

Facebook business Pages, which can serve as a social media storefront with a brand's address, hours, phone number and website, are effective for targeting parents of prospective students seeking timely information about admissions, tuition, housing, etc., with posts not limited to strict character counts and tools like Events, Appointments and Messenger.

> A Facebook Page is a public Facebook account that can be used by brands, organizations, artists and public figures. Businesses use Pages to share contact information, post updates, share content, promote events and releases, and—perhaps most importantly—connect with their Facebook audiences.
>
> (Newberry, 2021, para. 5)

For a company needing to provide real-time customer service, Twitter is a popular go-to for creating conversation and loyal customers via Mentions and DMs. "Twitter is an ideal platform for customers to turn to when they need assistance. It's fast-paced, public and geared toward conversation. It's where people go to make their voices heard" (Gomez, 2022, para. 4). Direct-to-consumers brands like retailers or financial services offering customer service to an international audience can use the popular global messaging app What's App. "For brands, WhatsApp presents an opportunity to personally connect with customers all over the world, providing timely support and real-time business updates" (Hill, 2022, para. 9).

See Chapter 3: Categories of Social Media for more information about the functionalities of specific social media.

Perspective From the Pros

By James Profetto

Social media is more than just the photos and videos you see on your timeline. How did they end up there? What's the reason for posting at 9 a.m. on Mondays but 2 p.m. on Thursdays? These questions and more are answered through social media strategy, which is a combination of content creation and metrics that matter to an organization—otherwise known as Key Performance Indicators (KPIs). There's also the specific tailoring of content for platforms based on your target audience. But to understand all of this, you must start from square one: What's your objective on social media, and what is your voice?

When you figure that out, you can then take time to study which platforms work best for what you're trying to achieve. If you have a tiny team, it's best not to overextend yourselves and open accounts on several platforms. Focus on one or two, and then see how you can optimize your workflow. Algorithms on each platform are unpredictable and change day to day, so it's key to understand that when you start from scratch, you're working against yourself. With proper planning, brand identity and knowing your voice, it'll be easier to draft a strategy that works for you and your audience.

But who is your audience? If you're a higher-ed institution, for example, you're catering to prospective and current students and alumni—but don't forget about moms and dads! Let's stick with this example. For prospective and current students, this audience skews younger (Gen Z and late 20s, early 30s), so Instagram is where you'll find success. But for alumni and professionals? Curate that type of content for LinkedIn and Twitter. Oh, and I'm not forgetting about our elders—I mean, our parent groups! They usually live on Facebook.

See, after you identify your core audience and couple that with your goals, you'll begin to see the content come into its own. However, it's not enough to just have this understanding—you'll need to have a personality. This is where your voice comes into play.

At Nova Southeastern University, we're the cool, knowledgeable professor. We understand our university the best and what positively resonates with our students, while also educating them on all things on and off campus that we're involved in. This gives us flexibility in our social media copy (a.k.a. captions). We can be playful, edgy at times and serious enough for crisis communication. We never lose track of who we are, though, and the reputation we've built among our audiences. Creating a brand hashtag and consistent aesthetic across all your platforms will help your audience know they're in the right place, too. Hashtags like #NSUSharks give our audience a sea of related content to explore. Cover images and logos that match each other and are curated properly for each platform help distinguish yourself from others, but also help your audience know that you care about your presentation.

That's a glimpse into what goes on for the public to see, but what goes on behind the scenes is equally—if not more—important. An organization cannot be successful unless it knows how to measure success. How do you measure yourself: is it engagement rate percentage, is it impressions or is both plus audience growth? Which days and times does your content perform best, and are there trends you need to jump on? Defining this and which KPIs are vital for your company helps you track which posts work and which don't. Your pain points are as just as vital as your wins because you can't grow without knowing where you failed. Keeping a monthly report card, where you measure your performance month-over-month, is what I do and will always encourage others to do, as well.

All of this is just a starting point for how you can set yourself up for success on social media and develop an effective strategy. There are going to be down days and sometimes weeks, but with proper planning and execution, success will always be right around the corner!

Tracking Your Success With Key Performance Indicators

We've identified our social media goals and created a social media lineup tied to priority publics, which also takes into account the best storytelling social platforms for communicating our message. Now, as James mentioned earlier, we need to be able to track the success of our social media program once we create one. How do we do this? With Key Performance Indicators, also known as KPIs. "A key performance indicator (KPI) is a metric tracked over time to determine progress towards a valuable business goal. Social media KPIs might include audience growth rate, amplification rate, and customer satisfaction score" (Hootsuite, n.d., para. 1).

Similar to how social media goals should be tied to business goals and priority publics, key performance indicators should be tied to social media goals.

> Social media KPIs are measurable metrics that reflect social media performance and prove social's ROI for a business. Put another way, tracking specific numbers allows your social team to ensure its social strategy is connecting with the target audience and that your brand is achieving its business goals. Plus, tracking social media KPIs makes reporting back to your boss easier—it's a reliable way to prove to your supervisors that your social media strategy is working.
>
> (Olafson, 2021, para. 2–3)

Organizations may set different KPIs for each social media channel it uses or specific KPIs for social media campaigns (see Chapter 10: Social Media Projects, Programs and Campaigns). Hootsuite lists the below as important KPIs for social strategists to consider when tracking success with social media goals and categorizes these KPIs by reach, engagement, conversion rates and customer satisfaction (Olafson, 2021):

Reach KPIs measure how many users come across your social media channels or are exposed to them. Examples of Reach KPIs include:

- **Impressions:** The number of times your post was visible in someone's feed or timeline. This doesn't necessarily mean the person who viewed the post noticed it or read it

- **Follower Count:** The number of followers your social channel has at a set time
- **Audience Growth Rate:** How follower count is changing over time
- **Reach:** The number of people who have seen a post since it went live
- **Potential Reach:** The number of people who *could* see a post during a reporting period
- **Social Share of Voice:** The number of people who mentioned your brand compared to the number of people mentioning your competitors

Engagement KPIs measure how users interact with your social media channels, including the quality of these interactions. For example, liking a post requires less effort from a follower than a comment or a share. Examples of Engagement KPIs include:

- **Likes:** The number of times followers interact with a social post by clicking the Like button within a given social media platform.
- **Comments:** The number of times your followers comment on your posts. Note that comments can have a positive *or* negative sentiment, so be careful how you measure this metric.
- **Applause Rate:** The number of positive interactions or approval interactions, including likes, shares, retweets, favoriting a post, etc.
- **Average Engagement Rate:** All the engagement a post receives divided by the total number of followers on your social channel.
- **Amplification Rate:** The rate of your followers who are sharing your content with their own followers.

Conversion KPIs measure how many social interactions turn into link clicks, purchases, inquiries, event RSVPs, newsletter sign-ups or other desired actions. Examples of Conversion KPIs include:

- **Conversion Rate:** The number of users who perform the actions tied to a social media Call to Action (CTA) compared to the total number of clicks on that given post. CTAs might include visits to your website, purchases, sign-ups to an email newsletter, etc.
- **Click-through Rate (CTR):** The percentage of people who viewed your post and clicked on the CTA it included.
- **Bounce Rate:** The percentage of visitors who clicked on a link in your social post but didn't take any action.
- **Cost per Click (CPC):** The amount you pay social media platforms per individual click on your sponsored (AKA paid) social media post.
- **Cost per Thousand Impressions (CPM):** The cost you pay every time 1,000 people scroll past your sponsored/paid social media post.

Customer Satisfaction KPIs measure the sentiment of user interactions, AKA how they think and feel about your brand.

- **Customer Testimonials:** Reviews submitted by your customers and posted on your social channels (e.g., Facebook reviews) or on social media review sites like Google online reviews, Yelp, TripAdvisor and Angi (formerly Angie's list).
- **Customer Satisfaction Score (CSAT):** Ratings measuring the customer satisfaction level of your product or service (e.g., rating scales from 1 to 10, Likert-type scales using "strongly agree" to "strongly disagree" or descriptors like poor, average or excellent).
- **Net Promoter Score:** Ratings measuring your followers' brand loyalty through polls or surveys. For example, "How likely are you to recommend this product to a friend?"

See the full article by Olafson (2021) in the Reference List for this chapter for user-friendly formulas for calculating many of these metrics, such as audience growth rate, post reach, potential reach, social share of voice, applause rate, average engagement rate, conversion rate, click-through rate and more. Note that many platforms will calculate a variety of metrics for you either with their free analytics tools or via their advertising managers when you create paid/sponsored posts.

Now that we've done a crash course into KPIs, let's revisit the hypothetical social media goals we mentioned earlier in the chapter: (1) attracting and engaging prospective students and their parents, (2) connecting with members of the media and (3) creating awareness for job opportunities at your institution.

For Goal #1, you could use Facebook Insights to examine the growth of your page via Page likes week to week coupled with demographic breakdown of your Page audience following by age to determine if you are reaching parents. Using Instagram Insights, you can look at the same metrics to see if you are reaching prospective students. While these metrics can reveal if you are "attracting" prospective students and their parents, you can look at individual posts on these platforms to identify trends in likes, shares and comments to determine if you're "engaging" these publics.

For Goal #2, you can measure "connecting" with media in a variety of ways. If the ultimate goal is to use social media to garner national media hits, you could report the number of media inquiries and/or actual media hits that resulted from direct messaging members of the media on Twitter or from tagging them in tweets. You could also report how many "interactions" you had with members of the media on Twitter within a certain period of time, breaking down these interactions by follows, mentions, replies, retweets, etc.

For Goal #3, you can measure the reach or impressions of job-related posts on LinkedIn, along with how many "interactions" resulted from those posts, whether it be likes, comments, shares or direct messages from interested applicants. During the interview process, you could also ask applicants how they learned about the job opening, making note of the percentage of applicants who learned about the opportunity via your social media efforts.

Once you've identified the KPIs you'll be using to track the success of your social media goals, you need to determine *how* you'll obtain those KPIs. One option is to gather KPIs yourself by examining your dashboard on a social platform or examining a specific piece of content. For example, you can check your dashboard to find your follower count or click on a piece of content to examine how many likes, shares or comments it received.

A second option is to use analytics tools provided through the platforms themselves. Facebook Insights, for example, allows users with a Facebook business Page to see analytics related to Page performance, such as weekly reach, Page visits, Page likes and audience broken down by age, gender and location. Most major social media platforms offer these built-in analytics tools (e.g., Instagram Insights, Twitter Analytics, LinkedIn Analytics and YouTube Analytics). A third option is to use a third-party program that provides performance analytics for a single social media channel or across multiple networks at once. Popular options include Sprout Social, Hootsuite and Google Analytics, among many others.

Finally, as James mentioned earlier, it's important to set a schedule for regularly tracking and reporting KPIs. Social media strategists can choose to this daily, weekly, monthly, etc. In my role as a public relations manager for a hotel and casino, we examined social media growth and engagement weekly during our team meetings with the marketing team. We also highlighted top-performing posts, discussed noteworthy customer reviews (good and bad), and examined our performance in relation to our competition. In James' role as a social media manager for a university, he compiles a monthly social media "report card" to communicate important metrics to his team, supervisors and university administration. Whatever method you select, keep the schedule consistent.

Chapter Summary

- Social media are one of the channels that public relations professionals use to build mutually beneficial relationships between an organization and its various publics.
- Creating a strategic social media lineup begins with defining your social media goals, which should align with your organization's business goals.
- Business goals, and therefore social media goals, are derived from an organization's mission and vision statements.
- Social media goals should be tied to priority publics that are defined using demographics and psychographics.

- A social media lineup should incorporate the social media channels that are most popular with your priority public(s).
- A social media lineup should also take into account the platforms that serve as the best storytelling tools for your organization.
- The success of a social media presence should be tracked using Key Performance Indicators, AKA KPIs.
- KPIs are categorized by Reach, Engagement, Conversion and Customer Satisfaction.
- KPIs can be obtained by manually checking your profile/dashboard and/or individual pieces of content or by using a channel's built-in analytics tool or a third-party analytics program.
- KPIs should be monitored and reported regularly (e.g., weekly or monthly).

Exercise 8.1

For the purpose of this exercise, select a hypothetical "client." This could be a student organization, a local business, a nonprofit, a multinational corporation or a public figure or celebrity, among other choices. Identify the mission statement and/or vision statement for your "client." Based on the mission statement and/or vision statement, what are the business goals for your client? With these business goals in mind, what should be the social media goals for your client's social media presence?

Exercise 8.2

Using the social media goals you identified for your "client," identify your priority publics and describe each public with demographics and psychographics. For psychographics, include any communication preferences (e.g., texting vs. calling) and the social media channels that are most widely used by that public.

Next, what are the social media channels that serve as the best storytelling tools for your client and why?

Finally, using the information you've gathered about your client's priority publics coupled with the strengths of specific storytelling tools in relation to your client's messaging, what is the social media lineup you recommend to your client and why?

Discussion Questions

1. In addition to considering the preferences of priority publics, social strategists need to consider the social media platforms that serve as the best storytelling tools for the clients they represent. Aside from social media, what other communication channels should a public relations practitioner consider using when telling an organization's story and why?

2. This chapter introduced Key Performance Indicators (KPIs) as a way to measure the success of a social media presence. In the "Perspective from the Pros" sidebar, social media manager James Profetto said he uses a monthly "report card" to share important metrics to his team and university administration. What are some other effective methods of communicating metrics to stakeholders?

References

Bobbitt, R., & Sullivan, R. (2014). *Developing the public relations campaign*. Pearson.

Cekala, W. (2021, March 3). Risks and rewards of social media recruiting: A 2021 study. *LiveCareer*. www.livecareer.com/resources/careers/planning/social-recruiting

Chen, J. (2021, September 2). Choosing the right social media channels for your business. *Sprout Social*. https://sproutsocial.com/insights/social-media-channels/

Cilluffo, A., & Fry, R. (2019, May 29). Gen Z, Millennials and Gen X outvoted older generations in 2018 midterms. *Pew Research Center*. www.pewresearch.org/fact-tank/2019/05/29/gen-z-millennials-and-gen-x-outvoted-older-generations-in-2018-midterms/

Duggan, M., Lenhart, A., Lampe, C., & Ellison, N. B. (2015, July 16). Parents and social media. *Pew Research Center*. www.pewresearch.org/internet/2015/07/16/main-findings-14/

Gomez, R. (2022, October 19). Twitter for customer service: 7 pro tips and examples. *Sprout Social*. https://sproutsocial.com/insights/twitter-customer-service/

Hill, C. (2022, August 11). 15+ social media platforms your brand should use in 2022. *Sprout Social*. https://sproutsocial.com/insights/social-media-platforms/

Hootsuite. (n.d.). *Key performance indicator (KPI)*. https://blog.hootsuite.com/social-media-definitions/key-performance-indicator-kpi/

Indeed Editorial Team. (2021, April 26). Demographics vs. psychographics in audience segmentation. *Indeed*. www.indeed.com/career-advice/career-development/demographics-vs-psychographics

Jurkowitz, M., & Gottfried, J. (2022). Twitter is the go-to social media site for U.S. journalists, but not for the public. *Pew Research Center*. www.pewresearch.org/fact-tank/2022/06/27/twitter-is-the-go-to-social-media-site-for-u-s-journalists-but-not-for-the-public/

Livingston, G., & Barroso, A. (2019, August 13). For U.S. teens today, summer means more schooling and less leisure time than in the past. *Pew Research Center*. www.pewresearch.org/fact-tank/2019/08/13/for-u-s-teens-today-summer-means-more-schooling-and-less-leisure-time-than-in-the-past/

Marsh, C., Guth, D. W., & Poovey Short, B. (2018). *Strategic writing: Multimedia writing for public relations, advertising and more*. Routledge.

MasterClass. (2021, December 13). Vision vs. mission statement: What's the difference? *MasterClass*. www.masterclass.com/articles/vision-vs-mission

McCoy, E. (2020, October 20). How to use visual storytelling in your marketing: 5 ways. *Social Media Examiner*. www.socialmediaexaminer.com/how-to-use-visual-storytelling-in-marketing-5-ways/

Newberry, C. (2021, July 15). How to create a Facebook business page in 7 easy steps. *Hootsuite*. https://blog.hootsuite.com/steps-to-create-a-facebook-business-page/

Olafson, K. (2021, May 17). 19 social media KPIs you should be tracking. *Hootsuite*. https://blog.hootsuite.com/social-media-kpis-key-performance-indicators/

Parker, K., & Igielnik, R. (2020, May 14). On the cusp of adulthood and facing an uncertain future: What we know about Gen Z so far. *Pew Research Center*. www.pewresearch.org/social-trends/2020/05/14/on-the-cusp-of-adulthood-and-facing-an-uncertain-future-what-we-know-about-gen-z-so-far-2/

Robehmed, N. (2019, March 5). At 21, Kylie Jenner becomes the youngest self-made billionaire ever. *Forbes*. www.forbes.com/sites/natalierobehmed/2019/03/05/at-21-kylie-jenner-becomes-the-youngest-self-made-billionaire-ever/?sh=1f3f495e2794

Schaeffer, K. (2019, August 23). Most U.S. teens who use cellphones do it to pass time, connect with others, learn new things. *Pew Research Center*. www.pewresearch.org/fact-tank/2019/08/23/most-u-s-teens-who-use-cellphones-do-it-to-pass-time-connect-with-others-learn-new-things/

Sons, T. (2022, October 31). Why your business should not be on every social media platform. *Newsweek*. www.newsweek.com/why-your-business-should-not-every-social-media-platform-1755424

Talbot, K. (2018, July 24). 5 social media lessons to learn from Kylie Jenner. *Forbes*. www.forbes.com/sites/katetalbot/2018/07/24/5-social-media-lessons-to-learn-from-kylie-jenner/?sh=645e87991677

Tyson, A., Kennedy, B., & Funk, C. (2021, May 26). Gen Z, Millennials stand out for climate change activism, social media engagement with issue. *Pew Research Center*. www.pewresearch.org/science/2021/05/26/gen-z-millennials-stand-out-for-climate-change-activism-social-media-engagement-with-issue/

Vogels, E. A., Gelles-Watnick, R., & Massarat, N. (2022, August 10). Teens, social media and technology 2022. *Pew Research Center*. www.pewresearch.org/internet/2022/08/10/teens-social-media-and-technology-2022/

Part 3

Social Media Practice and Strategy

9 Social Media Projects, Programs and Campaigns

Now that you've established a social media lineup, what do you do with it? In this chapter, we'll explore how to create a well-rounded approach using social media projects, programs and campaigns. In the next chapter, we'll look at strategies specifically pertaining to content and social branding.

What you can expect to learn in this chapter:

- The difference between social media projects, programs and campaigns
- How to incorporate projects, programs and campaigns into a social media strategy for a holistic approach
- The four-phase campaign process that its roots in public relations
- Types of persuasive campaigns, including political campaigns, commercial campaigns, reputation campaigns, educational or public awareness campaigns and social action campaigns
- Adaptations made to the public relations campaign model for social media

Projects, Programs and Campaigns

As mentioned in the previous chapter, this text examines social media as a function of public relations. Social media serves as one of the many communications tools that PR practitioners have in their toolboxes for managing the flow of information between an organization and its various publics in order to build and maintain mutually beneficial relationships.

When defining terms used in social media practice—such as projects, programs and campaigns—the field of public relations can provide guidance and clarity.

Project: A single and short-lived activity designed to meet an object. In public relations, this might be conducting an interview, drafting a press release, writing a bio sketch or planning a press conference, among many other activities. Social media projects, similarly, might include conducting a social media audit, crafting a Tweet or Facebook post, re-creating a TikTok trend, or responding to a customer's question via

DOI: 10.4324/9781003255734-12

DM. Projects are also referred to as "tactics" during the Implementation phase of campaigns (more on that later in this chapter).

Program: An ongoing activity dealing with several objectives associated with a goal. A PR "program" is your strategy or approach for the day-to-day operations of the job. Think of it as a job description. In public relations this might include everything from monitoring the news for media clips; environmental scanning for trends or brewing crises; maintaining an organization's website and Intranet for employees; responding to media inquiries; planning press conferences; creating PR materials such as news releases, media pitches and background materials; working with the advertising team to create copy as needed; working with higher-ups to develop and maintain organizational policies; coordinating photo and video shoots; planning and executing PR campaigns; managing the PR budget; community engagement; and much more. A social media "program," on the other hand, might include conducting regular social media audits of organizational social channels; conducting ongoing analyses of competitors on social media; creating and maintaining a social media content calendar; planning and executing social media campaigns; creating a variety of social media content, including blog articles, photos, videos, live streaming and more; weekly reporting of social media metrics to the team and marketing executives; monitoring the social media landscape for trends; working with departments across the organization to review and respond to comments and questions on social media; working with higher-ups and human resources to develop organizational policies regarding social media; working with social media ad platforms to develop targeted ads; identifying influencers to potentially partner with on social media; leading social media sessions during employee orientations; and much more.

Campaign: A campaign is a systematic set of activities, each with a specific and finite purpose, sustained over a length of time and dealing with objectives associated with a particular issue. PR campaigns follow a four-phase model that includes research, planning, implementation and evaluation. Unlike programs that run year-round, campaigns have a start date and an end date and seek to solve a problem or take advantage of an opportunity for an organization. For example, a PR campaign for Holy Cow Milks might run for three months leading up to the launch of its new flavored organic milk line. The "opportunity" is promoting the new product. Objectives associated with the campaign might include creating a digital media kit promoting the product, partnering with grocery stores and big-box retailers to hand out samples in stores, and working with the advertising team to develop a script and storyboard for a new commercial featuring the product. A social media campaign, on the other hand, might include updating the content calendar to incorporate organic content promoting the product, creating a series of social media ads targeting parents on

Facebook and Instagram, developing a custom Snapchat filter for customers to interact with in stores, and launching a social media contest asking customers for their help naming the product.

A successful, well-balanced social media strategy will incorporate projects, programs and campaigns, as all serve a different purpose/goal while also being interconnected. Projects are a one-time activity as part of an ongoing program or become tactics during a campaign. Social media programs involve planning campaigns as needed throughout the year to solve problems or take advantage of opportunities. Campaigns help social media programs reach a variety of business goals, whether that be increasing awareness or understanding for an organization, brand, product and/or service; driving sales; creating conversation; educating or persuading a public; combatting a crisis; and engaging in reputation management, among many other goals.

Social Spotlight

The COVID-19 pandemic affected all sectors of the U.S. economy in 2020, from restaurants and bars to airlines and hotels to nail salons and gyms. The arts and culture sector was also hit hard. "Between 2019 and 2020, the U.S. arts economy shark at nearly twice the rate of the economy as a whole: arts and cultural production fell by 6.4 percent when adjusted for inflation, compared with a 3.4 decline in the overall economy" (National Endowment for the Arts, 2022, para. 3). Certain arts industries experienced drastic declines, including the performing arts, museums, independent artists/writers/performers and motion picture and video production industries.

Amid closures and quarantines, the J. Paul Getty Museum, based in Los Angeles, created a clever social media campaign to keep museumgoers engaged from home. The museum used its Twitter account to challenge its followers to recreate a work of art with random objects (and even people) in their homes and then share their recreations on social media.

Getty shared followers' recreations side by side with the original artwork, creating playful conversation around art even during lockdowns. By mixing user-generated content with a fun and quirky challenge, the museum managed to keep its publics engaged without even opening its doors. "The posts showcased Getty's warmth and sense of humor, but also quietly showcased the impressive variety and scope of its collection. During a time where there wasn't much to report on social, user-generated content kept the content calendar full (not to mention it cost nothing and made fans happy in the process)" (McLachlan, 2022, para. 8).

The Public Relations Process

Social media campaigns have their roots in public relations campaigns, also known as the public relations process. The four-phase public relations process, as advocated by the Public Relations Society of America (PRSA), includes research, planning, implementation and evaluation and is often referred to as RPIE. It should be noted, however, that there are similar, accepted acronyms used for this process, such as RACE (Research and planning, Action, Communication, Evaluation), ROPE (Research, Objectives, Programming, Evaluation) and PIE (Planning, Implementation and Evaluation).

Regardless of the acronym used, the process used to guide any public relations plan should include the following (Universal Accreditation Board, 2015):

- Research/analysis of the situation
- Planning, goal/objective setting
- Implementation/execution/communication
- Evaluation

Before we examine how the social media campaign process was adapted from this four-phase model, it's important that we first have a basic understanding of what each of these phases entails from a PR perspective.

Research

According to the Universal Accreditation Board (2017):

> Research is the systematic gathering of information to describe and understand a situation, check assumptions about publics and perceptions, and determine the public relations consequences. Research is the foundation for effective strategic public relations planning. Research helps define the problem and publics.
>
> (p. 22)

When public relations campaigns are conducted by agencies, the research phase typically kicks off with an initial client interview to understand the problem or opportunity at hand and establish set goals for the campaign. When campaigns are conducted in-house (AKA within an organization), the public relations team will meet with relevant departments and executives to do the same.

Once the problem or opportunity has been identified and goals for the campaign have been established, the research phase begins with conducting secondary research, information gathered by someone else that is already published. An analysis of relevant secondary sources is the first step in describing and understanding a situation and defining priority publics.

Categories of secondary research analyzed during this first stage of information gathering might include (Bobbitt & Sullivan, 2014):

- Archival Research: External documents such as newsletters, annual reports and other publications or internal documents, such as memoranda, board meeting minutes, and information summarizing the results of previous campaigns
- Mass Media Sources: Articles from newspapers and magazines, as well as transcripts from radio and television broadcasts
- Historical Research and Case Studies: Problems or situations similar to the one facing the client or employer
- Databases and Internet Sources: Information such as demographic, economic, and scientific data, obtained through the web and internet sources
- Government Sources: Information such as demographic, economic, and scientific data provided by local, state and federal agencies
- University and Scientific Studies: Research results published by universities and other institutions

The background research then continues with identifying priority publics for the campaigns. Depending upon which author, text or industry organization you refer to for the PR process, the process of identifying priority publics could fall within the Research or Planning phase. The Public Relations Society of America, for example, identifies publics during the planning phase. Bobbitt and Sullivan (2014) identify publics as part of the Background Research process. Since identifying, defining and describing publics typically involve primary and secondary research, I have chosen to include this step as part of the Research Phase.

Publics are defined as "groups of people tied together by some common element" (Universal Accreditation Board, 2017, p. 23). We identify publics by asking questions like:

- Who do we want to reach?
- What do we want people in each public to do?
- What messages do we want to communicate to each public that will increase knowledge, change opinions, and/or encourage desired behavior?

Public relations practitioners identify and foster relationships with publics essential to the success or failure of organizations or clients. Some publics, such as residents of a specific neighborhood, advocates of certain

issues or fans of a sports team, are self-defined. Members are aware of their connection to others in the group. Other publics are identified by public relations practitioners. They often use demographics, psychographics, motivating self-interests, status of current relationships with an organization, location or other characteristics to define these publics.
(Universal Accreditation Board, 2017, p. 18)

Once we identify priority publics, we define and describe them using demographics and psychographics. Demographics typically group individuals by characteristics over which they have little or no control, for example, age, gender, race and ethnicity (Bobbitt & Sullivan, 2014). Other popular pieces of demographic data, that instead focus on characteristics that don't often change about individuals, include marital status, parental status, education, occupation, health, and income level. While demographics focus on characteristics that are usually fixed about an individual, psychographics, on the other hand, focus on characteristics that individuals can usually control, such as values, interests, attitudes, lifestyles, wants, needs, concerns, spending habits and hobbies (Indeed Editorial Team, 2021).

After completing secondary research and defining and describing publics with demographics and psychographics, the public relations practitioner needs to identify any gaps remaining in the research. What do we still not know or understand about the client, the problem/opportunity or the priority publics that are being targeted with the campaign?

Primary research can help answer these questions. Primary research refers to the process of getting information directly from the source and is sometimes called verification research because it often answers questions that could not be answered in the background research (Bobbitt & Sullivan, 2014). Research objectives refer to the questions raised by background research that you aim to answer with primary research. For example, "What is the perceived level of importance that Gen Z places on social review sites during the purchasing process?"

Primary research—such as focus groups, in-depth interviews, surveys, content analyses and more—can then be planned and executed to answer these questions.

Planning

During the planning phase, public relations professionals establish goals, objectives, strategies and tactics for the campaign.

- **Goals:** Broader, general outcomes the campaign aims to achieve (e.g., "To create awareness for and establish the Yellow Cab Co. as a leader in the mobile-based transportation space")

- **Objectives:** Specific and measurable indicators of whether or not a goal has been met (e.g., "To increase awareness of the Yellow Cab Co. by 50% among Millennials in South Florida"); objectives should be SMART (Specific, Measurable, Attainable, Realistic and Time-bound)
- **Strategies:** The road map/plan for how an objective will be achieved (e.g., "creating and launching social media ads for the Yellow Cab Co. targeting Millennials in South Florida on Instagram")
- **Tactics:** Specify elements or tools for accomplishing a strategy (e.g., "meet with graphic designer to discuss design concept for the series of social media ads")

Implementation

Public relations writing falls within the Implementation phase. Once we've assessed the situation during the Research phase and outlined our goals, objectives, strategies and tactics during the Planning phase, we are ready to execute the plan and communicate during the Implementation phase.

Our overarching goal, supporting objectives and strategies for the PR plan are carried out through tactics. *Tactics* are the "nuts-and-bolts part of the plan" and "describe the specific activities that put each strategy into operation and help to achieve the stated objectives" (Wilcox et al., 2016, p. 112). Whereas strategies typically refer to "the overall concept, approach, or general plan for the program designed to achieve an objective," tactics refer to "the actual events, media, and methods used to implement the strategy" (Broom & Sha, 2013, p. 273). Tactics are the most visible portion of a PR plan and "use various methods to reach target audiences with key messages" (Wilcox et al., 2016, p. 112).

The Implementation phase also includes logistics, which detail *how* the tactics will be executed, including staffing, budgeting and timing via a time-table or calendar.

Evaluation

At the conclusion of the campaign, we evaluate the effectiveness of the campaign using a variety of methods (Universal Accreditation Board, 2017):

- Revisiting the objectives to determine if they've been met
- Determining how members of each key public interpreted messages
- Identifying ways to improve and develop recommendations for the future
- Adjusting the plan, materials, messages and activities before moving forward
- Collecting and recording data/information to be used in the Research phase of the next campaign

Social Media Campaigns

As mentioned in the section above, the social media campaign process developed out of the four-phase public relations process. Kim (2021) defines the four phases of the social media campaign process as Listening, Strategic Design, Implementation and Monitoring, and Evaluation.

> Although the reality of the social world dictates a certain level of fluidity and uncertainty, sometimes even chaos, when engaging in social media campaigns organizations that utilize a strategic process to develop an effective framework for campaigns have a stronger capacity to leverage the potential of social media.
>
> (Kim, 2021, p. 21)

Listening

According to Kim (2021), "the first step in any social media campaign is to listen" (p. 21). Kim compares this phase to the Research phase. During the Listening phase, social strategists collect data that will form the foundation of the campaign with two key research elements called the foundational background and the social landscape.

Foundational Background

The foundational background allows a social strategist to gain an understanding of the organization itself and examines an organization's mission statement, organizational structure, communication audit, and policies and procedures.

The first step in formative mission is to identify the organization's mission and/or vision statements, values and strategic plans. "Social strategists recognize that each campaign, strategy and tactics in social media should relate to the brand's vision. Informed social media engagement relates to the core essence, or mission statement, of the brand" (Kim, 2021, p. 31).

After social strategists gain an understanding of the organization's purpose, goals and values, they next identify its organizational structure, including relevant participants from the organization, and acquire knowledge of how management is set up, how departments are structured, and who is responsible for each component. The examination of the organization structure should also examine organizational leadership, including whether top leaders (e.g., presidents and CEOs) are active on social media and whether they value its role in an organization's communications presence; key players who have an influence in terms of integrating social media into organizational life (e.g., the head of marketing, directors of PR and social media); key players who are tasked with maintaining and engaging with the organization's social media presence (e.g., social media managers, specialists and coordinators);

and skills possessed by the social media team (e.g., word artisans, content creators and data analysts). According to Kim (2021):

> Strategists use data from the organizational structure research to determine the level of support for social media integration into the core processes of a brand, as well as the appropriate type of social media team to create in order to help a brand thrive in the social environment.
>
> (p. 31)

The communication audit identifies all the channels that the organization uses to communicate with its publics. This analysis includes the communication platform used (e.g., a newsletter, website, community events, media relations efforts), the intended audience of the platform (e.g., employees, potential customers, alumni), the frequency of the communication (e.g., how often a website is updated or how often a social media channel is posted to), and the person/department responsible for managing the platform (e.g., the social media manager and the marketing department). "Data from communication audits display the tapestry of ways that key publics are being communicated with, informing key elements of message structure and timing within a campaign's design" (Kim, 2021, p. 31).

The foundational background concludes by examining all policies and procedures for the organization, including employee handbooks, brand guides, crises response plans, market research, and SEO and web analytic reports. This may also include policies and procedures specific to social media, such as social media manuals, social media policies for employees, and posting guidelines for users interacting with an organization's channels.

Social Landscape

Once social strategists gain an overall understanding of the organization itself, they need to next gain an understanding of who the organization in relation to social media. According to Kim (2021):

> In this phase of the listening (research) stage, the goal is to identify what conversations are taking place on social media that may be relevant to the brand, who is having those conversations, and ways that the organization might engage with that dialogue.
>
> (39)

The social landscape involves identifying:

- Key Listening Phrases: Includes specific and generic keywords associated with the organization to identify what conversations are taking place on social media about the organization and industry

- Conversation Platforms: Includes the social media channels/platforms where these conversations are taking place
- Brand Community Dialogue: Examines online communities for the brand and includes audience analysis, content analysis, community interaction (how the brand community is interacting with the organization) and brand dialogue (how the organization interacts with the brand community)
- Influencers: Identifies individuals who can drive conversations about the organization
- Competition: Identifies key competitors on social media and which social media channels they use

The listening phase concludes by using the information gathered during the foundational background and social landscape to conduct a SWOT exercise to identify the strengths, weaknesses, opportunities and threats for an organization. Kim (2021) describes this final step as sense-making.

> Sense-making is the final, crucial component of the listening phase. Often, people are eager to jump into developing a campaign after gathering so much data. But, unless the data are mined for information and that information is applied in meaningful ways to the context of a brand's social media needs, organizations will be unable to effectively leverage the power of social media for their brand.
>
> (Kim, 2021, p. 57)

Following the SWOT analysis, the social strategist crafts a problem or opportunity statement that will guide the social media campaign development.

Strategic Design

Armed with data that can inform the problem/opportunity statement, social strategists can create an overall strategy for the organization's social media during the Strategic Design phase. This phase closely mirrors the Planning phase during a PR campaign and develops campaign goals, SMART objectives, strategies and tactics.

The development of campaign goals is supplemented by the creation of social media vision statements. This begins with identifying the social media channels that are beneficial to the organization based on the research gathered during the Listening phase. The social strategist then creates a social media vision statement that will be incorporated as a regular part of the organization's social media presence. Vision statements include a description of each social media platform's purpose and how this purpose contributes to the organization's business goals. For example, "We will use Instagram for visual storytelling and to communicate campus culture in order to increase applications among prospective students."

Like some models offered for the public relations process, this phase also involves identifying audiences that are important to the success of the campaign. It's important to note that Kim (2021) uses the term "audiences" rather than "publics," the term advocated by the Public Relations Society of America. Kim (2021) defines audiences as "people who are somehow mutually involved or interdependent with particular organizations" (p. 87) a definition she credits to Cutlip and Center's *Effective Public Relations* (Broom & Sha, 2013). When identifying audiences, it's important to examine psychographics such as

Implementation and Monitoring

Like the Implementation phase of a public relations campaign, the Implementation and Monitoring phase of the social media campaign is the most visible phase. During this phase, strategists execute the program that was created and designed for social media. The implementation phase of a social media campaign includes two main components: implementing content using a content calendar and monitoring the impact of the campaign via "constant engagement with social communities" (Kim, 2021, p. 147). See Chapter 11. Content Strategies for more information about selecting and creating a content calendar.

> The actual *launching* of a social media campaign is only the beginning of what social media strategists need to focus on during the live portion of a campaign. Throughout the course of a campaign, brands should engage with their social media communities and continually monitor their progress toward SMART, outcome-based objectives of the campaign.
>
> (Kim, 2021, p. 155)

Kim (2021) offers several strategies for monitoring the effectiveness of a campaign:

- Opting into alerts that notify social strategists when something happens on an organization's channel (e.g., likes, comments, shares, direct messages) and responding when appropriate
- Using listening tools to monitor keywords and topics relevant to the organization
- Continually analyze the responses and interactions that are being gained as a result of the campaign
- Participate in conversations organically, as they occur in real-time
- Record any social media engagements or actions that serve as Key Progress Indicators (KPIs) for an organization, identify any influencers who were engaged, and identify the time decay of the post

Evaluation

The final step in a social media campaign is evaluating the effectiveness of the campaign. At the close of the campaign, strategists gather summative data and use this information not only to evaluate whether or not a campaign was successful but also to lay the foundation for future campaigns during the Listening phase.

Kim (2021) outlines three components of the evaluation phase:

- Preparation: Evaluation of a campaign's preparation during the Listening and Strategic Design phases to determine whether or not a strong foundation was in place prior to the launch of the campaign
- Implementation: Evaluation of the Implementation and Monitoring phase to determine whether information was delivered at the correct time, whether it reached the intended audience(s), and the nature of the engagement that occurred as a result
- Impact: Evaluation of the SMART objectives that were established during the Strategic Design phase to determine whether or not these objectives were met

---

Perspective From the Pros

By Tasha Yohan, MBA

Every influencer, layman and business, today has access to a megaphone through social media. How do organizations or brands stand out when there is so much noise to break through?

Projects, programs and campaigns are a component of a larger social media strategy—you can't have one without the others. By incorporating different elements, such as coordinated hashtag campaigns, paid social advertising or influencer programs, companies are able to create a successful holistic social media strategy.

So what's a great example of a social media program that stands out? Let's examine Spotify, the most popular music streaming service in the world. Launched in 2008, the company forever altered the way the masses consume music.

Each year, subscribers listen to billions of hours of music from artists all over the world. And each year, since 2016, Spotify gathers that data and compiles it into visually appealing and digestible statistics with a prompt to share your results on social media through its program known as Spotify Wrapped. The result is our feeds are flooded with the listening habits of our family, friends, coworkers and peers each December.

While Wrapped has become wildly successful for Spotify, there is another element to this that is fascinating to me as a marketing professional. Companies that we subscribe to, engage with and use are collecting massive amounts of data on us every year. But, the marketing team at Spotify has leveraged that data to generate content and community engagement with the brand. There are few, if any other, businesses I can think of that have done that and been as successful.

Chapter Summary

- Social media are one of the channels that public relations professionals use to build mutually beneficial relationships between an organization and its various publics.
- Social media projects are short-lived activities designed to meet an objective (e.g., crafting a tweet).
- Social media programs refer to ongoing activities supporting several objectives associated with a goal. Programs often refer to the day-to-day activities and duties that comprise an organization's year-round approach to social media management.
- Social media campaigns seek to address a problem or take advantage of an opportunity for an organization. Campaigns run for a set length of time and are not ongoing like social media programs.
- Social media campaigns have their roots in the public relations process, which includes the four phases of Research, Planning, Implementation and Evaluation.
- The social media campaign process has been adapted to include the four phases of Listening, Strategic Design, Implementation and Monitoring, and Evaluation.

Exercise 9.1

Select a student organization or a local nonprofit or business and imagine that you are its social media manager. You have been tasked with designing a social media campaign for the organization, and you need to complete the Listening Phase of the social media campaign process. First, begin with conducting Foundational Research by responding to the following prompts:

a) Mission Statement: What is the organization's mission and/or vision statement?
b) Organizational Structure: Does the organization have an organizational chart? How is leadership structured? Who are the "key players" who have influence over social media's role in the organization and who comprise the organization's social media team?

c)   Communication Audit: What channels does the organization use to communicate with its publics? Does the organization have a social media presence and, if so, what social media platforms does it use?

d)   Policies and Procedures: What policies/procedures does the organization have in place and how does it communicate them to its publics (e.g., employee handbook)? Does it have any policies or procedures specific to social media (e.g., social media guidelines)? If so, what are they?

Exercise 9.2

Next, complete the Social Landscape step of the Listening Phase by responding to the following prompts:

- Key Listening Phrases: What are specific and generic keywords associated with the organization that can be used to identify conversations that are taking place on social media about the organization and the industry it's in?
- Conversation Platforms: What are the social media channels/platforms where these conversations are mostly taking place?
- Brand Community Dialogue: How does the brand community interact with the organization on social media? What is the level of engagement (e.g., likes, shares and comments)? How does the organization interact with the brand community (if at all)?
- Influencers: Who are individuals who can drive conversations about the organization on social media?
- Competition: Who are the organization's key competitors on social media and which social media channels do these competitors use?

Discussion Questions

1.   This chapter examined the difference between social media projects, programs and campaigns. Locate a job listing for a social media specialist, manager or director position using a professional networking site like LinkedIn or Indeed.com. Based on the duties listed in the job description, how would you define/describe the organization's social media program (AKA the daily tasks that comprise the organization's ongoing approach to social media management)?

2.   The social spotlight in this chapter highlighted the success of a social media campaign conducted by the J. Paul Getty Museum. The campaign "problem" was keeping museumgoers engaged from home during museum closures caused by COVID. The problem was addressed with a clever social media campaign that challenged followers to re-create famous works of art using everyday household items and share their creations on social.

In your opinion, what is another successful social media campaign (past or present) that has a clearly defined problem or opportunity? How was the problem addressed via the social campaign, or how did the campaign take advantage of an opportunity?

References

Bobbitt, R., & Sullivan, R. (2014). *Developing the public relations campaign: A team-based approach*. Pearson Education, Inc.

Broom, G. M., & Sha, B.-L. (2013). *Cutlip & Center's effective public relations* (11th ed.). Pearson Education, Inc.

Indeed Editorial Team. (2021, April 26). Demographics vs. psychographics in audience segmentation. *Indeed*. www.indeed.com/career-advice/career-development/demographics-vs-psychographics

Kim, C. M. (2021). *Social media campaigns: Strategies for public relations and marketing*. Routledge.

McLachlan, S. (2022, January 4). 7 inspirational social media campaigns (Free template to plan your own). *Hootsuite*. https://blog.hootsuite.com/social-media-campaign-strategy/

National Endowment for the Arts. (2022, March 15). *New data show economic impact of COVID-19 on arts & culture sector*. www.arts.gov/news/press-releases/2022/new-data-show-economic-impact-covid-19-arts-culture-sector#:~:text=In%202020%2C%20arts%20and%20culture,decline%20in%20the%20overall%20economy

Universal Accreditation Board. (2015). *Study guide for the certificate in principles of public relations examination* (2nd ed.). Author.

Universal Accreditation Board. (2017). *Study guide for the examination for accreditation in public relations* (4th ed.). Author.

Wilcox, D. L., Cameron, G. T., & Reber, B. H. (2016). *Public relations: Strategies and tactics* (11th ed.). Pearson Education, Inc.

10 Content Strategies

In 1996, Bill Gates wrote an essay titled "Content is King," coining the now-famous phrase that still rings true today. While Gates used this phrase nearly three decades ago following the launch of the World Wide Web, today we often hear this phrase used in relation to social media. According to Olenski (2017):

> All of social media is basically content. . . . Could you imagine what Facebook, Twitter, LinkedIn, and Snapchat would be if they didn't have content? There would be blank spaces that no one would visit, because they have no need to.
>
> (para. 6–7)

You've drafted social media goals, launched your social media presence, and created a social strategy that strikes a balance with projects, programs and campaigns. Now you need to create content catered to your priority publics and individual channels.

What you can expect to learn in this chapter:

- What constitutes social media content and types of social media content
- How to pair content to specific platforms
- The difference between organic and paid social media content
- The difference between original, curated/shared content and user-generated content
- Different content goals (informational, educational, promotional, conversational and entertaining)
- How to select and create a content calendar
- What content to fill your calendar with
- Content strategies such as cadence, tagging, cross-promotion and influencer partnerships
- Strategies for promoting your social media presence

DOI: 10.4324/9781003255734-13

What Is Social Media Content?

Social media content, to put it simply, is what you share on your social media channels. Popular types of content include video, images, text-based posts, links, stories and live video, as well as content that combines these like images and videos coupled with captions. According to Hootsuite Academy (n.d.):

> When considering the value of content on social media, it's important to understand that "content" is a far-reaching term. It can include everything from gifs and images, to white papers and blog articles—as well as the accompanying copy in the social post.
>
> (para. 2)

Mailchimp (n.d.) identifies 12 types of content:

1. Written posts, blogs, articles, guides and more
   "These articles demonstrate your company's knowledge and expertise, which can help build your credibility and reputation" (para. 21).
2. Electronic books
   "An eBook tends to be longer and more detailed than blog posts, which helps showcase your industry expertise. Far fewer businesses take the time to produce an eBook compared to blogs" (para. 27).
3. Links to external content
   "If you don't have time to finish a blog post or your writer is on vacation, you can always link to relevant articles, resources, and websites from other sources that you trust. Industry leaders are also excellent resources for content" (para. 31).
4. Images
   "Visual content is much more digestible and engaging than long-form blogs and articles. Smartphone cameras are sophisticated enough to take stunning pictures, and apps help you quickly edit them, add filters to them, and more" (para. 36).
5. Videos
   "Capturing videos is easy and convenient—and they're more engaging than pictures. How-to guides, video tours, and product updates and demonstrations all make for great video content that can both drive traffic to your website and increase sales" (para. 41).
6. Video stories
   "Stories are images and short videos that last 24 hours before disappearing for good. . . . Keep users updated about events, offers, or other announcements—or give them a behind-the-scenes glimpse of your business. The possibilities are truly endless!" (para. 45).

7. Live videos

"Live videos are a great medium to bring events to audiences that aren't physically able to attend. Unlike stories, which are gone after 24 hours, you can still watch livestreams later" (para. 49).

8. Infographics

"Infographics use visuals to support explanations, statistics, and other written concepts. They are especially impactful for conveying complex ideas" (para. 55).

9. Testimonials and reviews

"People trust the opinions and experiences of others more than what a business says, which is why testimonials and reviews are so valuable" (para. 59).

10. Announcements

"Getting the word out about new products, events, livestreams, and other noteworthy things can help build hype and alert people about what's happening with your business. Audiences love having the inside scoop on their favorite stores and brands!" (para. 63).

11. Contests

"Because people like to win, social media contests are engaging and fun to host" (para. 67).

12. Holidays

"Many users love holiday-themed content, and it's easy for businesses like yours to piggyback on themes, traditions, and other holiday-specific concepts" (para. 72).

Pairing Content With Platforms

While creating a content strategy that includes a variety of types of content is important, it's equally important to pair content with the platforms they're best suited for. For example, content that focuses on the written word, like articles and captions that are on the longer side, are better suited for platforms that are informational in nature like blogs and social networking sites like Facebook and LinkedIn, which have generous character limits compared to the 280 characters we're capped to on Twitter.

Quick updates, announcements or breaking news are a good fit for microblogs like Twitter, which have strict character counts but are still informational in nature. For example, the media use Twitter to break timely news headlines, organizations use Twitter to communicate updates during a crisis, and brands use Twitter to live tweet play-by-plays during events.

Links are a great companion to articles and captions to direct readers to where they can find more information, such as your organization's website, making Facebook, LinkedIn and blogs a great choice. On YouTube, links can be included in a video description to direct viewers to more content, advertise a website or give credit to those who helped you make the video. Some platforms have special considerations to keep in mind with links. For example, captions for Instagram posts do not allow links to be hyperlinked (or clickable), so you have to direct readers to the click link that appears in your bio section. On Twitter, because of the character limits, you'll most likely need to use a URL shortener like Bitly, TinyURL or Google URLs. Most link shorteners will also allow you to view metrics like total clicks, which is useful in determining which channels are producing the most engagement with your content. When using "stories" across various platforms, you'll need to "attach" a link or use a link "sticker" for viewers to click on.

Photo and video content are geared toward content-sharing sites like Instagram, Snapchat, YouTube and TikTok. Instagram is especially photo-driven, serving as a popular choice for brands wanting to create visual storytelling through stories, posts and a carefully curated grid style (repeating rows of images) that appear on their profiles. Similarly, YouTube allows brands to create visual storytelling through curated "Playlists" for longer-form videos, and like many channels, has followed the success of TikTok's short-form videos, launching its own version called "Shorts" (Facebook and Instagram have "Reels").

With customer service communication, it's best to take these conversations out of the public arena on posts and comments and move them to platforms' private messaging platforms, for example, Messenger on Facebook and Instagram, Direct Message (DM) on Twitter or Messaging on LinkedIn. You can also choose to use platforms created for the sole purpose of messaging, like WhatsApp.

Organic Versus Paid Content

In addition to categorizing content by type, we can also further classify it by whether it's organic or paid content. "Organic" content is any free content shared on your social media channels, meaning, you didn't incur a cost to post it. Organic content includes original content you created yourself (sometimes referred to as "created" content); "curated" content, which is content from other brands or people that you share to your social media accounts; and user-generated content, which is content you share from your followers, fans, customers, etc.

Examples of original content include "Meet the Team" posts, real-life examples of how your product and/or service is used, relatable information and how-to guides (Zelefsky, 2022). Examples of curated content could be sharing someone else's post, sharing a link to someone else's blog post, or creating a roundup of quoted advice or best practices from industry experts. "Just like a museum curator's role is to choose the most important artifacts and artwork to display, your role as a content curator is to select only the best content to share with your audience" (Martin, 2022, para 8).

User-generated content (also called UGC or consumer-generated content) is any content—text, images, videos, reviews, testimonials, a podcast, etc.—created by your followers/customers that mentions your brand/organization and is posted on social media. Most UGC is from brand loyalists (AKA people passionate about your brand) who either submit UGC when you ask for it or because they've organically decided to share it. "UGC is used across all stages of the buyer's journey to help influence engagement and increase conversions. The customer-centric content can be used on social media and other channels, such as email, landing pages, or checkout pages" (Beveridge, 2022, para. 8).

UGC from employees (also known as EGC) is equally valuable, as it helps you tell your organization's story and create brand identity in an authentic way with a behind-the-scenes perspective. "Employee-generated content (EGC) shows the value and story behind your brand. For example, photos of employees packing or making up orders or a video of your team talking about why they love working for your company" (Beveridge, 2022, para. 7).

Organic content—including original content, curated content and UGC/EGC—can be seen by your followers, people who follow the hashtags you use, and followers of anyone who shares your post; however, relying on organic content alone could be problematic depending on your social media goals, as organic reach is much lower than one might expect. According to Zelefsky (2022):

> Unfortunately, with so many people and brands competing for attention on social media these days, organic reach has been declining. In fact, the average organic reach for a Facebook post is about 5.5% of your follower count with even less for brands with large followings.
>
> (para. 4)

Paid social media content, as opposed to organic content, is a form of advertising and involves "boosting" organic content that is already posted or creating a social media ad using a social channel's advertising platform like Facebook Ads Manager or Twitter Ads. Paid social content is popular because it's an affordable form of advertising that works with practically any ad budget, with some campaigns starting as low as $5.

Paid social media content is also effective in that it allows advertisers to target audiences using demographics. Facebook Ads, for example, allows advertisers to define audiences by location, age, gender, education, job title, interests, and behavior like prior purchases and device usage. Advertising campaigns can also help organizations hone in on specific goals like selling a product, gaining more followers or creating brand awareness.

When it comes down to organic versus paid content, neither is superior, as they serve different goals and audiences: organic content allows you to connect with existing followers and build brand identity while paid content allows you to reach a larger yet well-defined audience and meet specific goals. According to Zelefsky (2022):

> Rather than posting just to post, if you can create a balanced strategy and maintain social media pages that truly represent your brand well, you'll continue to reap the benefits of social media marketing and stand out from your competition.
>
> (para. 12)

Perspective from the Pros

By Michael North, Ph.D.

My students say no one uses Facebook anymore. Or if anyone does use Facebook, it's grandparents wishing happy birthday.

Of course, my students are wrong. They may not use Facebook, but almost three billion people do each month (Dixon, 2022). Say what you will about the Metaverse, but Facebook continues to do something right by providing billions of people a means to connect for personal or commercial purposes; share photos, videos, and news; and create content to educate and entertain. I'm no Facebook fan, but Facebook provides an effective guide to learn about content strategies among billions of users.

To increase engagement, you should integrate paid and organic content, feature video over static images, and respond to users' replies as soon as possible.

In its quest to make as much money as possible, Facebook designed its current algorithm to emphasize paid content. Organic content only reaches about 5% of a Facebook page's followers these days (Sehl, 2021), so you either pay to play or your content sits on the bench. Still, you don't have to break the bank by paying to promote all your content. Test your content strategies constantly, but you'll probably find that paid content reaches more users and the exact segment you're aiming to target while organic content can strengthen your brand by developing loyal users into brand ambassadors who engage in word-of-mouth communication (Cooper, 2021).

Once you find the proper balance between paid and organic content for your organization, you need content to post. In short, you should feature video over static images. Paid video ads reach more users, entice more clicks, and generate more sales leads than paid image ads (Grgurović, 2022). But it's not just any video. According to Sprout Social (2022), users engage the most with short videos followed by images, live videos, GIFs and memes, text, and then long videos. Again, test constantly to find the proper balance for your organization, but you'll likely find that short videos generate the most engagement.

And after you post your short video content, be prepared to respond quickly to users' replies. Users are more likely to reply if they think there's a chance the organization will respond (Sehl, 2021). You don't have to reply to every user. Instead, monitor replies for extreme negativity and for users with large followings. Then, step in and provide as much help as quickly as you can. Keep in mind this interaction is public, and while that may sound scary, see it as a chance to do great work in front of a huge audience. Turning a negative social media situation into a positive outcome can strengthen your organization's brand and impress the right people within your organization.

Posting paid and organic short video content and responding quickly to users leads to success on Facebook. These strategies can be adapted for other social media platforms as well. Test these strategies to finetune your organization's social media posts to increase engagement.

Creating a Content Calendar

Now that we've identified types of social media content, differentiated between organic and paid content, and strategized how to pair content to specific platforms, we now need to discuss how to plan content using a content calendar.

What is a content calendar? "A social media calendar is an overview of your upcoming social media posts, organized by date. Social marketers use content calendars to plan posts, manage campaigns, and review ongoing strategies" (Newberry & Cohen, 2022, para. 5).

Content calendars take a variety of forms: spreadsheets like Microsoft Excel or Google Sheets, shared calendar apps like Google Calendars or Apple's iCloud calendar, a social media management tool like Hootsuite or Sprout Social, or even a physical calendar like a desktop calendar or wall calendar.

A social media calendar typically contains the following elements for each post:

- The social channel(s) the content is being posted to
- The date and time the post will go live (or is scheduled to be posted)
- The caption/copy for the post
- Any visuals (photo, video, gif, infographic, illustration, etc.)
- Links to creative assets
- Links and tags to include
- Any platform-specific content (e.g., feed post, Story, Reel, poll and live stream)
- Any campaign(s) the content is affiliated with

Scheduling Content

Once you've selected the format of your social media calendar (digital vs. physical, shared calendar vs. social management tool, etc.), how do you fill it? You can start by scheduling organic, reoccurring content. For example:

- #mondaymotivation content showcasing inspirational quotes and/or stories related to your industry/sector

- #tiptuesday content offering helpful tips to your followers
- #wedndesdaywisdom content spotlighting advice from professionals in the field
- #tbt AKA throwback posts highlighting past events or milestones
- #featurefriday content showcasing organizational news/feature stories/accomplishments
- #saturdayspotlight showcasing the people behind your brand or user-generated content

Your weekly structure doesn't need to be branded by hashtags (although whatever content you feature should be accompanied by relevant hashtags for certain channels to gain greater exposure and engagement; see the Content Strategies section subsequently for more guidance on this). For example, perhaps you plan to do employee spotlights every Monday or

Your organic content also doesn't necessarily need to be scheduled five, six or even seven days a week (or multiple times a day for that matter), because it all depends on your audiences, goals and accepted cadence for each channel (more on this below).

In addition to any reoccurring content you plan to feature across your accounts, you'll want to add any upcoming events or announcements for your organization to the calendar, including one-time special events, annual events, product launches and new hires. Perhaps your organization hosts a holiday drive each winter, hosts a regular monthly event to recognize an employee of the month, plans to announce a new partnership, or prepares to roll out a new product or service. Social media strategists can work with the public relations and marketing departments to identify these dates.

Once you've added your regular reoccurring content and any upcoming events, you may want to consider adding in any holidays or nationally/globally recognized days that make sense for your organization. For example, International Coffee Day for a coffee company, National Day on Writing for an academic program offering courses in creative writing, or World Animal Day for a nonprofit focused on wildlife conservation.

Of course, there will also be unplanned, organic content that you can also add to the calendar as needed like media hits highlighting your organization (e.g., "Thanks @Timemag for naming us one of 2022's best inventions: [Link to article]"), awards or accolades (e.g., Did you hear? We've been named Social Media/Influencer Agency of the Year by @adage), user-generated content shared from fans and brand loyalists (e.g., "Thanks for sharing the love @clientname and choosing us for your home-security needs."), crisis communications (e.g., "Continue to follow us for timely updates about this product recall"), and trends you may want to piggyback on by creating similar content and joining the conversation (who remembers the #icebucketchallenge?).

Finally, add any paid content (AKA social media ads) to the calendar. Perhaps you plan to run a one-week social ad leading up to #GivingTuesday to encourage donations, or you want to run a reoccurring monthly ad counting down to a product launch. You may also want "boost" content (put a spend behind organic content) that you see is performing well. Put it all on the calendar.

Creating a Content Mix

How much of your calendar should be dedicated to organic content versus paid content? Your advertising budget will most likely dictate that decision, along with your specific social media goals and consideration for algorithm updates that make it more competitive to get eyeballs on your organic content.

While there is no formula for striking a perfect balance of types of content, Hootsuite offers the following advice and says social strategists should strive for a "social media rule of thirds" (Newberry & Cohen, 2022):

- One-third of your posts should promote your business or drive conversations.
- One-third of your posts should share curated content from industry thought leaders.
- One-third of your posts should involve personal interaction with your followers.

In addition to categorizing content by type and organic versus paid, you'll also want to consider the goal(s) of the content when creating a well-rounded content mix.

Content goals generally fall into five buckets:

- Content that **informs** (e.g., "Today is the last day to add or drop a class! Finalize your fall schedule here: LINK")
- Content that **educates or teaches (**e.g., Did you know? About 400 fatal crashes happen each year as a direct result of texting and driving. Learn more about how you can help prevent accidents due to distracting driving here: LINK")
- Content that **promotes a product or service (**e.g., "I scream, you scream, we all scream for ice cream! Stop by our stores starting Monday to sample our holiday-flavored ice creams.")
- Content that **entertains** (e.g., "See ya, 2022! Watch our video recap of our employees in action over the last year and how they're gearing up for the New Year!")
- Content that **creates conversations** (e.g., "This is our favorite spot on campus for a study break! What's yours?")

(Note: Chapter 11: Writing for Social Media also provides some examples of the above categories.)

According to the 80/20 rule prescribed by Hootsuite (Newberry & Cohen, 2022), 80% of your posts should seek to inform, educate or entertain, while 20% of your posts should be dedicated to promoting your business or driving conversations. Sprout Social (Aboulhosn, 2020) suggests, as a basic rule of thumb, to devote two-thirds of your posts to informational content and one-third or less to promotional content.

"A constant stream of overly promotional social media posts can alienate followers, making it essential to emphasize engagement over sales in your social media calendar" (Aboulhosn, 2020, para. 15).

Sprout Social also suggests strategizing your content mix by prioritizing what resonates with your audience. You can conduct a social media audit of previous content to see what content received high engagement, or if you're just getting started on social media, you can do an audit of a competitor in your industry.

"Social media is all about appealing to the people who follow your brand and providing them with value. That means testing different strategies and types of content to see what your audience likes best" (Aboulhosn, 2020, para. 10).

Social Spotlight

When it comes to content, Gen Z is saying "get real"—literally. The social media platform BeReal was launched in 2020 by French former GoPro employee Alexis Barreyat as an alternative to the highly curated social media platforms Instagram and TikTok perceived by some users to be inauthentic because of overly filtered content.

BeReal users are prompted to take a photo at a different time each day. When they receive the alert "Time to BeReal," they have two minutes from the time they open the app to snap a selfie of what they're up to. If users are late to respond to the prompt, the app marks their photo as late, encouraging them to post in the moment in a more realistic, less polished way. The prompts timing is unpredictable and changes every day. Photo filters are not allowed. There's also no ads or visible follower counts. Think of it as the anti-Instagram.

"BeReal, which prompts users once per day to snap and share a quick photo from wherever they happen to be, is topping app charts with a social media experience that prioritizes spontaneous connections over image-conscious curation" (Oremus, 2022, para. 2). With more than 22 million global downloads (mainly by Gen Zers), the success of the platform represents a shift away from highly curated, idealistic content to a desire for more candid, authentic and unfiltered— hence "real"—content. According to Ehlers (2022):

> BeReal's boom in popularity is likely due to a strong dislike of the curated and "fake" content that's often expected on mainstream platforms like Instagram and Facebook. The push to be genuine and show your friends what you're doing at the moment of the notification, instead of during the most interesting part of your day, is intended to keep younger users in the moment.
>
> (para. 2)

The app's success is now spawning copycats on other platforms. Tik-Tok announced a new feature called TikTok Now that gives users daily prompts to share impromptu photos or short videos, and Instagram confirmed it's developing a similar feature called IG Candid Challenges that sends a daily notification to users to capture and share a photo in two minutes.

Should this demand continue, brands may need to re-think their content strategy with younger followers, moving away from perfect marketing images to more in-the-moment imagery, such as user-generated content.

Content Strategies

In order to increase the reach of your posts and your audience's engagement with your content, consider incorporating the below content strategies into your content plan:

Cadence: Cadence refers to the "rhythm" or posting frequency to a social media channel. There is no set rule or agreed-upon method for how often to post on social media. According to Aboulhosn (2020):

> There's a lot of competing information on how often you should post on social media. Some professionals recommend posting as regularly as possible to stay top of mind. Others suggest only posting if you have high quality and valuable information to add to the conversation.
>
> (para. 17)

Sprout Social offers some suggestions for posting frequency across certain channels in order to maximize visibility (McLachlan & Cohen, 2023):

- Facebook: 1–2 posts per day
- Twitter: 1–5 tweets per day

- Instagram: 3–7 per week
- LinkedIn: 1–5 posts times per day

Tagging: Tagging (also called "mentions" on Twitter) refers to mentioning other accounts in your caption or Tweet by including the @ sign followed directly by their username. Tagged users will receive a notification that they've been mentioned in the caption, Tweet or story and can choose to interact with it by commenting (or "replying" on Twitter) or sharing the post, story or Tweet (called a "retweet").

Cross-promotion: Cross-promotion takes place two or more accounts form a marketing partnership and agree to share each other's content (usually for free) on their social media channels to have greater reach/exposure.

> Cross-promotion, simply, is companies helping each other market. They may run joint-advertising like Coca-Cola and McDonald's, recommend each other's products like VISA and JPMorgan Chase, or sell each other's products like Comcast and HBO.
>
> (Glotkin, 2020, para. 3)

Cross-posting: Cross-posting is the process of repurposing your content across multiple social channels. Posting similar content across your social presence can save time and resources but keep in mind that platforms have different requirements and content will need to be edited accordingly for each channel.

> Every social media platform is different. For example, Pinterest is awash with Pins, Twitter is full of Tweets, and Instagram is packed with Stories. So when you're crossposting, you need to be mindful of the differences between each social media platform and learn how to speak their language.
>
> (Beveridge, 2021, para. 11)

Influencer Marketing: Influencer marketing involves paying a person— an influencer—to promote your product or service to their followers on social media.

> Celebrity endorsements were the original form of influencer marketing. But in today's digital world, social content creators with niche audiences can often offer more value to brands. These smaller accounts often have very engaged followers on social media.
>
> (Newberry, 2022, para. 4)

Promoting Your Presence

You've strategized a channel lineup, selected a content calendar, created a content plan and launched your presence. But how do you get the word out to your priority publics that you're ready to connect on social media? Here are a few strategies you can try:

- Create an e-blast to use with your email lists (e.g., "Let's get social! Follow us on Facebook, Twitter, Instagram @holycowicecream").
- Add a line to your organization's email signature that includes your hyperlinked social icons.
- Add your social handles and branded hashtags to your marketing materials (e.g., flyers, posters and postcards) and merchandise/SWAG (e.g., t-shirts, water bottles, stickers and keychains).
- Use your "social media real estate" (e.g., cover images on Facebook, Twitter and YouTube, bio sections, and YouTube video descriptions) to promote your full social media lineup across your channels.
- Make your employees a part of the process! Incorporate your social handles/icons into orientation materials and create a social media policy for how employees can and should engage with your social channels.
- Create incentives for following or engaging (e.g., "Follow us for 10% off your next purchase with us!")

Chapter Summary

- Social media content is anything you share on your social media channels. Types of content include copy/captions, photos, videos, articles, links, infographics, testimonials, live videos and more.
- Content should be paired with platforms that the content is suited for (e.g., informational content/copy for blogs and social networking sites, photos and videos for content-sharing apps and visual storytelling platforms, testimonials for review sites, microblogs for breaking news or timely updates, and messaging apps for customer service).
- Organic content is content your organization posts to its social media channels that doesn't incur a cost, including original content, curated content and user-generated content. Paid content refers to content that has an advertising spend behind it, including social media ads and "boosted" content.
- Content can also be categorized as informational, educational, promotional, conversational and/or entertaining in nature.
- While there is no set formula for creating a well-balanced content mix, most experts agree there needs to be a balance of promotional content with other types of content and that content should be prioritized by what resonates with priority publics.

- A content calendar is a tool used to schedule, manage, and track social media content across social channels. A content calendar entry typically includes the platform(s) you're posting the content to, the date/time of the post, copy/caption, visual element (e.g., photo, video, infographic and gif), platform-specific information (e.g., post, Story and Reel), any relevant links and handles to tag, and any affiliated campaigns.
- Content strategies such as cadence, cross-posting, cross-promoting and influencer marketing can help increase visibility of and engagement with your posts.
- Strategies for promoting your social media presence include creating an e-blast, adding social icons to an email signature, adding handles and branded hashtags to marketing materials and SWAG, involving employees and more.

Exercise 10.1

Imagine you get hired as the social media manager for a toy company. The types of content that the company regularly produces include long-form written content, such as blog articles and employee spotlights, and how-to videos explaining how to build and use their products. In terms of pairing content to platforms, what social channels make the most sense for the company's social media lineup and why?

Exercise 10.2

Identify two to three leaders in the toy space/industry (AKA competitors) that have a presence on social media. Conduct a social media audit to determine which types of content perform the best. What are the types of content (e.g., written content, photos, videos, links, infographics and user-generated content) that garner the most engagement (likes, loves, shares, comments, etc.)? Are there any noticeable trends in terms of how the content strategy is balanced with informational, educational, promotional, conversational and entertaining content?

Discussion Questions

1. What are the pros and cons of creating and maintaining a physical content calendar? What are the pros and cons of creating and maintaining a digital content calendar like a shared calendar app or a third-party program like Hootsuite?
2. In addition to the methods mentioned in this chapter, what are some other ways you could promote a newly launched social media lineup.?

References

Aboulhosn, S. (2020, May 6). How to create a social media calendar that works. *Sprout Social*. https://sproutsocial.com/insights/social-media-calendar/

Beveridge, C. (2021, December 16). A guide to cross-posting on social media (without looking spammy). *Hootsuite*. https://blog.hootsuite.com/cross-promote-social-media/

Beveridge, C. (2022, January 13). What is user-generated content? And why is it important? *Hootsuite*. https://blog.hootsuite.com/user-generated-content-ugc/

Cooper, P. (2021, November 1). Paid vs. organic social media: How to integrate both into your strategy. *Hootsuite*. Retrieved November 25, 2022, from https://blog.hootsuite.com/organic-vs-paid-social-media/

Dixon, S. (2022, October 27). Facebook: Quarterly number of MAU (monthly active users) worldwide 2008–2022. *Statista*. Retrieved November 25, 2022, from www.statista.com/statistics/264810/number-of-monthly-active-facebook-users-worldwide/#:~:text=How%20many%20users%20does%20Facebook,used%20online%20social%20network%20worldwide

Elhers, K. (2022, October 31). FOMO: Should your brand hop new viral apps like BeReal? *Forbes*. www.forbes.com/sites/forbesagencycouncil/2022/10/31/fomo-should-your-brand-hop-on-new-viral-apps-like-bereal/?sh=2705a2c31e4b

Glotkin, I. (2020, August 3). What is cross-promotion? +8 examples. *LinkedIn*. www.linkedin.com/pulse/what-cross-promotion-8-examples-igor-glotkin/

Grgurović, M. (2022, August 18). Video vs. image ads: Why videos perform better than images. *Brid.TV*. Retrieved November 25, 2022, from www.brid.tv/video-vs-image-ads/#6-video-vs-image-ads-performance-on-facebook

Hootsuite Academy. (n.d.). *The value of social media content strategy*. https://education.hootsuite.com/pages/importance-of-a-social-media-content-strategy

Mailchimp. (n.d.). *Learn how to create social media content with a social content plan*. https://mailchimp.com/resources/top-12-types-of-social-media-content-to-create/

Martin, M. (2022, February 23). The complete guide to content curation in 2022: Tools, tips, ideas. *Hootsuite*. https://blog.hootsuite.com/beginners-guide-to-content-curation/

McLachlan, S., & Cohen, B. (2023, February 27). How often to post to social media in 2023. *Sprout Social*. https://blog.hootsuite.com/how-often-to-post-on-social-media/

Newberry, C. (2022, September 14). Influencer marketing guide: How to work with influencers. *Hootsuite*. https://blog.hootsuite.com/influencer-marketing/

Newberry, C., & Cohen, B. (2022, September 27). How to create a social media calendar [2022 guide]. *Hootsuite*. https://blog.hootsuite.com/how-to-create-a-social-media-content-calendar/

Olenski, S. (2017, June 21). Why content will always be king. *Forbes*. www.forbes.com/sites/steveolenski/2017/06/21/why-content-will-always-always-king/?sh=b86d6e5eb370

Oremus, W. (2022, September 17). BeReal is hotter than TikTok. So TikTok is copying it. *The Washington Post*. www.washingtonpost.com/technology/2022/09/17/bereal-copy-tiktok-instagram-snapchat/

Sehl, K. (2021, August 27). Organic reach is in decline—here's what you can do about it. *Hootsuite*. Retrieved November 24, 2022, from https://blog.hootsuite.com/organic-reach-declining/

Sprout Social. (2022, September 19). *Social media trends for 2022 and beyond*. Retrieved November 24, 2022, from https://sproutsocial.com/insights/index/

Zelefsky, V. (2022, May 6). The differences between paid and organic content on social media. *Forbes*. www.forbes.com/sites/forbescommunicationscouncil/2022/05/06/the-differences-between-paid-and-organic-content-on-social-media/?sh=87792fa1526a

11 Writing for Social Media

Writing for social media takes a multitude of forms from crafting compelling captions, to timely tweets, to keyword-driven video descriptions, to considerate comments and replies, to direct messages to customers, to in-depth blog posts, to strategically selected emojis to accompany snaps and stories, and more.

Whether you're conducting a one-time campaign or creating daily content as part of your organization's social media program, it's important to keep in mind that social media serves as an extension of an organization's communications presence, and, therefore, is held to the same standards as other channels of communication, such as advertising, public relations, marketing and sales. Whether it be a news release, a front-page ad, product packaging or a 15-second social media story, the communication should be clear, concise, honest, ethical, persuasive, on-brand and sensitive to all types of diversity while taking into account proper style, spelling, punctuation and grammar.

Social media is considered "controlled" media (vs. "uncontrolled"), meaning the sender controls the messaging, the frequency of the messaging, the tone and the decision to include, or not include, any multimedia elements, such as photos and videos, among other editorial choices. The messaging is not at the mercy of the media (like it is with "earned media" and publicity), and organizations have the ability to speak directly to its publics with the click of a button, which means the responsibility to get it right ultimately falls to the person posting.

Social media writing, specifically, should take into account the specific type or category of social media at hand and the inherent purpose of the platform, any accepted practices or "etiquette" for the platform (e.g., "Swipe up to learn more" vs. "Click link in bio"), and any special considerations or limitations that a platform may have, such as limiting a tweet to 280 characters or the fact that URLs do not hyperlink within Instagram captions. Furthermore, in terms of tone and voice, social media writing should be conversational and audience-driven to make those captions and comments really count.

DOI: 10.4324/9781003255734-14

In this chapter, we'll begin with some fundamental elements for successful social media writing, such as style, structure, tone and voice, and the use of handles and hashtags. Next, we'll explore strategies for writing across the most popular types of social media, such as social networking sites, blogs/microblogs, content-sharing sites and customer review sites. Finally, we'll review best practices for social media writing but also look at instances when we can, and should, break the rules.

What you can expect to learn in this chapter:

• What constitutes social media writing
• The purpose of social media writing
• Where social media writing fits into the social media process
• Basic fundamentals of writing for social media, such as style, structure, tone and voice
• How to incorporate hashtags and handles into captions and other forms of social media writing
• Considerations for writing across different types or categories of social media
• When it's OK, and encouraged, to break the rules
• A recap of best practices for social media writing

What Is Social Media Writing?

As mentioned at the beginning of this chapter, social media writing is so much more than a simple caption slapped with emojis and a long line of hashtags. Social media writing can take a myriad of forms, including but not limited to:

• Captions for posts, stories and snaps
• Tweets
• Creation and inclusion of handles and hashtags
• Blog posts
• Video descriptions and other forms of metadata
• Comments and replies to followers
• Direct messages/private messages to followers
• Social branding elements, such as a channel's "About" or "Bio" section
• Social media policies (e.g., posting policies for followers or policies for employees engaging with their organization's social media)

Social media writing can be multipurpose; it can be informational, promotional, conversational and/or entertaining, depending upon the goal of the writing.

• Informational: seeks to inform or educate
  Did you know that the roosterfish was once thought to be part of the jack family, but it's actually a totally unique species of its own? What makes it unique is that

its swim bladder penetrates its brain allowing it to amplify sound to track its prey! *#marinemonday*

- Promotional: promotes a product or service
  Here's the scoop! It's #NationalIceCreamDay, and we're ready to celebrate! Stop in our store today to get 50% off any of our signature scoops!
- Conversational: creates conversation
  Welcome back students! It's the first day of #fallsemester and we want to know. . . . What are you most looking forward to this academic year? Let us know in the comments below!
- Entertaining: provides entertainment value
  "Success is the sum of small efforts, repeated day in and day out."—Robert Collier #mondaymotivation

While social media writing can be versatile, its primary purpose is to communicate information that will influence priority audiences and persuade them to do something you want them to do, whether that be to "like" or "share" a piece of content, comment on a post, learn something, buy something, click a link, create conversation or any other action. Ensure that your social media writing is tied to organizational goals by including a call to action, also called a CTA.

Perspective From the Pros

By Michael North, Ph.D.

Effective social media writing uses repetition, gets to the point, and brings about a desired action.

In 1974, rock band Bad Company released its debut album titled "Bad Company." And one of that album's singles—you guessed it—was titled "Bad Company." Bad Company performed "Bad Company" on the album titled "Bad Company."

That's an example of good repetition. Repetition is an effective strategy to sear your keywords and key phrases into the minds of your organization's social media friends, followers and connections. Branding through consistent repetition is an old strategy, but it's particularly effective in today's digital world that's operated by search bars and algorithms.

Less tends to be more across today's social media platforms. Twitter is famous for its 280-character limit, but thanks to the size of smartphone screens and the length of our attention spans, getting to the point is appreciated by social media users. Trim your social media writing down to its essence.

Wall Street Journal columnist Peggy Noonan recommends to think "Fish" when writing: "Remember the waterfront shack with the sign

'Fresh Fish Sold Here.' Of course it's fresh, we're on the ocean. Of course it's for sale, we're not giving it away. Of course it's here, otherwise the sign would be somewhere else. The final sign: 'Fish.'"

Noonan's lesson should be applied to your social media writing. Challenge every word in your tweet or Instagram caption. Every word you choose to include should contribute toward bringing about the desired action.

And effective social media writing should bring about a desired action such as registering to vote, getting a vaccine, making a purchase decision or adopting a service. If your social media writing isn't working toward bringing about a desired action, then it's busy work. And busy work just contributes more noise to an already loud conversation.

We've read about developing "sticky" social media content. However, the gum on the bottom of your shoe is sticky. Sure, the gum stays with you, but it's annoying.

Instead, aim for influential content. Influential content isn't influencer content, which is often trite and easily forgotten. So what is influential? Synonyms for "influential" include persuasive, inspiring, pivotal, significant, noteworthy and powerful. Influential content makes people do something. Or at the very least, like, share or click a link to a landing page.

The Beach Boys, Elton John, Stevie Wonder, and the Rolling Stones released Billboard number-one albums in 1974. And so did Bad Company with its debut album titled "Bad Company," which was certified five times platinum by the RIAA. While "Can't Get Enough" and "Movin' On" were the album's highest-ranked songs on the Billboard Hot 100 list, the song "Bad Company" on the album "Bad Company" by the band Bad Company is the most memorable. Notice the repetition?

Repeat your simple message to bring about the desired behavior from social media users.

Social Media Writing and Its Place in the Social Media Process

Now that we've established what social media writing is and its purpose, we can take it a step further and pinpoint its place in the social media process. In Chapter 10, we examined the four-phase social media process that has its roots in public relations: Research (or Listening), Planning (or Strategic Design), Implementation and Evaluation.

Once we've assessed the situation during the Research phase and set our goal/objectives during the Planning phase, we are ready to execute the plan and communicate during the Implementation phase. It is in this phase—Implementation—where social media writing lives. Our overarching goal, supporting objectives and strategies for the social media campaign are carried out through tactics. Tactics are the "nuts-and-bolts part of the plan" and "describe the specific activities that put each strategy into operation and help to achieve the stated objectives" (Wilcox et al., 2016, p. 112).

In public relations, tactics are the most visible portion of a public relations plan and "use various methods to reach target audiences with key messages" (Wilcox et al., 2016, p. 112). From a PR standpoint, these key messages might involve news releases, media pitches, backgrounders, bio sketches, feature stories and other forms of PR writing. In social media, writing-related tactics could involve captions, comments, direct messages, social media bios, channel descriptions or any of the aforementioned forms of social media writing.

Style, Structure, Tone and Voice

Style

The style guide used within the field of communications, and therefore within social media, public relations, journalism, advertising and related fields, is The Associated Press Stylebook and Briefing on Media Law. "Updated regularly since its initial publication in 1953, the AP Stylebook is a must-have reference for writers, editors, students and professionals. It provides fundamental guidelines for spelling, language, punctuation, usage and journalistic style" (What Is the AP Stylebook?, n.d.). AP Style also provides guidance for writing about, and remaining sensitive to, all types of diversity, including race, ethnicity, gender, age, sexuality, disabilities, religion, mental illness, diseases and more.

The AP Stylebook contains special sections, such as punctuation, business, data journalism, polls and surveys, health and science, social media guidelines, religion, sports, food, fashion, media law, broadcast and more. The "AP Social Media Guidelines" section outlines how journalistic standards should be applied while using social media and provides general strategies that can be used across most social platforms. For example, AP Style recommends that handles/usernames be something "clear-cut and easy to remember" (Froke et al., 2020, p. 380).

Some basic AP Style guidelines that should be applied to all forms of communications writing, including social media writing, are outlined below:

- Numbers below 10 should be spelled out; for 10 and above, use numerals.
- Abbreviate Aug., Sept., Oct., Nov., Dec., Jan. and Feb. when they accompany a specific day of the month (e.g., "The first day of classes for the fall semester will take place on Aug. 22, 2021.")

- Spell out August, September, October, November, December, January and February when they stand alone or with only a year (e.g., "Classes will resume in August.")
- Spell out March, April, May, June and July in all instances.
- Abbreviate Ave., Blvd. and St. when they are used with numbered addresses (e.g., "1300 College Ave."), but spell them out when they stand alone (e.g., "Turn onto Adams Avenue").
- Spell out all other terms such as road, terrace and alley in all instances.
- Always spell out the days of the week (e.g., Monday, Tuesday, Wednesday and so on).
- Use one space between sentences.
- Titles should be capitalized when they appear directly before a person's name but lowercased when they appear after a name (e.g., "U.S. President Joe Biden" vs. "Joe Biden, president of the United States").
- When stating time of day, use figures except for "noon" and "midnight."
- Use a colon to separate hours from minutes ("11 a.m.," "3:30 p.m." and "9–11 a.m.").
- Lowercase "a.m." and "p.m." and use periods.
- Use the word "and" in writing and only use an ampersand (&) when it is part of a company's formal name or composition title.

(e.g., House & Garden)

For specific guidance referring to punctuation, see the special section titled "Punctuation" in the AP Stylebook.

For spelling questions not addressed by the Associated Press Stylebook, refer to Merriam-Webster's Dictionary.

Social Spotlight

The AP Stylebook is a great resource for social media writers in terms of spelling, language, punctuation, usage and journalistic style, but did you know it's also a great tool for social media strategy? The stylebook's dedicated section to social media and web-based reporting guidelines provides best practices for how journalists and other communications professionals can use social media professionally and ethically in their work. The guidelines address social media-related topics such as user-generated content, vetting and citing social media sources, and searching social media for breaking news and trending topics.

Structure

Inverted Pyramid Style is a method of structuring and summarizing writing and while it has its origins in journalism it can (and should) be applied to most forms of communications messaging, whether it be used when writing news releases, news stories, emails, social media captions or promotional text messages.

Sterin and Winston (2018) define the inverted pyramid as a "reporting structure wherein the most important facts are presented in the lead sentences, followed by more elaborate details that support those facts" (p. 472). Writing that follows inverted pyramid style states the "Who," "What," "Where," "When" and "Why"—also known as the five Ws—in the first one to two paragraphs. These first one to two paragraphs are referred to as the "nut graph." When applicable, the nut graph also includes the "How."

Inverted pyramid style is represented by an upside-down triangle, with the most important information appearing at the top of the triangle (five Ws), followed by important details, and then finishing with any general or background information.

Communications professionals rely on inverted pyramid style to summarize their writing, so that they don't "bury the lede" and keep readers guessing. So the next time you craft a blog post or type a tweet, remember to use inverted pyramid style, so that your followers don't lose interest and keep scrolling.

Tone and Voice

While journalistic writing and news reporting traditionally use a third-person point of view and avoid personal pronouns, such as "I," "we" and "you," there are instances, such as writing for social media, where this conversational tone is appropriate.

Social media, by definition, is intended to be social and conversational; therefore, using a second-person point of view ("you"-focused language) is appropriate and encouraged. Remember, we are speaking with—not at—followers and attempting to create conversation. When referring to your organization, say "we" instead of referring to the organization in the third person to make it feel more personable. In Chapter 13, we will examine strategies for engaging in effective customer service on social media to make the communication even more personal with messaging that addresses followers by their first names.

Social media writing and captions should be conversational to engage followers but should always remain factual. Language should be concise, audience-driven and considerate of the platform being used (e.g., Twitter has a 280-character limit for Tweets).

Handles and Hashtags

An accepted etiquette for crafting captions and other forms of social media writing is to include handles and hashtags within your writing. Before we look at an example of how handles and hashtags can be incorporated into social media writing, let's first define handles and hashtags. Below, we examine how the Associated Press Stylebook and Briefing on Media Law defines these two terms (Froke et al., 2020, p. 136):

- **Handle:** "a self-selected, public-facing username on a social network. May be used interchangeably with username."
- **Hashtag**: "a term starting with a number or hash sign (#) in a social network post. It conveys the subject of the post so that it can be easily found by users interested in that subject."

While handles refer to people, places or things, hashtags refer to topics and help provide context for your post. Hashtags can be created for special projects or events (e.g., #TheGreatBakeOff2020), for groups of people (e.g., #Classof2021), for hobbies and interests (e.g., #health #wellness #yoga), for cultural movements (e.g., #metoo) and for countless other areas of interest.

Hashtags always start with a "#" but won't work if you use spaces, punctuation or symbols. Sometimes, the first letters of words within a hashtag are capitalized for readability purposes—a practice that is more common with longer hashtags. Unlike spaces, punctuation or symbols, capitalization of certain letters won't hinder your hashtag.

Now that we know how to define and distinguish handles and hashtags, let's look at strategies for using them in our writing.

Let's say the pastry chef for the bakery called Bake My Day is named Bella Bossie, and she has an account on Instagram that uses the handle @ bellabakes. Her bakery has a separate Instagram account and uses the handle @bakemyday. Bella was recently named a nominee for a Chef Award in 2021 by the James Beard Foundation, which is represented by the handle @ beardfoundation on Instagram.

Imagine you are the social media manager for Bake My Day, and you want to craft a celebratory post on Instagram to bring awareness to Bella's achievement. First, try writing your caption without incorporating any handles or hashtags as you would for a news release, newsletter or email.

> *Congratulations to our head pastry chef Bella Bossie on being named a nominee for the prestigious Chef Awards hosted the James Beard Foundation. We are so proud of your sweet success!*

First, start with incorporating handles by simply swapping out any nouns (people, places or things) in the caption that have accounts, and therefore usernames, on Instagram. The caption would now look like this:

> *Congratulations to our head pastry chef @bellabakes on being named a nominee for the prestigious Chef Awards hosted by the @beardfoundation. We are so proud of your sweet success!*

Next, identify any words within the caption that might represent existing or popular hashtags on Instagram. Perhaps in researching this, we learn that the James Beard Foundation Chef Awards are a trending topic on Instagram represented by the hashtag #ChefAwards. Now, we substitute this hashtag and our caption looks like this:

> *Congratulations to our head pastry chef @bellabakes on being named a nominee for the prestigious #ChefAwards hosted by the @beardfoundation. We are so proud of your sweet success!*

Finally, we can add additional hashtags to the end of the caption to provide context and join similar conversations happening on social media.

> *Congratulations to our head pastry chef @bellabakes on being named a nominee for the prestigious #ChefAwards hosted by the @beardfoundation. We are so proud of your sweet success! #baking #pastries #desserts*

Now that we've seen handles and hashtags in action, you might be wondering, "Well, now I know to use them, but why do they matter?" Glad you asked. While including handles and hashtags in social media captions is an accepted practice for most social platforms, which is one important reason to use them, their true value lies in how they can create and increase engagement with your writing.

In our example above, the final version of the caption tags @bellabakes and @beardfoundation, will alert these accounts that they've been tagged in a post. These accounts can choose to share the post on their accounts, which will give the post greater reach and exposure to potential new followers. The hashtags will index the post, so that it becomes visible to anyone searching #ChefAwards, #baking, #pastries or #dessert, creating the opportunity for conversation and to connect with potential followers.

Communicating Across Categories of Social Media

Communications professionals are tasked with writing for all types of social media operated by an organization. A typical day on the job might involve posting an important news update to the company's Facebook page, answering consumers' questions on Twitter, live streaming an event on Instagram live, crafting a Q&A with an exec for a blog post, creating a how-to video for the company's YouTube channel, responding to a customer complaint on Yelp, or promoting a job opportunity on LinkedIn.

In order to write effective social media content, it's your job to know the inherent purpose of any social sites your organization has a presence on in order to use them strategically with content. Whereas Facebook posts are typically informational in nature, tweets tend to be used for updates or breaking news. Instagram, Snapchat and YouTube tell stories through photos and videos, while blog posts explore a topic in great detail through the written word. Yelp, Angie's List and TripAdvisor are for creating and sharing reviews, and Pinterest allows users to curate content around specific topics. And so on.

Social media managers also need to be privy to the "rules of the road" for social media sites, including any limitations, so that they can adjust their writing accordingly. For example, while Facebook's character limit for posts is in the tens of thousands, tweets are limited to 280 characters. Instagram does not hyperlink URLs in captions or comments, but it does allow users to include a clickable link in user bios (e.g., "Click link in bio to learn more"). On Snapchat, we instead attach links to snaps and direct "friends" to "swipe up."

It's also important to know the lingo associated with different social sites. Facebook, Instagram and LinkedIn have "posts," Twitter has "tweets," Snapchat has "snaps" and Pinterest has "pins." Facebook and LinkedIn have "pages" to differentiate from personal profiles, YouTube has "channels" that categorize content by "playlists," Pinterest has "boards" and Snapchat has "stories." Facebook and Instagram now have "stories," too. Facebook pages have "followers," but Facebook profiles have "friends." LinkedIn profiles have "connections," LinkedIn pages have "followers," and YouTube channels have "subscribers."

In addition to "lingo" associated with each social media site, it's important to keep in mind the etiquette or accepted practices for a respective platform. For example, while a longer caption might be appropriate on a social networking site like Facebook, several paragraphs of copy might turn someone off on a content-sharing site like Instagram, where the content should be the focus. Social etiquette also includes any user features associated with the specific platform, such as "Swipe up" (Snapchat) versus "Click link in bio" (Instagram) versus "Double Tap" (Instagram ads).

For a full breakdown of the most widely used social media sites, check out Dave Kerpen's book "Likeable Social Media, Third Edition: How to Delight Your Customers, Create an Irresistible Brand, & Be Generally Amazing on All Social Networks that Matter" (2019).

Breaking the Rules

As the saying goes, "Rules are meant to be broken." Due to the fact that certain social media sites do have limitations, such as character counts, there are specific instances when we can break the "rules of the road" when it comes to social media writing:

- When character limits make it difficult to communicate a full message, consider using accepted acronyms or abbreviations for the platform to shorten the amount of characters used. On Twitter, for example, "TY" is often used in place of "thank you" and social platforms like Facebook and Instagram are recognized by "FB" and "TW," respectively. "DM" refers to "Direct Message."

How sweet it is to be loved by you! Today we reached one million followers. TY for the love! Make sure to follow us on our other social channels @bakemyday on FB and IG. Check out our spring menu at bakemyday.com and feel free to DM us with questions. #sweetsuccess

- While all communications writing should strive to use correct spelling, punctuation, grammar and style, there are instances where we can use slang with popular sayings and phrases in order to create conversation. *How 'bout them Canes? #hurricanes #football #umiami*

Best Practices

Now that we've defined social media writing and explored style, form, tone, voice, handles, hashtags and special channel considerations, let's revisit and round up some basic best practices for writing across all social media channels that can provide a strong foundation for all types of social media writing:

- **Strike a Balance:** Social media content should provide different types of value for followers. Content can be informational, promotional, conversational or simply entertaining. Ensure that your content strategy strikes a balance to create maximum value for your followers.
- **Include a Call to Action:** Ensure that social media messaging is tied back to organizational goals by including a call to action, such as "learn more" and "apply today."
- **Use AP Style:** Associated Press (AP Style) is the accepted style used within the field of communication and should be applied to all forms of social media writing when possible.
- **Don't Bury the Lede:** Use Inverted Pyramid Style to streamline and organize your messaging.
- **Voice and Tone:** Social media is meant to be social. Write in second person and use pronouns such as "you" and "we" to make your messaging conversational.
- **Incorporate Hashtags and Handles:** Increase engagement by tagging relevant handles and join/create conversations by incorporating hashtags.
- **Consider Channel Limitations:** Social media writing should take into account any special considerations or limitations for the specific social platform at hand, such as character limits or captions that don't have hyperlinking capabilities.
- **Stick to Social Etiquette:** Learn the social etiquette of the social platforms you're creating content for, so that you don't make a social faux pas and turn off followers.

Chapter Summary

- Social media writing is much more than just captions; it can be customer service (comments and direct messages to followers), channel "bios," blog posts, video descriptions and other forms of metadata, the creation of handles, hashtags, social media policies and more.
- Social media writing should create value for followers and should be a blend of content that is informational, promotional, conversational and entertaining.
- Social media writing should be tied back to organizational goals and should contain a CTA (call to action).
- Social media writing has a specific style (AP Style), structure (inverted pyramid), tone (conversational) and voice (second person, you-focused language).
- Incorporating handles and hashtags into captions can increase engagement and exposure to new followers.
- When communicating across different categories/types of social media, keep in mind a platform's inherent purpose, its "rules of the road" or accepted etiquette and any language/lingo associated with the platform.
- Know the rules but break them when necessary, for example, when character counts limit your messaging or when using slang would be more conversational.

Exercise 11.1

Imagine that you are the social media manager for the bakery Bake My Day. Using the information below, craft three captions: one for the bakery's Facebook page, one for its Twitter account and one for its Instagram account. Use inverted pyramid to structure the information from most important to least important and include a clear call to action. Keep in mind that Twitter posts are limited to 280 characters and that Instagram captions do not hyperlink URLs included in them.

- All featured flavors are gluten-free and use organic ingredients.
- Customers can visit www.bakemyday.com to sign up for email alerts and receive 50% off their first purchase.
- Bake My Day is preparing to launch its "Summer Sweets" menu on June 1 featuring new flavors of its gourmet cupcakes.
- Featured flavors include strawberry shortcake, carrot cake, coconut cream and piña colada.

Discussion Questions

1. This chapter introduced Associated Press Style and how it serves as the accepted style guide in the field of communications. When it comes to social media, there are certain instances when we can and should break

the rules, for example, when adhering to character limits/counts or using conversational language. What are some other social media situations that might require us to break the AP Style rules?

2. What are some ethical concerns to take into consideration for tagging accounts via their handles in social media posts? For example, would it be ethical and/or appropriate for journalists to tag subjects of their news/feature stories when promoting their work on social media?

References

Froke, P., Bratton, A. J., McMillan, J., Sarkar, P., Schwartz, J., & Vadarevu, R. (2020). *The Associated Press stylebook 2020–2022 and briefing on media law*. The Associated Press.

Kerpen, D. (2019). *Likeable social media: How to delight your customers, create and irresistible brand, and be amazing on Facebook, Twitter, LinkedIn, Instagram, Pinterest, and more.* McGraw-Hill.

Sterin, C. S., & Winston, T. (2018). *Mass media revolution* (3rd ed.). Routledge.

What Is the AP Stylebook? (n.d.). www.apstylebook.com/help?query=USAGE#/questions/210938-What-is-the-AP-Stylebook

Wilcox, D. L., Cameron, G. T., & Reber, B. H. (2016). *Public relations: Strategies and tactics* (11th ed.). Pearson Education, Inc.

Recommended Reading/Resources

Social Media Marketing & Management Dashboard. (2020, October 7). *How to use hashtags: A quick and simple guide for every network.* https://blog.hootsuite.com/how-to-use-hashtags/

Twitter. (n.d.-a). Glossary. *Twitter.* https://help.twitter.com/en/glossary

Twitter. (n.d.-b). Speak the language of Twitter | Twitter help. *Twitter.* https://help.twitter.com/en/twitter-guide/twitter-101/speak-the-language-of-twitter-twitter-help

Zote, J. (2020, August 7). 130 most important social media acronyms and slang you should know. *Sprout Social.* https://sproutsocial.com/insights/social-media-acronyms/

12 Customer Service and Crisis Management

Organizations use social media for a plethora of reasons: to advertise and market products and services, connect with potential customers or create conversation with existing ones, crowdsource ideas, communicate company culture, keep an eye on the competition, and much more.

From a public relations standpoint, organizations can use social media to build and maintain mutually beneficial relationships with their publics. In an effort to create two-way communication with these publics, organizations can use social media for customer service and crisis management.

What you can expect to learn in this chapter:

- How to define social media customer service and social media crisis management
- How organizations use social media for customer service and crisis management/communications
- The social platforms/channels most used for customer service and crisis management
- How organizations can be proactive, rather than reactive, when it comes to customer service and crisis management
- Social strategies for strong customer service and crisis management

What Is Social Media Customer Service?

Customer service has come a long way since the introduction of the 1–800 number. According to Hootsuite, "Social media customer service is the practice of using social tools to resolve customer questions or concerns. Social customer support is highly effective because it allows customers to reach your team on the platforms they already use" (Newberry, 2021, para. 1). Customer service inquiries might include anything from product availability to payment options to shipping times. Customers might also use social media to report service outages or provide feedback about products or the purchasing process. The volume of customer support requests can also be influenced by product launches or promotions, which can lead to

DOI: 10.4324/9781003255734-15

an influx of sales and, therefore, more opportunities for inbound questions. According to Solis and Breakenridge (2009):

> Social media represents an entirely new way to reach customers and connect with them directly. It adds an outbound channel that complements inbound customer service, traditional PR, direct marketing, and advertising, placing companies and their customers on a level playing field to discuss topics as peers.
>
> (p. 204)

Social media provide a way not only for organizations to provide customer service to their publics but also for members of these publics to connect and help one another.

> If you provide a place for consumers to connect and to gripe, to share information and to learn and to grow, people will realize you are committed to them and the community you are fostering, and they will return that commitment to you. So now when someone unfamiliar with your company comes to the community, a potentially huge new prospect, and posts a question, another member of the community might answer the prospect's question before you have time to. Or when an unsatisfied customer comes to the Facebook page to complain, the community is likely to rally behind you without your even having to ask.
>
> (Kerpen, 2019, p. 88)

Customers are increasingly turning to social media to meet their customer service needs. According to Sprout Social, the number of consumers who preferred using social messaging for customer service jumped 110% from 2020 to 2021 alone. Lanier (2022) wrote:

> What does it mean to have exceptional customer service? Automated phone systems? Website chatbots? Help guides? These ease your customer support teams' workload, but they don't always cater to the needs of your customers—especially if they have a unique or urgent issue. When this happens, they don't want to click through a series of irrelevant options or read through useless FAQs. They want to speak to a human as soon as possible, and guess where they go to achieve this? Social media.
>
> (para. 1–2)

Platforms Used for Social Customer Service

Similar to how an organization's social media lineup—the channels that it uses as a part of its regular social media presence—takes into account where priority publics already are on social media, an organization's decision of which social media platforms to use for customer service should do the same.

> Most companies already have websites, chatbots, and phone support, so what's different about social media customer service? Accessibility. You want to interact with your customers where they spend most of their time and where they feel most comfortable reaching out. For most people, that means communicating with businesses on the same platforms they communicate with everyone else.
>
> (Porter, n.d.)

The size of the organization and, therefore, its capabilities, might also influence which social tools to use. "A single-location bakery might make do with free tools while a multinational brand needs a more robust solution" (Barnhart, 2021, para. 23).

While the social channels an organization uses for customer service will largely be dictated by its publics' preferences and/or the size of the organization, there are also certain social platforms that stand out for their popularity in the customer service arena.

Twitter

Twitter is live and geared toward conversation, which makes it a popular choice for providing customer service. Its public nature means that customers and potential customers can see how an organization interacts with its consumer base, and the Direct Message feature also allows organizations to take conversations out of the public arena when needed. Organizations can use Twitter for live offline events, conversations in which people want to address specific individuals and a group at once, or to host live chats, contests and promotions.

"Many brands use Twitter as an alternate customer service channel. According to advertisers on Twitter, more than 80 percent of social customer service requests happen on Twitter. And Salesforce calls Twitter the 'New 1–800 Number for Customer Service'" (Lua, n.d., para. 38).

Kerpen (2019) names Target, Apple, Lyft, Forrester and Starbucks News as five companies that use Twitter well for customer service.

Facebook and WhatsApp

According to Sprout Social, more than half of brands report that private/direct messaging plays a role in their customer care strategy. Facebook is the number one platform where consumers follow brands, so using Facebook Messenger, Facebook's dedicated messaging app and platform is an easy way to connect with them (Lanier, 2022). "If your customers are on Facebook, then you should be too" (Lanier, 2022, para. 34). In 2021, over 1.3 billion people around the world used Messenger to stay connected with friends, families and businesses. The app supports text messaging, voice and video calls and is free to use for anyone with a Facebook account and internet connection (Sehl, 2021).

Facebook's inbox compiles Messenger, Facebook posts and Instagram comments into one view. Facebook Messenger also offers a free chatbot service, which can be useful to organizations with a high volume of the same type of questions (Barnhart, 2021). Other benefits of Facebook Messenger include (Meta, n.d.):

- The ability to respond to inquiries from story replies, comments and messages from posts on Instagram
- The Facebook Chat Plugin makes it easy for people to start conversations with your organization while browsing your website
- The ability to add a "Send Message" call-to-action to your Facebook Page or Page posts
- The ability to create ads that click to Messenger
- The ability to add hyperlinks to emails, messages, social media posts and more
- QR codes make it easy to start conversations in Messenger from offline locations such as in-store signage, product packaging, direct mail and more

Facebook Messenger is also a great option for conversations that belong out of the public eye.

> Maybe a customer has a question that they are shy to ask publicly. For example, Stayfree Africa uses Facebook Messenger as a safe space for customers to talk about their periods. Or, maybe a customer had a negative experience that you would rather resolve privately.
>
> (Sehl, 2021, para. 21)

WhatsApp is a free private messaging and calling app that was acquired by Facebook in 2014. With two billion users, it's the third most-used social media platform, behind Facebook and YouTube (Lua, n.d.; Newberry, 2022). Organizations can create a WhatsApp business profile with information that makes it easy for users to connect with them both on and off the app. A business profile provides credibility and sets expectations for how users can interact with the organization on the app. The WhatsApp Business app was developed for small businesses that personally manage conversations with customers, while the WhatsApp Business Platform is geared toward medium to large businesses communicating with customers at scale. Features of WhatsApp Business include (Newberry, 2022):

- A business profile with the organization's contact information
- Quick replies to use when responding to common questions
- Labels that can differentiate users (e.g., customers vs. leads)
- Automated away messages and new customer greeting messages

Strategies for Social Customer Service

Popular strategies for providing excellent customer service include catering customer service channels to your publics, monitoring conversations about your brand, maintaining a high response rate and fast response time, taking conversations offline when necessary, creating a handle dedicated to customer service requests, incorporating customer service information into your social media guidelines, being proactive in anticipating customer service requests, getting creative with customer service solutions, and having a holistic approach to social media customer care that involves all departments within an organization.

Catering Customer Service Channels to Your Publics

As mentioned earlier in the chapter, providing strong customer service on social media begins with meeting your publics where they already are. "If your customers are on Facebook, then you should be too" (Lanier, 2022, para. 34). According to Hootsuite:

> For your social customer care to be effective, you've got to use the channels where your audience already spends their time. Monitor social platforms to see where people are already talking about your company online. This will give you a good sense of what channels to prioritize for your social media customer service.
>
> (Newberry, 2021, para. 39–40)

Monitor Conversations About Your Brand

Don't expect to always be alerted about conversations happening on social media about your organization. Many users mention brands (positively and negatively) without tagging them. Some of these conversations may warrant a response. Using social listening tools, like a platform's search function or an app dedicated to social listening like Mention, can help organizations to be proactive by monitoring mentions, so that they can intervene when there are issues or simply share a kind compliment.

Another benefit of social media customer service is that you can find people who have concerns but don't complain directly to you. Let's face it, people are much more likely to Tweet about a negative experience than they are to search out a business' direct support line and make a complaint. But now, their issues don't need to go unanswered.

(Porter, n.d., para. 11)

Maintain a High Response Rate/Fast Response Time

Having a presence on social media is a great start for organizations wanting to connect with priority publics but maintaining a high response rate and fast response time will take a social presence to the next level.

When possible, organizations should always respond to questions, comments and even compliments. Potential customers reaching out for support who don't receive a response (or a timely response) may move on to the competition.

> People asking questions of your brand on social media may or may not be your customers (yet). Answering all questions on social channels shows that you have responsive customer service. This proves to potential customers that you care about your clients' needs.
>
> (Newberry, 2021, para. 26)

Sprout Social reported that more than 75% of consumers expect a reply within 24 hours on social media (Lanier, 2022). While the golden rule or standard for responding is typically 24 hours, the expected response time can also vary by industry, product or service.

> At one time, taking a day or more to respond to a customer was acceptable. But now most demand instant access and gratification. And if you're considered a high-priced product or service, then you definitely must respond quickly. One report shows customers who pay more for a service expect a higher level of social customer care.
>
> (Lanier, 2022, para. 29)

Take Conversations Offline When Necessary

While public-facing conversations between an organization and its followers certainly can be beneficial, there are some conversations that are better had in private. When customer service interactions take a turn for the worse, it's best to direct users to private messaging options to continue the conversation offline. For example, Facebook has Messenger and Instagram Direct Messaging. "In the digital world, 'DM' usually stands for 'Direct Message.' A DM is a private mode of communication between social media users. When you send a direct message, only you and the recipient can see the content" (Sprout Social, n.d., para. 1).

Direct messages aren't just for customer service interactions that have gone awry. Organizations can also use DM to connect with partner organizations, potential influencers, brand ambassadors and prospects. "Direct messaging is a powerful tool in a brand's ability to build relationships with customers. DMs are private, intimate and personalized" (Sprout Social, n.d., para. 3).

Create a Dedicated Handle for Customer Service

While social media channels are typically managed by an organization's marketing team, setting up a separate account and handle for an organization's customer care team could create faster response times.

> Your customer service team can likely address client questions faster and in more detail than your social marketing team can. . . . That's why it can be a good idea for brands to use a separate social account to offer social media customer service solutions. For example, Hootsuite uses @ Hootsuite_Help, which is run by the support team.
>
> (Newberry, 2021, para. 4)

A separate customer service account also benefits the organization.

> While it's great to have this two-way communication with customers, a customer service-filled feed can distract from other campaigns and promotions your brand is trying to highlight. This is why some brands stand up separate Twitter accounts dedicated to customer care.
>
> (Lanier, 2022, para. 40)

Incorporate Customer Service Information Into Social Media Guidelines

Organizations can manage customer service expectations on social media by incorporating customer service information, like typical response times for each channel, into their social media guidelines. Answers to frequently asked questions and protocols for escalating customer issues are other valuable pieces of service-related information organizations might want to consider including.

> Your social customer service may not be available 24/7, and that's okay. You just need to set customer expectations appropriately. Make your social customer service hours of availability clear. Let customers know when you're going offline. Provide links to self-help solutions. Direct them how to reach other customer service channels (like your call center) in the meantime.
>
> (Newberry, 2021, para. 30–31)

Be Proactive

If users regularly pose the same or similar questions, organizations can be proactive in anticipating these questions and create self-service information resources. Educational content like how-to videos and best practices posts/blogs and updates about any known service issues can help cut down on the volume of support/customer care requests. Some platforms, like Instagram, offer "quicky reply" features that allow organizations to pre-write answers to common questions for quick responses.

Be Creative

Customer service-driven social media channels can be used for more than just resolving problems, complaints and questions. They can also be used to surprise and delight your priority publics. For example, Morton's The Steakhouse once famously delivered a full dinner delivered by a tuxedo-clad sever to a man at Newark Liberty International Airport after he jokingly tweeted @Mortons on Twitter about wanting a porterhouse steak upon his arrival.

> Customer service can include anything that makes your customers feel more connected to your brand. It should make them more comfortable buying, using, and recommending your products.
>
> (Newberry, 2021, para. 20)

Have a Holistic Approach to Customer Care

Creating a dedicated account and handle for customer care is an easy way to incorporate an organization's customer service department into its social media program, but what about the rest of the organization's departments? Rather than letting PR, marketing or customer service departments have sole ownership over social media, a more strategic, holistic approach involves all areas within an organization. According to Quesenberry (2021):

> As customer service activity moves to social media, companies must be prepared. To be effective, marketing and its advertising and public relations partners must work with customer service. The customer doesn't distinguish between company departments and business disciplines and will seek engagement with all in the same channel.
>
> (p. 334)

Social Spotlight

If there's a secret to customer service success on Twitter, eyeglasses and sunglasses retailer Warby Parker may have cracked the code. Twitter Business named the retailer as one of "4 brands that take Twitter customer service to the next level" (Alton, n.d.).

The company created a dedicated handle (@WarbyParkerHelp) and launched the hashtag campaign #HomeTryOn to encourage customers to try on different pairs of glasses and Tweet customer service for expert advice. If Warby Parker's social media team couldn't communicate the information in 140 characters or less (prior to Twitter's increase to 280 characters), the team would shoot videos of themselves answering questions and tweet customers a link to the video uploaded to their YouTube channel.

Warby Parker found that customer service tweets that included a video were retweeted 65 times more frequently than other tweets from the company (Leiser, 2012). Warby Parker Co-founder Dave Gilboa told LinkedIn:

> Customers were so blown away that we are going to these lengths to meet their needs that they tweet about it and tell dozens of other people. That's been a win-win in thinking about customer service as a marketing channel.
>
> (Leiser, 2012, para. 6)

Warby Parker's success with customer service shows that going the extra mile with creative solutions pays off.

> It's a great proof point that there are still countless new ways to think about how to leverage social media to help solve problems for customers. Great service is simple—be fast, friendly and helpful. Social media is perfect for that philosophy.
>
> (Leiser, 2012, para. 7)

What Is Social Media Crisis Management?

A social media crisis is any activity on a social platform that may impact the organization in a negative way. It's more than an isolated mean comment or customer complaint; however, it's a situation that has the potential to snowball into a flood of negative responses or permanently damage relationships with an organization's publics.

> In other words, a social media crisis is when there's a major change in the online conversation about your brand: an action that has sparked anger, disappointment, or distrust on a wide scale. If left unaddressed, it could have major long-term consequences for your brand.
>
> (McLachlan & Dawley, 2022, para. 8)

Situations that could lead to a social media crisis include (McLachlan & Dawley, 2022):

- Insensitive or out-of-touch comments
- Hypocritical posts
- Poor employee behavior
- Product failures
- Customer dissatisfaction

Beyond these, hate speech, discriminatory posts, profane or lewd language, and the like can clearly cause a problem that not only creates a social media crisis but results in the organization, brand and/or public figure getting banned from a social platform altogether for violating its guidelines. For example, former U.S. president Donald Trump was banned or suspended from Facebook, Instagram, Twitter, YouTube and Snapchat following the Jan. 6, 2021, insurrection at the Capitol. Platforms cited hate speech, the spread of misinformation, and the risk of inciting violence as their reason for removing Trump, either temporarily or permanently. Meta cofounder Mark Zuckerberg wrote in a Facebook post:

> We believe the risks of allowing the President to continue to use our service during this period are simply too great. Therefore, we are extending the block we have placed on his Facebook and Instagram accounts indefinitely and for at least the next two weeks until the peaceful transition of power is complete.
>
> (2021, para. 5)

In 2022, Ye, the rapper and fashion designer formerly known as Kanye West, was locked out of his Twitter and Instagram accounts following antisemitic posts, and several fashion brands, including Adidas, severed deals with him. Some speculated that his attempt to purchase Parler, the social media platform popular with right-wing audiences, was also affected by his antisemitic commentary, although the company that owns Parler stated it "mutually agreed" to terminate the deal. "At the start of October, he was a billionaire music artist and businessman, and had deals with some of the world's biggest brands. Fast-forward just two months, and most of those no longer apply" (BBC News, 2022, para. 1–2).

Quesenberry (2021) notes that it's important to distinguish between a social media crisis and a traditional crisis, stating, "a social media crisis is caused by messages, situations, or responses that occur on social media platforms themselves," whereas "traditional crises happen offline and are discussed in social media" (p. 342). A real-world crisis or emergency situation, for example, would constitute a traditional crisis. Both types of crises may require an organization to respond on social media.

Crisis Management Platforms and Messaging

Where you respond and what you say during a social media crisis (or traditional crisis) should depend on your audience. According to Sprout Social (n.d.):

> Know your audience. Are they primarily customers? Students? Employees? Local community members? Think about what their questions, concerns and needs are right now. Providing content that speaks directly to these considerations ensures your social presence remains relevant and valuable during a difficult time.
>
> (para. 15)

In addition to catering messaging to those affected by the crisis, an organization also needs to consider pausing any regularly occurring content that may come across as insensitive or out of touch. Posting previously scheduled #mondaymotivation or #wednesdaywisdom content during a social media crisis or traditional crisis will most likely not resonate with followers or, worse, could add fuel to the fire, if it appears an organization isn't taking the matter seriously.

For social media crises that call for a public apology, messaging can, and does, take different forms from the written word to video or even audio across a variety of platforms. Whether an organization utilizes Facebook posts, Instagram captions, Stories showcasing screenshots of the Notes app, scripted YouTube videos, a 280-character tweet or any or means, what matters is to deliver an apology where it will be seen by those you are trying to reach.

During a traditional crisis or emergency situation, Twitter's fast-paced, news-driven nature makes it a popular option for organizations needing to communicate minute-by-minute updates. According to *TIME* magazine:

> Since it launched in 2006, Twitter has played an increasingly significant role as a trustworthy source of information in times of crisis. In emergency situations, many government officials, journalists, local authorities, and community leaders broadcast essential information and updates about what's going on. The public can read those tweets—on the platform itself or on other platforms as they're shared by local media.
>
> (McCluskey, 2022, para. 6)

Best Practices for Crisis Management on Social Media

When it comes to crises, one thing is certain—no brand, business or public figure is perfect, so experiencing some sort of social media crisis or faux pas is probably inevitable. The good news is there are some strategies that can help to navigate a social media storm.

> Time moves at a different pace on social media. One minute, your brand is a beloved internet meme. The next, you're the target of some

blazing online ire. Because no matter how careful and cautious you are with your content, a social media crisis always has the potential to strike. Luckily, a social media crisis doesn't have to mean the end of your brand's reputation.

(McLachlan & Dawley, 2022, para. 1–2)

Kerpen (2019) offers the following strategies for combatting strategies when they strike:

- Say you're sorry:

  Being able to say 'I'm sorry' when you make a mistake goes a long way toward making up for your error. Companies are made up of people, and everyone makes mistakes sometimes, so it's inevitable that companies are bound to do something to upset or otherwise anger their customers occasionally. The issue, and what's particularly frustrating, is when companies don't apologize and take care of the problem with speed.

  (p. 209)

  Kerpen recommends that an apology come from the highest-ranking person at an organization, such as a president or CEO, and usually video when possible since it humanizes the organization in a way that that the written word can't, for example, through a press release, blog post or website update.
- Have a plan in place:

  You know your company will make mistakes, but you don't know when they will come, what they will be, and whom they will offend. The best to do now, then, is to plan for the unplanned.

  (p. 210)

  Having a social media crisis plan in place will allow the organization to act quickly when situations arise—big and small—and will dictate who will respond, how they will respond, and what language to use.
- Practice the plan:

  Once you have a plan established, conduct a fire drill or two to see how well your organization responds.

  (p. 218)

- Listen closely:

  Make sure you are listening in closely and keeping watch on the online conversation about your company—even on weekends and holidays.

  (p. 218)

Organizations can opt into platforms' alerts letting them know when they are tagged in a post or when there is engagement on their channels. They can also conduct manual searches on each channel or use services dedicated to social listening, like Hootsuite or Mention, that can help monitor mentions of the brand.

Perspective From the Pros

By Tasha Yohan, MBA

As a social media manager, how do you know when a mishap turns into a crisis? A crisis will generally be a viral reaction that can negatively impact the reputation of your brand or organization.

Take Tide, the laundry detergent company, for example. When the brand launched Tide Pods, tweens started the Tide Pod challenge on social media. Quickly, calls to poison control spiked, and there was an increase in hospital visits for children who ingested the product. However, the company was able to properly handle the situation, further protecting its reputation, by swiftly responding on social media and with an accompanying awareness campaign.

Tide recruited four-time Super Bowl Champion Rob Gronkowski to assist in creating a roughly filmed video for social use to deter adolescents from eating laundry pods. By working with a sports athlete who resonated with that age group, they had great success in spreading the message. So, while the clip appears as though it may have been filmed with a phone, the quickness in turning around this production was essential in a situation where a fast reaction mattered.

The social media campaign was supplemented with PSA commercials on television and additional information on its product packaging. And, while no one could have predicted that eating Tide Pods was going to become a viral social media challenge, the company did an excellent job efficiently pulling together this campaign.

The key takeaway from this case is that social media is unpredictable and while not every crisis is the same, there are still crucial steps you need to execute:

- Plan for the unexpected
- React in a timely manner
- Give accurate and honest information
- Monitor social media and respond appropriately, as needed

Chapter Summary

- Social media customer service is the practice of using social tools to resolve customer questions or concerns.
- The platforms an organization decides to use for customer service should be dictated by audience preferences (where they already spend time on social media) and may be influenced by the size/capabilities of the organization.
- Social platforms that are popular for customer service include Twitter, Facebook Messenger and WhatsApp.
- Social media interactions can be public or private depending on the nature of the conversation. Using Direct Messaging features and private messaging apps are ways to take the conversation out of the public eye.
- Strategies for providing strong customer service include monitoring conversations about your brand, maintaining a high response rate and fast response time, taking conversations offline when necessary, creating a handle dedicated to customer service requests, incorporating customer service information into your social media guidelines, being proactive in anticipating customer service requests, getting creative with customer service solutions, and having a holistic approach to social media customer care that involves all departments within an organization.
- A social media crisis is any activity on a social platform that may impact the organization in a negative way.
- A social media crisis refers to a situation that takes place on social media platforms, whereas a traditional crisis is a situation that takes place offline and is discussed on social media.
- What an organization says and the platforms it uses to deliver any messaging during a social media crisis should be catered to its priority audiences/those most affected by the social media crisis.
- Twitter is a popular option for communicating to publics during a traditional crisis since its live, public nature makes it an ideal choice for communicating in-the-moment updates.
- Strategies for combatting a social media crisis include having a plan in place (e.g., a crisis plan included in the organization's social media guidelines), practicing the plan with routine fire drills, and listening closely to the conversation about your organization to be as proactive as possible.

Exercise 12.1

Earlier in this chapter, we discussed how Morton's The Steakhouse used social media customer service to surprise and delight one of its customers and how Warby Parker tweeted personalized videos of its employees to assist customers trying on glasses from home. Locate an example of an organization that has used its social channels to provide exceptional customer service. What platform(s) does the organization use to connect with its publics, and how did social media allow it to go and beyond?

Exercise 12.2

Locate an apology issued by an organization on social media in response to either a social media crisis or a traditional crisis and respond to the following prompts:

a. Was the situation that prompted a public apology a social media crisis or a traditional crisis? Why?
b. What format did the apology take (e.g., video apology, written post and audio recording)?
c. What social platform(s) was used to deliver the apology?
d. Do these platforms properly reflect the affected parties and/or priority publics for the organization?

Discussion Questions

1. A holistic approach to social media customer service means including departments other than PR, marketing, advertising and customer care in the process. What are some other departments within an organization that might play an integral role in social media customer care?
2. This chapter distinguishes a social media crisis from a traditional crisis. How might the tone and/or messaging be different when responding to a social media crisis versus a traditional crisis on social media?

References

Alton, L. (n.d.). Creative roundup: 4 brands that take Twitter customer service to the next level. *Twitter Business.* https://business.twitter.com/en/blog/creative-roundup-customer-service.html

Barnhart, B. (2021, May 12). How top brands handle social media customer service and support. *Sprout Social.* https://sproutsocial.com/insights/social-customer-care/

BBC News. (2022, December 2). *Kanye West Twitter ban: A timeline of the rapper's downfall.* www.bbc.com/news/newsbeat-63833338

Kerpen, D. (2019). *Likeable social media: How to delight your customers, create an irresistible brand, and be generally amazing on all social networks that matter.* McGraw-Hill.

Lanier, S. (2022, October 27). The social media customer service statistics brands need to know in 2022. *Sprout Social.* https://sproutsocial.com/insights/social-media-customer-service-statistics/

Leiser, J. (2012, November 19). Warby Parker's customer service secret. *LinkedIn.* www.linkedin.com/pulse/20121119183756-20738463-warby-parker-s-customer-service-secret/

Lua, A. (n.d.). 20 top social media sites to consider for your brand in 2023. *Buffer.* https://buffer.com/library/social-media-sites/#16-reddit-430-million-maus

McCluskey, M. (2022, November 17). Twitter was once vital in a crisis. The UVA shooting shows it won't be able to replace. *Time.* https://time.com/6233609/uva-shooting-twitter-crisis/

McLachlan, S., & Dawley, S. (2022, June 2). How to manage a social media crisis and save your job: 9 tips. *Sprout Social.* https://blog.hootsuite.com/social-media-crisis-management/

Meta. (n.d.). *Customer service on messenger.* https://developers.facebook.com/products/messenger/customer-care/

Newberry, C. (2021, February 4). Social media customer service: Tips and tools to do it right. *Hootsuite.* https://blog.hootsuite.com/social-media-customer-service/

Newberry, C. (2022, March 21). How to use WhatsApp for customer service: 9 tips. *Hootsuite.* https://blog.hootsuite.com/whatsapp-customer-service/

Porter, S. (n.d.). How Twitter has become a key customer support channel. *Twitter Business.* https://business.twitter.com/en/blog/how-twitter-has-become-a-key-customer-support-channel.html

Quesenberry, K. A. (2021). *Social media strategy: Marketing, advertising, and public relations in the consumer revolution.* Rowman & Littlefield.

Sehl, K. (2021, June 25). Facebook Messenger: The complete guide for business. *Hootsuite.* https://blog.hootsuite.com/facebook-messenger/

Solis, B., & Breakenridge, D. (2009). *Putting the public back in public relations: How social media is reinventing the aging business of PR.* FT Press.

Sprout Social. (n.d.). *Direct Message (DM).* https://sproutsocial.com/glossary/direct-message-dm/

Zuckerberg, M. (2021, January 7). The shocking events of the last 24 hours clearly demonstrate that President Donald Trump intends to use his remaining time. *Facebook.* www.facebook.com/zuck/posts/10112681480907401

13 Social Media Policies, Laws and Ethics

You've identified priority publics, launched a strategic channel lineup, created a content calendar, crafted content, and put a customer service and crisis communications plan in place. What's left to do? You now need to outline the rules of the road for users interacting with your channels and even members within your organization who might want to participate, such as employees. Social media policies developed for internal and external publics can set an organization up for success by dictating appropriate behavior on its social media channels.

In addition, members of the organization who are tasked with creating and maintaining social media channels for the brand need to be knowledgeable of legal and ethical considerations that come into play when managing a social media presence, as well as any specific policies/guidelines established by individual platforms.

What you can expect to learn in this chapter:

- How to define a social media policy
- The benefits of creating and maintaining a social media policy
- Different types of social media policies, such as social media guidelines and community guidelines
- Steps to take before writing a social media policy
- Types of content to include in a social media policy
- Best practices for communicating a social media policy to an organization's publics
- Legal and ethical concerns for managing a social media presence

What Is a Social Media Policy?

According to Hootsuite:

> A social media policy is an official company document that provides guidelines and requirements for your organization's social media use. It covers your brand's official channels, as well as how employees use social media, both personally and professionally. The policy applies

DOI: 10.4324/9781003255734-16

to everyone from the CEO to summer interns, so it needs to be easy to understand. It can be part of a wider social media marketing strategy, or it can live with onboarding materials and other company policies.

(Newberry & Cooper, 2021, para. 2–3)

Even organizations without a single social channel need a social media policy due to the fact that its employees are most likely active on social media and can benefit from guidance in terms of how to interact with and represent the organization when using their personal accounts.

Organizations can use social media policies to maintain brand identity across social media channels, protect themselves from legal and regulatory challenges, and facilitate diversity and inclusion (Newberry & Cooper, 2021).

While the terms "social media policy," "social media guidelines" and "community guidelines" sound synonymous, they each have a distinct purpose and are tailored to different publics.

According to McLachlan (2022), "A social media policy is a comprehensive document that describes in detail how the company and its employees use social media. These policies are intended to protect a brand from legal risk, and maintain its reputation on social media" (para. 10).

Social media guidelines, on the other hand, are more instructional in nature and have the goal of teaching internal publics, such as employees, how to interact with an organization's social media, along with how to appropriately represent the organization on their personal social media channels. "Social media guidelines are suggestions for how employees of a company should represent themselves and the company on their personal social media accounts. Think of social media guidelines as an employee manual for social media best practices" (McLachlan, 2022, para. 5–6).

Community guidelines are also instructional in nature but are geared toward external publics that interact with your social media channels and content. These guidelines outline what types of behavior are acceptable and, mostly, not acceptable when interacting with an organization's channels.

A fourth, related term, "social media style guide," has the goal of protecting and maintaining the organization's brand identity on social media.

Community Guidelines

In addition to (or as part of) developing a large, more comprehensive social media policy, an organization should develop two types of social media guidelines: guidelines for the community (the public) and guidelines for internal publics like employees. Community guidelines set the rules for public engagement with an organization's social media presence.

Community guidelines are created by organizations *and* by individual social platforms that set the rules of the road for their respective channels. Twitter (n.d.), for example, has "The Twitter Rules" published on its website. Rules included in its community guidelines are focused on four key areas:

- Safety: Twitter bans any threatening of or promotion of violence, terrorism, child sexual exploitation, abuse/harassment, hateful conduct, perpetrators of violent attacks, suicide or self-harm, sensitive media (such as graphic violence and adult content) and/or illegal or certain regulated goods or services.
- Privacy: Twitter bans the publishing or posting of other people's private information (e.g., home phone numbers and addresses) without their express authorization and permission. It also bans any non-consensual nudity.
- Authenticity: Twitter bans platform manipulation and spam, including "behavior that manipulates or disrupts people's experience on Twitter" and "posting or sharing content that may suppress participation or mislead people about when, where, or how to participate in a civic process" (para. 13–14). It also bans the impersonation of individuals, groups or organizations, the use of a fake identity that disrupts the Twitter experience, synthetic and manipulated media, and the violation of others' intellectual property rights.
- Third-party Advertising: Twitter bans the submission, posting and/or display of any video content that includes third-party advertising, "such as a pre-roll video ads or sponsorship graphics," without the platform's prior consent (para. 19)

The rules also contain a section titled "Enforcement and Appeals" that outlines potential consequences for violating the platform's policies and procedures for appeals.

Organizations and social platforms can post these community guidelines on their websites and/or directly on their social media channels. Ferris State University (n.d.), for example, has its "Social Media Interaction Rules" posted to its website and Facebook page. The university encourages others to use these guidelines as a template for developing their own. "We recommend that you post rules of interaction for your platform. This document allows you to delete or hide posts that contain unacceptable comments or posts that do not relate to your content" (Ferris State University, n.d., para. 1).

Social Media Guidelines for Employees

As mentioned earlier, social media guidelines are different from a social media policy in that they are more instructional in nature and serve as best practices for how internal publics can properly interact with organizational social media or represent the organization on their own personal accounts.

Social media guidelines are not intended to stifle communication; on the contrary, they are meant to empower it through education. "Every single employee (yes, including Maurice in accounting) is a potential online brand ambassador. Sharing social media guidelines is your chance to provide the whole team with tools to help them hype you up positively, inclusively, and respectfully" (McLachlan, 2022, para. 14).

In addition to employees, social media guidelines can be developed for different types of internal publics, such as leadership (AKA the C-suite), or from an academic standpoint, faculty and students. The University of North Georgia (n.d.), for example, has its "Social Media Policies & Guidelines" posted to its website for students, faculty and staff.

> The University of North Georgia recognizes the value of social as a significant tool for the creation and dissemination of news and information about the university. UNG has assembled the guidelines on this page to help you use social media platforms effectively. The university expects everyone participating in social media on behalf of the university to understand and follow these guidelines. These guidelines evolve as social media evolves.
>
> (para. 1–2)

Social media guidelines can exist as part of an organization's full social media policy and/or they can exist as separate documents. They can also be incorporated into handbooks, orientations and trainings, among other options. According to Kim (2021):

> Reading through the organization's employee handbook will provide a lot of insight into the culture of the organization. It should also clarify expectations of employees, responsibilities for employees, and, potentially, any information that already exists about how employees are trained on interacting via social media.
>
> (p. 37)

McLachlan (2022) suggests including the following information in any social media guidelines:

- Official Accounts: A listing of the organization's official social media accounts and branded hashtags so that employees can follow and join the conversation when appropriate.
- Disclosure and Transparency: If employees indicate on their personal social media accounts that they work for the organization, they should consider adding a disclosure to their profile/bio section that their content/opinions are not the official viewpoints of the organization (e.g., "thoughts = my own").

In the United States, if employees plan to discuss organization-related matters in their social media content, it is required by the Federal Trade Commission (FTC) that employees identify themselves as working for the organization in these posts.

- Privacy: Reminders about information that is private and confidential, such as private information about coworkers, financial disclosures, upcoming products, private communications, research and development intel, and other sensitive information.
- Cyber Safety: A review of cyber-security basics that can help avoid cyber threats and phishing scams.
- Harassment: Guidelines can remind employees to be kind on social media and also provide support and guidance if they experience any form of harassment on social media.
- Inclusivity: Best practices for promoting inclusivity, such as the use of inclusive pronouns, descriptive captions for images, diverse imagery and icons (e.g., gender- or race-neutral emojis), accessible text, and plain language.
- Legal Considerations: Reminders to employees to respect intellectual property, copyright, trademark and other relevant laws.
- Do's and Don'ts: A quick reference list of do's and don'ts for employees to turn to when engaging on social media.

How to Create a Social Media Policy

The process of creating a social media policy should include steps to prepare for the development of the policy, the writing of the policy, a strategy for communicating the policy to organizational publics, and a plan for re-evaluating the plan as needed and as social media evolves.

Preparing to Develop a Social Media Policy

Breakenridge (2012) suggests the following steps when preparing to develop an organizational social media policy:

- Obtaining the support of organizational leadership/higher-ups
- Conducting a social media audit to identify any strengths and weaknesses of the organization's existing social media presence
- Assembling a team to assist in policy development, including members of various departments, such as PR, marketing, IT, legal, human resources and others
- Researching strong examples of social media policies from other organizations
- Dividing the writing responsibilities

- Setting up an internal sharing system for the team to use when collaborating
- Establishing deadlines for completing the policy
- Creating a strategy for communicating the policy to various publics
- Scheduling future planning sessions for re-evaluating and updating the plan as needed

Writing a Social Media Policy

Common types of content highlighted in an organizational social media policy include (Newberry & Cooper, 2021):

- Roles and Responsibilities: An overview of which departments/employees manage organizational social media channels and contact information for these people, so that employees know whom to contact when they have questions.
- Security Protocols: An overview of social media security risks/protocols, such as the maintenance and updating of platform passwords, the use of personal social accounts on office computers, whom to contact when there is a security breach, and more.
- A Plan of Action for a Security or PR Crisis: A social media crisis management plan with an up-to-date emergency contact list, including social media managers, legal and PR professionals, and relevant leadership/C-suite executives; guidelines for identifying the scope of the crisis; an internal communications plan; and an approval process for response
- An Outline of How to Comply with the Law: Compliance information at the local, state, national, and international levels, such as copyright law, management of confidential/private information, and required disclaimers for testimonials or marketing claims. This section can also include industry-specific regulations, for example, reminders about FERPA for an academic institution
- Guidance for Employees' Personal Social Media Channels: Best practices for sharing content affiliated with the organization and/or showcasing elements related to the organization (e.g., uniforms) and rules for properly disclosing employment when posting about the organization
- Employee Advocacy Guidelines: Best practices for how employees can serve as advocates/spokespeople for the organization on social media

As mentioned earlier, a social media policy can also contain community guidelines and social media style/brand guidelines.

While these pieces of content are popular choices for inclusion, social media policies should also take into account organizational needs and industry-specific considerations.

Communicating a Social Media Policy

Once an organization has developed a social media policy, it next needs to strategize how to communicate its contents to relevant publics, like its employees and social media communities, and how to best motivate them to comply.

> By following the previous steps, you're on your way to having a social media policy for your organization; however, you're only halfway there. The other half of the equation is to think about how you're going to roll out the policy for both the employees and the public, communicate the value, and then measure participation

First, an organization needs to decide where its social media policy will live. Some options include the organization's external website, its intranet, shared drives, and employee handbook, among many others. Next, it needs to develop a plan for rolling out the policy. What communication channels will the organization use to announce the new policy (or periodic updates to it)? The policy could be introduced via email, trainings or standing meetings, a newsletter or any other means best suited to organizational publics. Finally, the organization needs to consider how it can motivate its employees to comply.

Breakenridge (2012) offers these best practices for introducing employees to social media policies while inspiring them to embrace them:

- Develop a two- or three-page summary of the full social media policy that can serve as quick and easy way for employees to reference key takeaways.
- Present the policy using an interactive format like a PowerPoint presentation or Flip Book instead of a lengthy Word document.
- Create a quiz or a quick way to evaluate if employees have read and understood the policy.
- Survey employees about their general knowledge of social media to determine what content areas might require more instruction and training.
- Develop training classes (online or in person) to acquaint employees with the policy and educate them on how to interact with organizational social channels and/or serve as brand ambassadors on their personal channels.
- Create an internal newsletter focused on social media and upcoming campaigns.
- Reward social media participation as a part of employee recognition or rewards programs.

Updating a Social Media Policy

Social media policies should be reviewed, re-evaluated and updated regularly, since the social media landscape is ever-evolving, and organizational needs and practices related to social media will also change. For example, the organization may decide to incorporate a new social media channel into its regular lineup, create new campaigns tying into its social media presence, issue new rules or policies pertaining to social media, or create new social media positions (coordinator vs. specialist vs. manager vs. director), among other updates. State and federal laws relating to privacy, confidentiality, copyright, and any industry-specific regulations should also be re-examined to ensure they are current. The team assembled to develop the social media policy should establish future planning sessions to keep the policy timely and effective.

Compliance Considerations

Legal considerations related to social media typically fall under conversations of compliance. According to Sprout Social (n.d.):

> Compliance means rules and guidelines—guidelines that can't be ignored, causing employers to take a polarizing approach to anything associated with potential infraction exposure. But business processes should never be driven by fear, in fact, this usually ends up having the opposite effect than was intended. The compliance component needs to be proactively addressed. It should be at the core of your social media policy and fueling your growth, instead of being something that stifles it.
>
> (para. 8–9)

Organizations in highly regulated spaces particularly need to be aware of rules in their respective industries, so they understand what can safely be shared online and also communicate that information to their publics.

In the United States, some of the regulatory bodies that may need to be considered include:

- U.S. Department of Education: Administers and enforces student privacy laws such as the Family Educational Rights and Privacy Act (FERPA) and the Protection of Pupil Rights Amendment (PPRA) (U.S. Department of Education, n.d.)
- U.S. Food and Drug Administration: Protects the public health by "ensuring the safety, efficacy, and security of human and veterinary drugs, biological products, and medical devices; and ensuring the safety of our nation's food supply, cosmetics, and products that emit radiation" (U.S. Food & Drug Administration, n.d.)
- The Federal Trade Commission (FTC): Protects consumers and competition by preventing anticompetitive, deceptive, and unfair business practices through law enforcement, advocacy, and education (Federal Trade Commission, n.d.)

- The Financial Industry Regulatory Authority (FINRA): A government-authorized not-for-profit organization that oversees U.S. broker-dealers and aims to protect investors and safeguard market integrity (FINRA, n.d.)
- The U.S. Office for Civil Rights: Enforces the Health Insurance Portability and Accountability Act of 1996 (HIPPA) Privacy and Security Rules, a federal law that required the creation of national standards to protect sensitive patient health information from being disclosed without the patient's consent or knowledge (Centers for Disease Control and Prevention, n.d.; U.S. Department of Health & Human Services, 2019)
- The Securities and Exchange Commission (SEC): Protects investors, maintains fair, orderly, and efficient markets, facilitates capital formation, and strives "to promote a market environment that is worthy of the public's trust" (U.S. Securities and Exchange Commission, n.d., para. 1)

According to Quesenberry (2021), government organizations outside of the United States that regulate social media include Canada's Competition Bureau, the Competition and Markets Authority (CMA), the Australian Competition and Consumer Commission (ACCC), the European Commission in the EU, and the International Consumer Protection and Enforcement Network (ICPEN). Examples of regulations strategists may need to be aware of outside of the United States include the EU General Data Protection Regulation (GDPR), Europe's data privacy and security law, and/or Canada's Anti-Spam Legislation (CASL), which protect consumers and businesses from the misuse of digital technology, including spam and other electronic threats.

While legal/compliance matters can be broad and varied, most can be categorized into the following four categories (Newberry, 2022):

- Privacy and Data Protection: Requirements that generally limit who marketers can contact and how they collect and store data
- Confidentiality: Requirements related to confidentiality for specific industries, such as FERPA and PPRA in education and HIPAA in healthcare
- Marketing Claims: Marketing and advertising rules from regulatory bodies such as the FTC (e.g., endorsements and testimonials) and FDA (e.g., claims related to food, beverage and supplements)
- Access and Archiving: Requirements that aim to ensure access to critical information, such as the U.S. Freedom of Information Act (FOIA) and other records laws that ensure public access to government records

In order to stay compliant on social media, Newberry (2022) recommends that organizations utilize in-house compliance experts in order to understand the regulations for their respective industry; controlling access to social media accounts by limiting who has platform passwords or the ability to create content; monitoring social accounts for any comments that require a response or reporting to regulatory bodies; archiving communications when necessary; creating a pre-approved content library that includes easy-to-access compliant social content, templates and assets; including social media compliance training a part of the onboarding process; and creating appropriate social media compliance policies.

It's important to note that platforms may also have their own policies/rules that organizations also need to consider. For example, Instagram's "Promotion Guidelines" outline rules related to giveaways, contests and other promotions.

Social Spotlight

We all know that violating social media rules can result in temporary and/or permanent bans from channels (e.g., Ye and Trump), but the consequences can also be costly ones. In 2022, Kim Kardashian was fined $1.26 million by the U.S. Securities and Exchange Commission after she promoted the crypto asset company EthereumMax on Instagram and failed to disclose that she was paid $250,000 for the post.

The SEC found that Kardashian violated the anti-touting provision of federal securities laws. In addition to paying the fine, she was ordered to forfeit the $250,000 payment plus interest. She also agreed to not promote any crypto securities for three years (Isidore & Egan, 2022).

In a press release issued by the SEC, SEC Chair Gary Gensler said:

> This case is a reminder that, when celebrities or influencers endorse investment opportunities, including crypto asset securities, it doesn't mean that those investment products are right for all investors. We encourage investors to consider an investment's potential risks and opportunities in light of their own financial goals. Ms. Kardashian's case also serves as a reminder to celebrities and others that the law requires them to disclose to the public when and how much they are paid to promote investing in securities.
>
> (U.S. Securities and Exchange Commission, 2022)

Kardashian isn't the only celebrity to be fined for a crypto-related situation. CNN reported that boxer Floyd Mayweather Jr. and music producer DJ Khaled each paid fines for pushing crypto in 2018, and that actor Steven Segal paid more than $300,000 in penalties for the same offense in 2020 (Isidore & Egan, 2022).

Ethical Considerations

Whereas compliance deals with regulations and the law, ethical concerns pertain to matters of "good," "bad," "right," and "wrong." Organizations should be familiar with their own industry's code of ethics. In the United States, social strategists can consult professional organizations in the fields of communications and marketing such as the Public Relations Society of America (PRSA), the Society of Professional Journalists (SPJ), the American Marketing Association (AMA), the American Advertising Federation (AAF) and the Institute for Advertising Ethics (IAE), among others.

Outside of the United States, social strategists can consult professional organizations such as the Marketing Agencies Association (MAA), the Advertising Association (AA), and the Public Relations and Communications Association (PRCA) in the UK; the Canadian Association of Marketing Professionals (CAMP), the Association of Canadian Advertisers (ACA), and the Canadian Public Relations Society (CPRS); and the Australian Association of National Advertisers (AANA), the Australian Marketing Institute (AMI), and the Public Relations Institute of Australia (PRIA), among many others.

Perspective from the Pros

By Kimberly Cohane, Ph.D.

As digital marketers become aware of ways to automate online communications, bot or social bot usage has been increasing exponentially. Bots are autonomous or semi-autonomous computer programs or scripts that run on social networks and can mick human behavior by replying to posts and sharing information. Bots can be useful by automating weather or emergency updates. However, bots can be misused to inflate account follower numbers, create artificial engagement, leave negative reviews, share misinformation, amplify unverified information, and share links to suspicious websites. Bots can be harmful to online communities and potentially distract your online users from engaging with your content and brand messaging.

You can curate a better experience for your online community by removing harmful bots. Is the same account replying to your posts or your followers with similar or spammy messaging? If so, you can run a few checks to see if it's a bot account.

5 Ways to "Spot a Bot":

1. Look for typos and grammar issues in their content.
2. Check the bio photo and bio text. Are they using an actual photo? Do a Google Reverse Image Search to see if they're using a common stock photo or a commonly used image.

3. If you're on Twitter, use sites like Followerwonk, Botometer, and Bot Sentinel to analyze an account and look at the bot scores.
4. How many followers do they have? Bot accounts tend to have lower follower accounts compared to human user accounts.
5. Using these previously mentioned tools, check to see if the account exhibits unusual behavior. Do they post at odd times or only on certain days of the week? Do they retweet hundreds of times all day? If it seems humanly impossible, it might be a bot.

Handle Bots Like a Pro:

1. If you suspect you have bot accounts engaging with your content or followers, the first option is to ignore them. If you interact with them, it may encourage more engagement. Sometimes, it's best to ignore them.
2. However, if they persist and cause disruptions in your online space, you can block them. Most social media networks have a block feature to prevent them from seeing or finding your account. This will stop the account from engaging with your content and create a barrier to your community.
3. Finally, you can report them. Using bots may go against a social networks' terms of service. If your report is accepted, the bot account may be suspended or banned.

Bots may be here to stay for a while. As digital marketers, you can prepare for this by understanding what bots are, how they work, and how to manage them if they create issues for your online community and brand.

Chapter Summary

- Social media policies, employee guidelines, community guidelines and social media style/brand guidelines are distinct documents with different goals and publics.
- When preparing to develop a social media policy, organizations should obtain the support of leadership, conduct a social media audit to identify any strengths or weaknesses, research strong examples of social media policies, and assemble a team to assist in the policy development that is comprised of members of different departments.
- Organizations can communicate their social media policies to their publics using a variety of communications channels such as their external websites, their intranets, their social media channels, handbooks, orientations, trainings, newsletters and more.

- Social media policies should be reviewed, re-evaluated and updated regularly since the social media landscape is ever-evolving and organizational needs will change.
- Organizations in highly regulated spaces particularly need to be aware of rules in their respective industries, so they understand what can safely be shared online and also communicate that information to their publics.
- When dealing with ethical matters, organizations should consult the code of conduct for professional organizations in their respective industries.

Exercise 13.1

Imagine you are the social media director for the flavored-milk company Holy Cow Milks, and you've been tasked with leading the development of a social media policy. Locate a strong example of a social media policy for an organization in the food/beverage space. What are the content areas covered by this social media policy? How might the content need to be adjusted/adapted for Holy Cow Milks? What compliance rules and/or regulatory agencies need to be included?

Exercise 13.2

Holy Cow Milks has decided to partner with a social media influencer to promote its line of organic flavored milk to parents on Facebook. What are some legal and/or ethical concerns that should be considered for the partnership? Does Facebook, specifically, have any rules relating to paid partnerships? If so, what are they?

Discussion Questions

1. Some employees may view social media guidelines as a means of controlling or stifling communication. As the social media manager for Holy Cow Milks, how would you counter this viewpoint and what key points would you emphasize in communicating the value that a social media policy has to an organization *and* its employees?
2. Journalists often promote their work on social media. For example, many journalists post their published news stories to Twitter. Is it ethical for journalists to tag the subjects of their stories when promoting their work? Why or why not?

References

Breakenridge, D. K. (2012). *Social media and public relations: Eight new practices for the PR professional*. Pearson Education, Inc.

Centers for Disease Control and Prevention. (n.d.). *Health Insurance Portability and Accountability Act of 1996 (HIPPA)*. www.cdc.gov/phlp/publications/topic/hipaa.html

Federal Trade Commission. (n.d.). *About the FTC.* www.ftc.gov/

Ferris State University. (n.d.). *Social media interaction rules example.* https://www.ferris. edu/social/rules.htm#:~:text=Be%20respectful%20to%20others.,Check%20your%20 facts

FINRA. (n.d.). *About FINRA.* www.finra.org/about

Isidore, C., & Egan, M. (2022, October 3). Kim Kardashian charged by SEC, agrees to pay $1.3 million fine. *CNN Business.* www.cnn.com/2022/10/03/investing/kim-kardashian-sec-fine/index.html

Kim, C. M. (2021). *Social media campaigns: Strategies for public relations and marketing.* Taylor & Francis.

McLachlan, S. (2022, November 30). How to create effective social media guidelines for your business. *Hootsuite.* https://blog.hootsuite.com/social-media-guidelines/

Newberry, C. (2022, May 24). Social media compliance: Everything you need to know in 2023. *Hootsuite.* https://blog.hootsuite.com/social-media-compliance/

Newberry, C., & Cooper, P. (2021, September 29). *Hootsuite.* https://blog.hootsuite. com/social-media-policy-for-employees/

Quesenberry, K. A. (2021). *Social media strategy: Marketing, advertising, and public relations in the consumer revolution.* Rowman & Littlefield.

Sprout Social. (n.d.). *Navigating social media compliance across regulated industries.* https:// sproutsocial.com/insights/guides/social-media-compliance/

Twitter. (n.d.). *The Twitter rules.* https://help.twitter.com/en/rules-and-policies/ twitter-rules

University of North Georgia. (n.d.). *Social media policy & guidelines.* https://ung.edu/ social-media/resources/policy-guidelines.php

U.S. Department of Education. (n.d.). *Student privacy at the U.S. Department of Education.* https://studentprivacy.ed.gov/

U.S. Department of Health & Human Services. (2019). *Who enforces the health information privacy and security standards established under the Health Insurance Portability and Account-ability Act (HIPAA)?* www.hhs.gov/hipaa/for-professionals/faq/2019/who-enforces-hipaa/index.html#:~:text=Answer%3A,concerns%20about%20protected%20health%20 information

U.S. Food & Drug Administration. (n.d.). *What we do.* www.fda.gov/about-fda/ what-we-do

U.S. Securities and Exchange Commission. (n.d.). *About the SEC.* www.sec.gov/about

U.S. Securities and Exchange Commission. (2022, October 3). *SEC charges Kim Kardashian for unlawfully touting crypto security* [Press release]. www.sec.gov/news/ press-release/2022-183

Conclusion

The creation of the World Wide Web in 1989 by Tim Berners-Lee forever changed the way that we connect and communicate as a society. As the internet evolved from a passive media experience to an active one, we were introduced to early forms of social media like online Bulletin Board Systems (BBS). The explosion of the internet in the mid-to-late 1990s brought us blogs, Wikis, Match.com (1995), memes, Craigslist (1995), Angie's List (1995), ebay (2005), AOL Instant Messenger (1997) and Social Networking Sites starting with SixDegrees.com (1997). We watched as millions of users exchanged MP3s for the first time online with the music-sharing site Napster (1999), then watched as its demise in 2001 paved the way for Apple's iTunes (2001) and, later, music-streaming services like Spotify and Pandora.

The success of Social Networking Sites like LinkedIn (2002), MySpace (2003) and Facebook (2004) in the early 2000s led to the launch of other categories of social media, such as website and blog builders like WordPress (2003); photo-sharing sites like Flickr (2004); online review sites like Yelp (2004); content-sharing sites like YouTube (2005), and Tumblr (2007); e-commerce sites like Etsy (2005); and microblogs like Twitter (2006).

The hashtag was born in 2007 on Twitter (Samur, 2018) when early adopters used it to organize their tweets and quickly went from being the symbol we associate with phone numbers to a social media staple. We used it to let people where we're posting from (#staycation), what we're posting about (#fakenews), how we're feeling (#YOLO), who we're with (#squad), what we're eating (#brunch), what we're wearing (#OOTD) and what inspires us (#mondaymotivation). It wasn't long before the hashtag was used for news and crisis communication with the 2007 #sandiegofire and creating social and political change with #Egypt and #ArabSpring.

In 2008, President Barack Obama became the first president of the social media age—using social media in a variety of ways during his two terms in office. He was the first to have @POTUS on Twitter, the first to go live on Facebook from the Oval Office, the first to answer questions from citizens on YouTube, and the first to use a filter on Snapchat (Schulman, 2016).

A year later, China launched Weibo (2009) and banned Facebook and Twitter, FarmVille (2009) was named one of *TIME* magazine's "world's worst inventions," and we started to "check in" with Foursquare (2009). Grindr (2009) joined the location-based trend and connected gay and bisexual men, becoming the first geosocial networking app.

2010 introduced Instagram and photo filters and "pinning" with Pinterest. 2011 taught us how to "Snap." Not far behind, Vine (2013) became the original short-form video platform with its six-second clips. Following Ellen DeGeneres' Oscar selfie that was re-tweeted more than three million times, Twitter deemed 2014 the "Year of the Selfie," "Serial" set the gold standard for true crime podcasts, and Facebook introduced its Safety Check feature, so we could mark ourselves safe during a crisis situation.

Social media captions and our digital culture were forever altered again with the widespread adoption of emojis, AKA emoticons. In 2015, Oxford Dictionaries declared the Word of the Year was not a word—it was an emoji (the "face with tears of joy" emoji to be specific).

In 2016, Instagram piggybacked on the success of disappearing content and Snapchat Stories, launching its own version of Stories, which then spawned "Fleets" on Twitter, and the copycat wars with platforms racing to keep up with each other's functionalities were born. The success of Tik-Tok spawned Reels on Instagram and Spotlight on Snapchat, and we all scratched our heads trying to keep up.

We learned what #MAGA meant during the 2016 U.S. presidential election and watched Facebook come under fire for its biggest data leak in history when Cambridge Analytica acquired the private data of tens of millions of users to benefit the Republican Party.

The #MeToo hashtag rose to prominence in 2017 and was used hundreds of thousands of times when users shared their personal stories of harassment and abuse following revelations of alleged sexual harassment and assault by Hollywood producer Harvey Weinstein.

In 2018, Instagram reached two billion users and cemented a culture where filters and FaceTune became the norm, and Parler popped up as a "free speech-driven" space and became popular among conservatives who disagreed with rules around content on other apps.

When users pushed back against the highly curated, polished content that has become all too commonplace on visual storytelling apps, BeReal launched in 2020 as an alternative and as the anti-Instagram app. 2020 also brought a global pandemic, a racial reckoning (#BlackLivesMatter), and one of the most heated and divisive presidential elections in U.S. history. Donald Trump was banned from Facebook, Twitter and YouTube following the insurrection at the Capitol and concerns that his presence on social media would incite more violence. A new social app—Clubhouse—changed the way we create and consume content with social audio.

In 2021, a whistleblower for Facebook leaked thousands of internal documents, and in the wake of the scandal, the company announced a new name—Meta—to describe its vision for working and playing in a virtual world. A true-crime-obsessed generation on TikTok became wannabe detectives with content creators sharing their theories and feelings about the case.

Elon Musk purchased Twitter for a whopping $44 billion in 2022, promptly fired members of its C-Suite, re-instated Trump's account, and confused us all when he changed the meaning of the blue verified check. Ye, the artist formerly known as Kanye West, put the social spotlight on hate speech when Twitter restricted his account after he posted an antisemitic tweet.

And just like that, we're in a new era again with some of the once all-powerful social media giants facing an uncertain future. Meta is in decline with widescale layoffs and losses in profit, and its Instagram app is under fire for damaging the self-esteem of adolescent teenage girls, creating conversation around social media harming mental health. Twitter is in chaos facing an uncertain future with Elon Musk as its "Chief Twit," with once-loyal users leaving in a mass exodus for a new platform called Mastodon that could be defunct or the most popular social platform by the publication of this text. Social media platforms across the board have been forced to navigate rules regarding free speech while banned public figures simply start their own social platforms (Trump and Truth Social) or consider purchasing an existing one (Ye and Parler). TikTok has been labeled as a security threat by the U.S. government over concerns that the Chinese-owned video app could weaponize the data its collects by influencing users or controlling their devices.

If the past three decades since the launch of the internet have taught us anything, it's that the future of social media is unknown and unpredictable. The only thing that is for sure is that the media we use for the practice of being social will continue to change, along with the reasons we use social media, whether it be to connect, create identity, communicate during a crisis, influence an election, solve a crime, share and receive reviews, start a home renovation, escape from our everyday lives or anything else.

References

Samur, A. (2018). The history of social media: 29+ key moments. *Hootsuite*. https://blog.hootsuite.com/history-social-media/#:~:text=Friendster%20(2002),people%20with%20friends%20in%20common

Schulman, K. (2016). *The digital transition: How the presidential transition works in the social media age*. https://obamawhitehouse.archives.gov/blog/2016/10/31/digital-transition-how-presidential-transition-works-social-media-age

Index

Note: Numbers in **bold** indicate tables and those in ***bold-italics*** boxes.

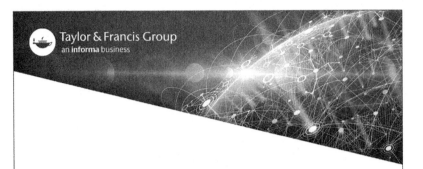

Printed in the United States
by Baker & Taylor Publisher Services